PENNSYLVANIA SPECULATOR AND PATRIOT

*This volume was published with the
cooperation and support of the Pennsylvania
Historical and Museum Commission in its
continuing attempt to preserve the history
of the people of the Commonwealth.*

PENNSYLVANIA SPECULATOR AND PATRIOT

THE ENTREPRENEURIAL JOHN NICHOLSON, 1757-1800

Robert D. Arbuckle

THE PENNSYLVANIA STATE UNIVERSITY PRESS

University Park and London

Copyright © 1975 The Pennsylvania State University

All rights reserved

Printed in the United States of America

Designed by Andrew Vargo

Library of Congress Cataloging in Publication Data

Arbuckle, Robert D
    Pennsylvania speculator and patriot: the entre-
preneurial John Nicholson, 1757–1800.

    Bibliography: p. 235
      1. Nicholson, John, 1757–1800. I. Title.
HC102.5.N5A7   332'.092'4 [B]   74-3446
ISBN 0-271-01168-8

To Lorraine

CONTENTS

ACKNOWLEDGMENTS

I wish to express my sincere thanks to many persons for assistance in the preparation of this study. All of the directors and librarians of the institutions listed in the bibliography offered invaluable aid, but a special word of thanks is due Miss Martha Simonetti, Associate Archivist, Pennsylvania State Archives, Harrisburg, Pennsylvania, for her assistance with the Nicholson Papers and for her permission to read them while they were being prepared for microfilming.

Sincere thanks also must be extended to Mr. Albert Miller and his staff of the New Kensington Campus Library of The Pennsylvania State University for their aid in filling numerous requests for inter-library loan materials; to the librarians of the Carnegie Library, Pittsburgh, and to those of the Hillman Library of the University of Pittsburgh for their assistance.

I wish also to express my appreciation to those who aided in the preparation of this work. Two of my former mentors at The Pennsylvania State University deserve special mention. Dr. Philip S. Klein read the manuscript and his incisive comments helped me to avoid some errors. My deepest thanks goes to Dr. Neil A. McNall who introduced me to John Nicholson, guided the preparation of a master's and doctoral thesis on this subject, and offered invaluable assistance in the preparation of this study with his sound criticisms and knowledgeable comments.

Finally, no words can express my gratitude to the person to whom this volume is dedicated.

1
THE
SPECULATIVE
IMPULSE

Historians have often explored in detail the political, social, and international aspects of the Confederation period and the Federalist era in the United States, but the economic aspects, including land speculation and the activities of individual promoters and speculators, have been neglected. John Nicholson was an early promoter-speculator in the United States. He was driven by the profit motive—a universal trait that has been particularly pervasive in this country since its discovery. It has been responsible for many facets of the nation's development, not the least of which was the founding of most cities and towns.

John Nicholson was a product of the American economic environment, which stressed the Puritan ethic of success and its concomitant, the speculative urge. He is a classic example of a man whose life was affected by this contagious impulse—attempting one economic activity, such as land speculation, and then engaging in such peripheral operations as the export trade, iron manufacturing, textile production, city development, or steam-boat promotion—confident that his next venture would be the great one that would bring all his enterprises to successful fruition. Listed in the ranks of those who were activated by this impulse in the 1790s are such significant figures of American history as James Wilson, Alexander Hamilton, Robert Morris, Aaron Burr, and Edmund Randolph. Indeed America itself was founded partly as a result of a promotional impulse, and it has provided the appropriate environment for the speculator and entrepreneur ever since 1492. John Nicholson and others like him had the motivation to exploit this fertile field.

Each era in the growth of the United States has provided the American with a speculative path, but only resourcefulness, ingenuity, and good fortune enabled him to achieve his goal at the end of this hazardous road. The speculative path that Nicholson followed most often in his heyday from 1780 to 1800 was land. Land consti-

1

tuted a prime base for wealth and social status in the colonial and early national periods of America and, when available cheaply, offered the speculator an enticing sphere for investment. George Washington was among the prominent individuals of the era who saw the advantages to be gained from land speculation and wrote in 1767 that the only way to make a profit and obtain relief from the burden of debt was "by taking up and purchasing at very low rates the rich backland. Any person who neglects the present opportunity of hunting out good lands . . . in order to keep others from settling them will never regain it. . . ."[1] Nicholson in a similar manner said, "every settler in a New Country gives a value to all the circumjacent land . . . a person who owns only a Single Tract, when he improves it or causes it to be improved is indirectly giving half of his labor to others [speculators]. . . ."[2]

In addition to indigenous participants, numerous foreign travelers commented on this mania for land speculation. A Frenchman in 1796 called the United States "the land of speculation." Thomas Cooper, an Englishman seeking land on which to establish a settlement in 1793, came to Nicholson with his queries and commented that "the staple of America at present consists of Land, and the immediate products of land; and herein seems to be the most pleasant and most certain, and the most profitable means of employment for Capital, to an almost indefinite extent."[3]

Nicholson moved down this speculative road with an enthusiasm seldom equaled in the history of the United States. He and other land speculators played an important role in the long involved epic of the march of America westward.[4] The speculator was both hero and villain in the opening of frontier areas—hero because his land purchases and advertisements gave stimulus, however artificial, to other purchases and settlements, and villain because of his tendency to keep the genuine settler from the best lands. Another foreign traveler, Isaac Weld, described some of the land speculators' methods when he said that most of the original sales to settlers by the speculators were at a price that merely covered the original cost and the expense of administration. Scattered throughout the settlements, however, were tracts of land reserved by the speculator for sale when the values rose because of the initial settlements.[5] Weld's description aptly fitted Nicholson and his partner Robert Morris, "the Financier of the Revolution."

Nicholson and Morris may be considered speculative symbols of the 1790s, the period labeled the "Federalist Decade." They also were the years of Nicholson's uncontrolled speculations. Though his land dealings extended into many other states and territories of the United States, Pennsylvania, his home state, was to be the scene of much of his endeavor. Before his death in 1800, he controlled over four million acres in the Keystone State and had accumulated debts of over twelve million dollars. Most of this debt was acquired in pursuit of land enterprises, but some of it resulted from peripheral speculative activities, which were, however, inextricably related to land speculations. For example, he was instrumental in helping to establish the capital of the United States at Washington, D.C., and was responsible for building many of the early houses and manufacturing enterprises there—in his case, a speculative venture undertaken in hope of raising funds to salvage his own depressed land companies. Another outgrowth of such enterprises was his effort to establish a manufacturing center at the Falls of the Schuylkill River near Philadelphia similar to the ill-fated Paterson, New Jersey, complex promoted by Alexander Hamilton and the Society for Useful Manufactures. Land speculation precipitated his promotions of iron works, lead mines, pot and pearl ash manufactures, road and internal improvement projects, emigrant aid society sponsorships, flour trade enterprises, and numerous other activities.

His fame as a promoter became so widespread that he was constantly besieged by budding manufacturers, inventors, and others seeking his assistance. One wrote, "this place [Washington] appears to offer encouragement for a Tan Yard and should you be willing to take a share in one—tho a Stranger to you I will venture to assist." Another, Jacob Glause, wanted to establish a lattice works and asked Nicholson if he would furnish the capital, and a third wanted funds so that he could publish musical works.[6] Nicholson possessed the amazing ability to engage simultaneously in many different enterprises while creditors constantly harassed him. He himself gave a clue as to how he was able to do this:

> when I reflect that William Penn, the founder of Penna. was once unable to pay his Coachman wages [of] £20 & obliged him to accept payment of a Square in the City of Philadelphia which would now sell for about 2 Millions [sic] Dollars—I think by hanging on I shall be very rich after paying all my debts.[7]

John Nicholson constantly attempted to realize his speculative dream and in the process made significant contributions to the growth and development of the new nation. The purpose of this volume is to reveal his role in the economic history of Pennsylvania and the nation during the early national period. Although most of

3

Nicholson's operations occurred simultaneously, his speculative and entrepreneurial activities are discussed separately in the chapters that follow. Early American speculation and business have never been adequately explored by historians, and I hope case study will provide a better understanding of the economic activities of the era by exploring John Nicholson's role in American capitalistic enterprise.

2
THE BASES OF NICHOLSON'S SPECULATIONS: HIS ROLE AS A GOVERNMENT OFFICIAL

John Nicholson was born somewhere in Wales about the year 1757.[1] The exact date of his family's emigration to America cannot be found, but he came with his mother Sarah, his father William, and his brothers and sisters Samuel, Reuben, Jane, Elizabeth, and Arabella. During the pre-revolutionary years his family resided in Chamberstown (presently Chambersburg) and Carlisle, Pennsylvania.[2] During the Revolution, John left the family confines and established a residence in Cumberland County, while his brother Samuel, who later would become a minor business partner with John, took up residence near Shippensburg after the Revolution. After the outbreak of the Revolution, Nicholson joined the Continental Army and served as a sergeant in the First Pennsylvania Regiment.[3]

Nicholson must have been endowed with a capacity for finances because in October 1778 he was appointed a clerk in the Chamber of Accounts of the Board of Treasury of the Continental Congress. Among his duties were validating pay claims for government officers paid by rank and inspecting the account books of officers in the war office. Nicholson defended officers who he thought had been treated unjustly and on one occasion influenced the auditors to validate the claim of Brigadier General J. Gist.[4] Nicholson and the other clerks had so much work to do that the staff of the Treasury Board had to be enlarged in January 1780 in order to expedite the accounts of discharged soldiers. Not only were soldiers not being paid properly but Nicholson himself wrote to a friend stating that Congress allowed him $7,000 in back pay but that he thought they still owed him about $3,000.[5]

While serving with the Treasury Board, Nicholson constantly received complaints revealing the discontent and dissatisfaction that

5

existed in the military during the Revolutionary War. Captain John Henderson of the ship *South Carolina* said that private citizens were receiving more pay for their services than the soldiers: "If the British Army were treated [in such a manner] a general disertion would be the Consequence. I overheard one soldier lately tell another that [General Benedict] Arnold was a 3 year 20 Dollar Man and [this] made him Desert to the Regulars."[6]

During his employment with the Chamber of Accounts, Nicholson became involved in a controversy—the first of many during his short lifetime. Francis Hopkinson, treasurer of loans, charged the Board of Treasury and its clerks with altering records and neglecting their duties. The clerks attended a hearing, and Nicholson, acting as spokesman for the group, criticized Hopkinson's work as treasurer of loans. The latter retaliated by asking for Nicholson's dismissal in 1780, but he was able to hold this position until 8 March 1781 when he resigned to accept a position as one of two auditors of accounts for the Commonwealth of Pennsylvania.[7]

While Nicholson was employed in the service of the central government, he made many contacts with persons who would later be associated with him in business ventures and speculations. It was probably during this period that Nicholson became acquainted with the Gibson family. John Gibson, Sr., was auditor general of the United States and commissioner of the Board of Treasury in 1779–80, and John Gibson, Jr., would later become secretary of many of Nicholson's land companies as well as a partner in some of them. Daniel Brodhead, a military leader from Pennsylvania, entered the finance office of Robert Morris as clerk on 28 August 1781, and he too would become a close associate, especially in land speculation schemes. Since Robert Morris was chairman of the Secret Committee of Trade of the Continental Congress and superintendent of finance under the Articles of Confederation, it was probably in this interval that Nicholson and he began their twenty-year association in public business, private trading ventures, and speculations in public lands, securities, and city development. In their early years of contact, Morris and Nicholson did not always agree, especially when acting in their official capacities. This was most evident after Nicholson had begun his work for the Commonwealth of Pennsylvania in 1781. In this era Nicholson was a protégé of Joseph Reed, leader of the Radical faction in Pennsylvania politics and an opponent of the conservatives, one of whose leaders was Robert Morris. As president of the Supreme Executive Council, Reed helped to secure Nicholson's appointment to the auditor's position. Reed and Nicholson had become friends while frequently visiting army camps together in 1779–80. During this time Reed had introduced Nicholson to several of the general officers.

In addition to his position as auditor, Nicholson was appointed on 23 April 1781 commissioner to pay depreciation certificates to soldiers of the Pennsylvania line, and on 5 July 1781 he assumed the duties of an auditor to settle accounts of guards and miners at army camps. However, the office that made him the virtual financial dictator of the state was that of comptroller-general. He was appointed to this position on 8 November 1782 by the Supreme Executive Council, vested with the executive power under the Pennsylvania Constitution of 1776, and used this office for personal advantage. To understand the environment which produced Nicholson and the functions of the offices and the uses he made of them, a brief review of various parts of the land laws and the land system of Pennsylvania before 1800, as well as some of the national economic policies that had a bearing on Nicholson's activities, is necessary.

After war erupted between England and her colonies and the Declaration of Independence was written, the people of the Commonwealth of Pennsylvania viewed the ownership of unlocated and unappropriated lands by the Penns as inconsistent with the republicanism of their age. Heeding the demands of her citizens, the assembly passed a divesting act on 28 June 1779 which vested "the estates of the late Proprietaries . . . in the Commonwealth." This law appropriated 130,000 pounds sterling to be given to the Penn family as compensation for the proprietary manors, but they received no payment for the additional twenty-two million acres appropriated by the state, which the Penns valued at one million pounds sterling. After the war, the sum appropriated was paid to the Penn family.[8]

The divesting act placed the legislature in control of the disposal of public lands, and the legislature of 1779 authorized the appointment of officers to supervise land transactions. In 1781 the General Assembly passed a law providing for the appointment of a secretary of the Land Office, a receiver-general, and a surveyor-general to supervise land affairs. The president of Pennsylvania, Joseph Reed, under whose administration the Divesting Act was passed, commissioned these officers for five-year terms. At the time the legislature was faced with the task of ridding the state of its huge war debt and the sale of lands provided an excellent source of funds. In addition, the soldiers of Pennsylvania had been promised bonuses for aiding the revolutionary cause and land could also be used for this purpose.

State assumption of congressional debts began in 1780 when the

Pennsylvania Speculator and Patriot: John Nicholson

Continental Congress was unable to fulfill all of its financial obligations. In April 1780 Congress asked the states to compensate their troops in the Continental Army for back pay not received and to make up losses which the soldiers had suffered for having been paid in depreciated currency. The states then began to settle the accounts by issuing state certificates for money due. As a result Pennsylvania amassed a debt of $1,845,000 by 1787. On 18 December 1780 the legislature passed the Depreciation Law, a measure which set aside two tracts of land for the purpose of compensating Pennsylvania's soldiers. A provision of the act authorized the naming of two auditors, Nicholson was appointed to one of these positions. One of his duties was to handle depreciation claims and certificates. In most states, including Pennsylvania, depreciation certificates remained the largest item in state debts after the Revolutionary War.

Since the troops of the Pennsylvania line had been paid in continental certificates, which decreased in value as the war continued, a depreciation pay scale was established, and Nicholson, as one of the auditors, was to compute the losses which had occurred over a three and one-half year period, 1777–80. If a soldier wished to purchase land from the state, he could submit his depreciation certificates to the land office, and they would be accepted at the calculated value in lieu of specie in payment for the land. If the soldier died, his heirs were entitled to receive his certificates. Nicholson visited several army posts validating and distributing depreciation certificates and wrote President Reed that the depreciation due the Pennsylvania line would be "a very great sum." Several times he ran out of applications because of the great demand at the offices he established in Carlisle, Yellow Springs, York, and Lancaster. Nicholson was constantly seeking more funds with which to pay depreciation claims not only from Reed but also from Reed's successor, President John Dickinson.

In addition to the depreciation claims of soldiers, Pennsylvania and the other states also faced the problem of satisfying their citizens who held federal certificates or bonds. Congress had no money to pay these debts, and the certificates and bonds were depreciating in value just as had continental money. President Reed said that Pennsylvania farmers refused to plant surpluses for market because they were taken by the government for use by the Continental Army and worthless continental certificates were given in exchange.[9] Citizens of Pennsylvania then refused to pay state taxes to be used for continental purposes unless the state accepted these certificates. Congress provided some relief in 1780 when it reduced the outstanding loan certificates to their specie value according to a table of depreciation, but by this time the state had absorbed much of the federal certificate debt and had even assigned county officials the task of impressing the specific supplies required by Congress.

The national government also issued indents or certificates of interest to its creditors. Those creditors who lived in Pennsylvania were not satisfied with congressional indents so the legislature of Pennsylvania passed a bill early in 1785 which provided for an emission of 100,000 pounds in currency to pay interest on all public securities held by citizens of the state. Tax revenues and proceeds from the sale of unappropriated lands were to be used in support of the issue. Nicholson, as comptroller-general, supervised security and indent payments. Pennsylvania already had begun to receive military and civilian final settlement certificates as payments for unappropriated lands.

The Radical majority responsible for passing these measures in Pennsylvania wanted to increase the independence of the state. Robert Morris, as superintendent of finance under the Articles of Confederation, opposed these measures, as did President Dickinson who feared that these measures would aid speculators. The indents paid were six percent which Dickinson said would yield speculators about forty to fifty percent profit on their investment. As president of the Supreme Executive Council, he pleaded for discrimination to be made between original holders of the certificates and the mere speculators, but to no avail. It is not difficult to understand why Nicholson supported the above measures. He was the officer chiefly responsible for implementing them and thus was in an excellent position to engage in speculation in these certificates and the lands that could be obtained with them. This is precisely what he did as evidenced by the fact that his friend Andrew Russell was taking out warrants in fictitious names from a list Nicholson had given him.[10] Nicholson had earlier helped Russell obtain a job in the Treasury Office.

In 1786 Pennsylvania formally assumed public securities of the national government held by Pennsylvanians, calling in $5,168,000 and giving her citizens "new loan" state securities in exchange. Then in 1787, Pennsylvania issued new loan certificates in exchange for federal loan certificates which her citizens had purchased in New Jersey and Delaware bringing the total assumption to $6,045,126. Nicholson was the most prominent individual in the state engaging in speculation of new loan certificates, and his official position again was the major reason. When impeachment proceedings were

9

launched in 1793 against Nicholson, the major charge was that he had used his office to obtain new loan certificates illegally. Nevertheless, he reported to Governor Thomas Mifflin in 1790 that "the accounts of the important and almost unlimited trust reposed in me of Granting New Loan Certificates hath been settled. . . ." He wanted the report of his activities in regard to the certificates published in order to prove his innocence.[11]

The Commonwealth of Pennsylvania set aside tracts of land which could be obtained in exchange for certificates of various kinds, and Nicholson again was in a position to take advantage of the situation. In March 1783, a tract of 720,000 acres known as the Depreciation Lands, located in what are now Beaver, Allegheny, Butler, Armstrong, and Lawrence counties, was set aside. To induce further enlistments in the Revolutionary cause, in March 1780 the assembly had offered lands as a bonus. Soldiers were given certificates to unspecified lands in a donation tract which they could claim when the war terminated. These lands between the Allegheny and Ohio rivers and the Mahoning Creek included all of the counties mentioned above plus the counties of Crawford and Mercer and parts of Warren, Erie, and Venango. The location and quality of the specific claims were determined by lottery and the allotments were to be made according to the following schedule:

Major-generals to captains	500 acres
Ensigns, chaplains, and surgeons	300 acres
Sergeants and quartermasters	250 acres
Corporals and privates	200 acres[12]

The soldier, after paying surveying fees, was given a patent attesting to the ownership of the land. Both tracts totaled 14,125 square miles, about five-sixteenths of the state, and Nicholson was to assume ownership of much of this.

Nicholson's future partner, Robert Morris, was in opposition to many of these state policies, especially after his appointment to the new office of superintendent of finance on 20 February 1781. Morris was somewhat reluctant to accept the post because of personal business reasons, but Alexander Hamilton and others helped to persuade him with statements like "I know of no other in America who unites so many advantages and of course every impediment to your acceptance is to me a subject of chagrin."[13] Morris was very much in favor of centralized congressional finance and his policies would be opposed by Joseph Reed, John Nicholson, and other Radicals of Pennsylvania who wanted finances to remain under state control. The Congress of the Articles of Confederation was under conservative control by 1781, and the appointment of so many conservatives (like Robert Morris, Gouverneur Morris, Robert Livingston, and Philip Schuyler) to important posts prompted Joseph Reed and Arthur Lee to suspect that a cabal was in progress. Lee wrote, "Toryism is triumphant here. They have displaced every Whig but the President." Robert Morris began to dominate the Congress, and Reed said that Congress was at his mercy.[14] An example of the dispute between Morris and the Pennsylvania Radicals occurred when Morris asked for an impost tax and urged the state legislatures to permit one so that the national government could pay its creditors. There was much debate over the measure but eventually the states refused the request, so Morris said he would not pay the interest on loan certificates held by United States citizens and urged creditors to put pressure on the states to pass the impost. The Pennsylvania legislature then notified the Congress of its objection to the stoppage of interest and threatened to pay her own citizens by withholding money from the central government, which they did, effective 21 March 1783. Morris was foiled and threatened to resign, which would have pleased Reed, Nicholson, and others who wanted local autonomy. With the end of the war the centralizing influence subsided and the settlement of army accounts and creditor payments was left largely to the states enabling officers like Nicholson to profit from the situation.

One of Nicholson's duties upon his appointment by the Supreme Executive Council to the office of comptroller-general in 1782 was to validate depreciation claims, a useful task for one wanting to buy up such claims for the purpose of speculation. Another of his tasks was certifying those entitled to land warrants in the Donation Tract and fixing the quantity each man was to receive on the basis of his rank. These donation and depreciation reservations were divided into districts which were surveyed into lots of 200–250 acres by deputy surveyors, many of whom worked for Nicholson. He therefore knew where the best tracts were located, who received the largest grants, and, consequently, who to approach to obtain warrants for a nominal sum.

Not only was he supervising the disposal of state lands and issuing depreciation certificates, but he was also charged with collecting all unpaid taxes and liquidating the debts and claims of the commonwealth. In addition to these duties, Nicholson had the task of disposing of Loyalist estates confiscated by the state, such as those of Joseph Galloway, and thus had another opportunity for speculation. His powers were further enhanced by the following duties: settling bills of credit accounts for carrying on the War; disposition of proprietary lands; disposition of certificates issued in 1780 for provisions and horses for the army; settlement of interest notes issued to citizens for cash loaned the state and national governments; handling of new loan certificates and certificates for funded debt given for debts due when there was not enough money to discharge them. As though these responsibilities were not enough, in 1787 he was made escheator-general which placed him in charge of the disposal of confiscated estates and of those that had reverted to the state when there were no legal heirs, another means of acquiring lands cheaply. It is easy to understand why Nicholson would oppose too much interference by the central government and Robert Morris.

Even though his activities while serving in the capacity of comptroller-general were later found to be less than honorable—and in this he behaved no differently than other Pennsylvanians like Robert Morris, William Bingham, Thomas Mifflin and comparable individuals in other states—Pennsylvania, under his direction, took the lead among the states in stabilizing her fiscal situation after the Revolution. If Robert Morris and Nicholson could have followed the latter's fiscal policy in their private affairs as well as they did in those of a public nature, their eventual plight might have been averted, for Nicholson stated that "a strict adherence to the promises of the State and a fulfillment of her obligations, is the only way to secure confidence and credit. . . ."[15]

Nicholson was comptroller-general from 1782 to 1794 and during this time he supervised the dispensation of $27,000,000 in public funds. When he assumed office, there was a backlog of uncollected state taxes. The situation was complicated further by the constant removal of excise officers with every overturn in politics. It was the comptroller's job to collect taxes, to supervise the dispensation of depreciation and donation certificates, and generally to bring order to state finances, and Nicholson's achievements in this position were remarkable when one considers that he had no assistants to help him during his first two years in office. Even after he received some clerical help, the accounts were so voluminous that they filled two rooms in the Pennsylvania State House in Philadelphia, then the state capital, and in 1786 Nicholson had to ask the Supreme Executive Council for more space.

For all this time and effort he was paid 500 pounds per year, which was gradually raised to 800 pounds per year by the time he left office in 1794. Nicholson was expected to pay the expenses of his office out of this and on one occasion complained to President John Dickinson that "surely it cannot be they [the expenses] should be defrayed out of the salary of 500 pounds per annum. . . ."[16] These circumstances were probably contributing factors in his use of his office for personal aggrandizement.

Even though Nicholson was burdened with work, he found time in these early days for personal indulgence and activities. He studied French and Dutch, both of which would be useful in his business enterprises, and learned dancing and fencing, which he felt were necessary to be among the elite of Philadelphia society. He also read widely on a variety of topics which would be beneficial in polite circles. He made a catalog of his books in 1780, including Rohault's *System of Natural Philosophy*, Mill's *Lexicon on Greek and Latin*, Martin's *Introduction to the Newtonian Philosophy*, and Steuben's *Military Maneuvers*.

The consistent business-like approach to life exemplified in Nicholson's manuscripts and letters is striking, but in matters pertaining to Hannah Duncan, who became Mrs. John Nicholson, there was a touch of sentimentality. On 9 November 1781 he wrote, "My Dearest girl . . . let me plead the sincerity of my heart, the strength & length of my passion, the flattering prospects of happiness in a married state and my anxieties to expedite the happy love. . . ."[17] Hannah surrendered to John's solicitations and agreed to marry him in the spring of 1782. He was so happy that he concluded his next letter with "farewell my Dear Hannah and believe me it is with tears in my eyes."[18] But Hannah knew from the outset that John's first love was business when he wrote informing her that he was receiving 500 pounds per year as comptroller-general—the office, he said, might be his for life—and that he was selecting a house on Arch Street in Philadelphia close to his business and official affairs which she could furnish when she came to town. In the same letter he wrote that he would come to her father's Lancaster County farm, marry her quickly, and then return because "the State would be injured if I stay away too long." On 28 April 1782 he informed her that he was taking the next Tuesday off to marry her. He asked her to only have one female friend to act as the bridesmaid to save time.[19]

Because of the primacy of business matters over those of the heart, there was evidence that Nicholson's personal life was not a happy one. His wife frequently left her husband in Philadelphia and took the children to her parents' home. On 25 September 1784 he wrote that he was very lonely for her and his son Billy. He had not seen them for two weeks, and he said, "I'll not put on clean sheets until you come. . . . If Billy can speak any ask him if he is willing and wishes to go home to his papa. If he says yes or *Umph* kiss the Dear little fellow." The next year found her gone again, and despite his frequent pleas, she remained away. He said that during the day business could preoccupy him but the night "shows me how lonely and disconsolate a creature I am when you are gone."[20] She did return often enough in these and later years to bear John a large family. Before 1790 he had three sons and a daughter—William, John Jr., Seth, and Anna. After 1790 Samuel, James, Joseph, and Sally were added to the Nicholson progeny.

There is strong evidence to suggest that in the 1790s, when Nicholson's speculative activities were at their peak and consuming most of his time, the love Hannah once had for him was gone, for she was frequently absent from Philadelphia. She sometimes stayed with her sister in New York for months at a time. On one occasion a Quaker, Stephen Collins, had seen Hannah in New York. John wrote, "he was going to tell me he had for me your *love* or your *Compliments* or something but he drew back I suppose out of respect for the truth. . . ."[21] But Nicholson still loved his wife. He loved her as much as his complicated, business-riddled life allowed him to love anyone. In 1793 he wrote,

> remember New York is not your home, you have no permanent abiding place there. . . . However I claim you and not before your time, you are happy and I am so in the reflection that you are. The time will come sooner or later when I shall see you if we both live . . . women want their husbands a little sometimes, and after wandering and raking, for *every woman is at heart a rake,* you will all return.[22]

Despite the strained feelings that existed, the family remained together until John's death in 1800.

Nicholson's chief preoccupations as comptroller-general were his attempts to solve the state's financial problems. He devised several plans for the liquidation of the state debt. To raise funds he developed a plan for the state-owned land in the city of Philadelphia, providing for its survey and division into lots which were then sold to individuals. This brought 75,000 pounds into the state treasury. By an act passed 8 April 1786, the revenue from the sale was to be used for redeeming the certificates of debt of the state, and this was done. In 1784 his office conducted a lottery which brought in $42,000, and half of this sum was used for road improvements in the state.[23]

He also made a supreme effort to raise funds by collecting delinquent taxes due the state. He replaced many of the old county treasurers whom he partly blamed for not being diligent in their collections. The new treasurers wrote to him complaining that one of their major problems was that people opposed paying taxes of any kind and that when constables seized their farm goods for not paying, no one in the country would buy the confiscated goods. They also accused some of the former collectors of pocketing funds, and Nicholson ordered suits to be brought against the suspects to try to remedy the situation. To persuade the people to pay their taxes, he personally traveled into the interior counties of the state and published articles explaining the need for funds. His policies began to bear fruit by 1787. One of his tax collectors wrote, "I have rode through two-thirds of the county [Cumberland] and am happy to inform you that a disposition for payment Seemed universally to prevail, the people only prayed time to make sale of their produce to enable them to comply."[24]

Nicholson had a reputation for diligently doing his work and for showing compassion for those with whom he was dealing. Many soldiers wrote thanking him for settling their depreciation accounts, and he made certain that widows of soldiers received the certificates that would have gone to their husbands. He put pressure on the Pennsylvania delegates to the Congress under the Articles of Confederation to get the latter to pay money due officers of the Pennsylvania line, and he personally went to the Board of Treasury on behalf of Major John Story, commissioner of accounts for the Commonwealth of Pennsylvania, and his clerks, Samuel Osgood, Arthur Lee, and Walter Livingston, to help clear them of charges of misuse of office. He discharged his duties with such impartiality that in at least one instance he brought charges against a former friend.

There was also evidence to suggest that as comptroller-general Nicholson rejected attempted bribes to obtain favors for individuals. John Nixon, later president of the Bank of Pennsylvania, wanted Nicholson to accept a present. Nicholson responded, "Altho I feel myself highly honored by the valuable offer you have made me yet my situation as a public officer permits me not to suffer myself to accept a present especially in a case where I have had any public business to transact. . . ."[25]

There is no evidence that Nicholson accepted bribes or gifts while serving in his official capacities, but there is evidence that he disseminated gifts to Indians during his state tenure in order to maintain peaceful relations and also to facilitate his land operations. To ensure that the Indians in Pennsylvania remained peaceful, the state and Nicholson were anxious that the army posts be maintained properly. Nicholson must have had supervisory powers over these army posts because Captain James McLean of the Pennsylvania Guard found some of his guards absent from their posts and wrote to Nicholson asking what he should do with them "as the want of proper instructions puts it out of my power to inflict punishment adequate to their crimes."[26]

Perhaps Nicholson's major problem while serving in the position of comptroller-general was in trying to bring order to the chaotic condition that existed in matters concerning national-state finance. He was in charge of supervising the assumption of Pennsylvania's Revolutionary War debts by the national government. He believed that the central government's creditors should be paid, but he also believed that the states, which already had paid their citizens much of the debt owed by the Confederation government, should be compensated. For example, in 1786–87 the state gave to her revolutionary veterans 460,450 acres. Calculated at $80 per one hundred acres, the state thus gave away lands worth $386,360, and Nicholson's books reveal that the national government later assumed this debt with six percent interest amounting to $412,563.[27] He thought assumptions of this sort were proper and just, but when the new federal government under the Constitution was debating the assumption of state debts as part of Alexander Hamilton's financial programs, he vigorously opposed most of the Hamiltonian formulas for both official and personal reasons.

In an article of protest to the editor of the *Pennsylvania Packet*, which he signed "A Pennsylvanian," Nicholson explained that one-third of the depreciation debt in the hands of the original holders in Pennsylvania had been paid off at the value of money in 1781. The interest on the remaining two-thirds was funded by the state excise tax. The depreciation lands and the confiscated estates were set aside by the state as a sinking fund for the whole amount. According to their value in 1781, the certificates held by Pennsylvania citizens had been accepted into the treasury of the state in payment for taxes. The interest on these certificates had also been paid since 1781. In addition, all of the certificates had been receivable in the land office of the state in payment for lands. Nicholson maintained that one-half of the total amount of certificates held by citizens of Pennsylvania had already been taken up by the state in the sale of lands, city lots, confiscated estate sales, and the like.

Now Congress proposed to assume state debts totaling twenty-five million dollars with the citizens of all the states bearing the cost of funding through the payment of taxes. Pennsylvania, under Nicholson's direction, had already paid off much of her debt. Furthermore, the port of Philadelphia, through the collection of import duties, contributed one-fourth of the revenue collected by the United States at that time. So in effect, about six million dollars of the assumed debt of the states was being paid for by the port of Philadelphia. As matters stood, the taxpayers of Pennsylvania under the assumption plan would be paying six million dollars for the benefit of the other states. The comptroller concluded by saying that if Pennsylvania were a debtor state there would be no objection. But she was not a debtor state; she was mostly a creditor state—and, he might have added, thanks to his efforts. Advocates of the plan said that adjustments would be made to compensate Pennsylvania for this, but Nicholson maintained this was a distant prospect, and many with whom he had spoken said it would never occur. So Nicholson recommended that each state pay its own debts.

Nicholson's personal opposition to federal assumption can be gleaned from the following statement:

> The payment of the State debt of Pennsylvania, in its present form, by receiving the certificates in the land office may be considered as an accommodation to the landed interest. . . . [Under] the proposed assumption, the debt will not only be increased in the proposition of Six to one, but the payment must be in Cash caused by new federal taxes. The payments also to the land office of the State must in future be in money instead of Certificates.[28]

Since Nicholson was a major speculator in state and national certificates and frequently used them in payment for land purchases, his personal opposition to federal assumption under Hamilton's scheme is easily understandable.

Nicholson carefully watched the situation as it developed in Congress through such informants as General William Irvine who wrote from New York telling him that the Assumption Bill "will be divided in Committee of the whole but how is uncertain." The Assumption Bill was passed, and being a resourceful person, Nicholson began to speculate in both the debt of Pennsylvania and the debt of the United States.

Despite Nicholson's facility in utilizing changing situations for his own benefit, his reputation as an astute and diligent financier was widely acknowledged. On one occasion he had taken the extremely disorganized accounts of three auditors from Northampton County and put them in order. One of the auditors, Joseph Horsfield, wrote and said he was simply amazed at Nicholson's skill and concluded with, "I wish I had you only one day." Another individual wrote to Nicholson with some queries about certificates because he was the only individual with a "perfect knowledge of all paper matters respecting Pennsylvania."[29]

It is interesting to note that Nicholson became so scrupulous in his work that he even put pressure on Robert Morris to settle an outstanding account with Pennsylvania respecting supplies which Morris bought for the state in 1781. Morris owed $4,800 but claimed that this money had been expended for the general use of the national government. The case was eventually taken to court and Morris was cleared. Nicholson and Morris were not very friendly in the early 1780s, and this may help explain why Nicholson attempted to embarrass the financier. Nicholson constantly complained to the central finance office headed by Morris, and Morris retaliated by stating that the financial officers of Pennsylvania were not following orders. He accused some Pennsylvania officers—not mentioning Nicholson by name—of taking advantage of the weak and unprotected and working in collusion with certain individuals, entitling them to more money than their services to the country warranted. He could only have meant Nicholson by this statement since Nicholson was the chief officer responsible for validating claims in Pennsylvania. In fact, as late as 1791 Nicholson was still requesting and receiving from Joseph Nourse, register of the United States Treasury, statements of the accounts of "the Honorable Robert Morris, late Superintendent of Finance."[30]

Nicholson was in a position of great power and influence and it was natural that he would create many enemies while serving as comptroller-general. Most of these were political enemies who would retaliate by trying to remove him from office twice. One of these enemies was Christian Febiger, the treasurer of Pennsylvania. David Rittenhouse, Nicholson's friend and political ally, had been treasurer in the 1780s but due to a shift in political fortunes in the state, which will be discussed later, he resigned on 9 November 1789. Febiger, his successor, accused Rittenhouse of malpractice, and Nicholson defended Rittenhouse by accusing Febiger of being lax in performing his duties.[31] Febiger would later be the one to bring charges against Nicholson resulting in an impeachment trial in 1793.

Another of his political enemies was Samuel Miles. The comptroller reported mistakes and irregularities discovered in settling the accounts of public officers handling state monies to the assembly. Such a report was submitted on Miles, a Revolutionary War colonel, a member of the Council of Censors and the Supreme Executive Council, a leading Republican, and a political opponent of Nicholson who was a Constitutionalist. The legislature, dominated by Nicholson's opponents, exonerated Miles of the charges, and a committee of the house proposed removing the comptroller-general from office. The action, so obviously political, failed. Nicholson disclaimed any political motivation of his own in this affair when he wrote, "the good character Col. Miles had so long sustained & his high reputation with all parties and persons made it a painful task for me to reveal the defects of human nature and believe me it was with reluctance I did it. What I have done is the result of cool, calm and unbiased reason."[32]

This cool, calm, if not entirely unbiased, approach helped him fulfill his duties as the state's leading financial officer very successfully. Reviewing the work of the comptroller, the *Freeman's Journal* commented in 1790 that

> all accounts and demands are liquidated with a diligence and an ability that is of the most important advantage to the state. A chaos of old papers have been waded through with immense patience and many errors of the former auditors and committees of assembly discovered.[33]

By 1790 Nicholson had settled 24,000 outstanding accounts and issued 21,000 depreciation certificates. "The errors corrected and recovered for the state and which otherwise would have been lost, I would deem a handsome annual compensation for my services."[34]

However, the use of his office for personal gain more than repaid the services he rendered the state. This had political repercussions that resulted in his resignation from the office of Comptroller-General.

3
THE BASES OF NICHOLSON'S SPECULATIONS: THE USE OF OFFICIAL POSITIONS AND CONTACTS

The new nation emerged from the Revolutionary War and found foreign trade heavily handicapped due to the severance of ties with Britain. Since investment in foreign trade was somewhat unattractive, much of the available commercial capital was diverted into investment in land and to other enterprises that seemed to offer greater prospects of profits. Anyone advantageously situated to exploit the available areas of investment could thus hope to amass considerable wealth. Nicholson was such an individual, but he was by no means the only one in the era who used his office to increase his fortune. The propensity toward exploitation was national and was displayed in the actions of men like William Duer, Alexander Macomb, and William Constable of New York, Oliver Phelps and Jeremiah Wadsworth of Connecticut, and Nathaniel Gorham and Andrew Craigie of Massachusetts. During the Revolutionary War, Jeremiah Wadsworth was censured by the Continental Congress for expenditures made under his supervision as commissary general for which he could not account, and he and Oliver Phelps, Massachusetts superintendent of army purchases, awarded themselves beef contracts. Craigie, apothecary general of the Continental forces, tried to establish a private medical supply house.[1]

That Robert Morris of Pennsylvania financed the Revolution out of his own pocket has recently been discovered to be a myth. It was, in fact, the other way around; Morris diverted at least $80,000 to his own purposes while serving as finance superintendent. William Bingham, another active speculator of the period from Pennsylvania, used his office as American commissioner to Martinique for private

20

gain, as did Nicholson's friend from the Keystone state, Thomas Mifflin, who was court-martialed but not convicted for profiteering while serving as quartermaster general during the Revolutionary War. The office of comptroller-general of Pennsylvania afforded opportunities for personal gain to a man with ambition, and Nicholson took advantage of this position.

The state provided him with an opportunity when it extinguished the Indian title to an area which was to embrace eighteen of the northwestern counties of Pennsylvania. After the expeditions of General John Sullivan and Daniel Brodhead in 1779, the Senecas under Cornplanter knew that further resistance to white encroachments would be futile. As a result, after a conference at Fort Stanwix in October 1784, Indian title to five-sixteenths of the present state of Pennsylvania was acquired for 5,393 pounds, 16 shillings, and 7 pence. One of the real tragedies of the persistent speculative urge of the whites had been aptly expressed by Teedyuscung, a leader of the Delaware Tribe, in a statement made in 1757 at the Treaty of Easton, when he said, "The land is the cause of our Differences, that is our being unhappily turned out of the land; . . . they do not act well nor do the Indians justice. . . . We on our parts gather up the leaves that have been sprinkled with blood, we gather up the blood, the bodies and the bones, but when we look round, we see no place where to put them."[2]

The land speculators—Nicholson in particular—took the lead in securing the best of these ceded lands within the state for personal gain. One of his duties as comptroller-general was to certify veterans entitled to depreciation and donation lands. This function and the chaotic land situation that existed in the state eventually helped him acquire over four million acres of the Keystone state.

In the confederation and early national periods, the general procedures for securing land were similar in the various states where a firm and thorough survey did not antedate the sale of the land. Sales of land were authorized under a law of the state which provided for the opening of a land office. Officials in the land office then determined the conditions of the sale. Persons who wanted to buy came to the land office, paid the price or the downpayment on the number of acres they wanted, and obtained an order, called a warrant, for the state surveyors to survey the stipulated acreage. The survey was then made at the buyer's expense, and the buyer naturally would instruct the surveyor to pick the best lands of those offered for sale. In the event that there were two individuals seeking the same land, the oldest warrants obtained preference. The surveyor drew maps of the lands called plats and deposited these with his report on their quality in the land office. Then the title was issued to the purchaser. This sounds like a simple procedure, but as Charles Maurice, Prince de Talleyrand, commented when he visited the United States in the 1790s, "the conflicting surveys and the resulting sale to several persons of the same property are monstrosities which happen every day...."[3] Contributing to the confusion in Pennsylvania was the fact that the Land Office was never sure which lands were occupied and which were not and so the prospective buyer had to assume the added responsibility of making certain that the land he sought was unoccupied. Other problems were caused through the use by the state of undescriptive warrants which did not specify the particular piece of land to be surveyed but merely ordered the surveyor to survey any spot within a widely designated area, such as the Depreciation Land Tract. Indeed, under the Act of April 3, 1792, if warrants were granted for lands later found to be rightfully claimed by others, the person holding these warrants could then locate on any vacant lands within the state.[4] These practices resulted in the conflicting claims observed by Talleyrand, and Nicholson was involved in many such disputes.

When controversies did develop, the parties had to take their cases before a body known as the Board of Property. This board, originally organized under the Penns to settle land title disputes, was reestablished by the state under the Act of April 5, 1782. The Board of Property had the power to hear all controversies on which caveats —legal notices or writs which prevent an officer from acting until all litigants are heard—had been filed, and it was also given authority to examine cases pertaining to escheats, which are legal writs that revert land to the state as the original proprietor when the legal owner fails to hold the property.

Under the law of 1782, the president and vice-president of the Supreme Executive Council of Pennsylvania, as well as the secretary of the Land Office, the surveyor-general, and the receiver-general constituted the Board of Property. Since Nicholson was a major state officer, he knew all of these individuals and had business connections with some of them during his tenure as comptroller-general. The president of Pennsylvania in 1788—and first governor of Pennsylvania under the new state constitution of 1790—was Thomas Mifflin, a close friend and business associate of Nicholson's. The surveyor-general from 1789 to 1800, during the peak of Nicholson's speculative activities, was Daniel Brodhead, a close friend who would later collaborate with the comptroller-general in using their offices for mutual benefit. The secretary of the Land Office, for much of Nicholson's tenure, was Tench Coxe, fellow speculator and business associate.

With the Board of Property staffed with many of his allies, Nicholson had an excellent chance to win most of the cases in which he was involved that were brought before this body. On one occasion, Samuel Wallis and he both claimed 135,350 acres in Luzerne County and 60,000 acres in Northumberland County. Wallis brought a caveat against Nicholson on 19 March 1793 and again on 7 June 1794. The board decided in Nicholson's favor, but Wallis still had recourse to the courts, as the board's decisions could be appealed. Nicholson, with the aid of Robert Morris, bought off Wallis in 1795. Later, when Wallis tried to reclaim these lands, Nicholson persuaded Jared Ingersoll, attorney-general of the state, to issue ejectment notices against him.

Nicholson was also disputing lands with another speculator of the era, James Wilson, signer of the Declaration of Independence and one of the authors of the United States Constitution. Wilson, like Nicholson, overextended himself in land speculation and suffered bankruptcy. Wilson had over one million acres west of the Alleghenies, and he clashed with Nicholson who claimed lands equal to the size of Connecticut and Rhode Island in the same vicinity. One instance involved 200,000 acres in overlapping claims, and Nicholson offered to buy Wilson out to avoid a contest. Wilson agreed because at this point in his career he owed almost everyone money, including Nicholson, and Nicholson paid for part of the land with Wilson's notes. On another occasion, Wilson and he claimed the same land in Huntingdon County. The dispute was brought before the Board of Property and Nicholson's claim was upheld.[5] Wilson was losing on all fronts near the end of his life and had to take up residence in debtors' prison. In 1796, Nicholson commented that he was glad to hear that Wilson was "at liberty again" and that he felt sorry for him. Nicholson held many of his notes, but he refused to bring suit against Wilson because he did not want to aggravate his own plight.[6]

In addition to Nicholson's most favorable position with the Board of Property, he could also use his post as escheator-general for personal advantage. Mifflin helped him to achieve this position in 1787, and he held onto this office even after he resigned as comptroller in 1794. This position gave him authority to supervise the disposal of confiscated estates, including those of Loyalists and estates which reverted to the state when no legal heirs existed. Not only was Nicholson escheator-general, but Mifflin helped to have his brother Samuel appointed deputy escheator-general! These circumstances placed

Nicholson in a very advantageous position since he would be the officer responsible for sending the data to the Board of Property in cases dealing with escheats. And since his brother was his deputy there would be no effective check on his reports.

He used the experience gained in the office of escheator-general in establishing a private business to handle escheats. One that he administered was the estate of Dr. Barnabas Binney. The Binneys had been on very friendly terms with the Nicholsons while the doctor was alive. However, after Binney's death his heirs began to question Nicholson about his handling of the family estate. Nicholson's lawyer, James Gibson, informed him that he might be called to account for the management of the estate, and this is exactly what happened. He was constantly being prodded by Susan Binney, the doctor's daughter, and Dr. Marshall Spring, her stepfather, about the estate; they accused Nicholson of diverting part of it for his own use and threatened suits against him in the 1790s for its recovery. He kept stalling on the issue and told Susan, "Minors need not concern themselves with the business end of it."[7] Eventually, in 1796, a proceeding was brought, but by this time it was ony one of nine hundred suits which had been brought against Nicholson.

Another of his duties as comptroller-general was to supply the Land Office with lists of those entitled to depreciation and donation lands. It was simple to insert fictitious names or to get others to take out warrants for him for a small transfer payment. This practice could be expanded further if one had a working agreement with those responsible for running the Land Office, and with Daniel Brodhead in control of this office, Nicholson had the necessary connection. There were several counties in which warrants were registered in Nicholson's name. Although the acreage in each case is small when you consider that all of it went to one individual, the aggregate acreage involved becomes impressive. It was difficult to discover how much land was acquired by Nicholson in this way because of the numerous fictitious names that were used, but he acquired land using his own name in the following counties:

Northumberland, February 22, 1785, 400 acres
Bedford, March 10, 1795, 400 acres
Luzerne, July 9, 1787, 400 acres
Northumberland, September 7, 1789, 400 acres
Huntingdon, July 27, 1792, 400 acres[8]

Furthermore, a man by the name of William Barker took out several warrants, representing 7,000 acres, in his name for Nicholson's use; a

Mr. Gross bought up donation lands for him using assumed names, and John Young offered him 50,000 acres in Fayette County if he wanted them.[9]

Under the law, surveyors of depreciation and donation lands were not to favor military men, whatever their rank, with better quality lands, but a surveyor could easily be persuaded to do otherwise. It is interesting to note that among the surveyors who laid off depreciation lands were Samuel Nicholson and Daniel Leet, a man who later became a manager of one of Morris's and Nicholson's land companies. John Armstrong, Jr., secretary of the Executive Council of Pennsylvania in 1783, cautioned John Lukens, the surveyor-general, against abuse of trust by the surveyors. He reported that efforts were made to conceal the true value of lands. But this warning was to no avail since surveyors made the best deals that they could get with the various speculators. Under Pennsylvania law, deputy surveyors had to be bonded, and often speculators would pay their bonding fees in return for favors. In addition to Samuel Nicholson and Daniel Leet, Major Thomas Robinson was working in this capacity for Nicholson in Northumberland County. On one occasion, he warned Nicholson that three or four rivals of his were out to claim the lands Nicholson wanted and cautioned him to lose no time in making his entries in the Land Office and sending up the orders for survey. Later Robinson bought up the soldiers' claims and sent the list of warrants which totaled 2,500 acres to Nicholson so that surveys could be made. In 1785, Nicholson took out warrants for lands claimed by another, so Robinson bought other land and paid the expense of having Nicholson's warrants altered. Another surveyor, Ennion Williams, doubled as Nicholson's land agent in the Westmoreland County area.[10]

When surveyors such as these worked for speculators like Nicholson and concealed the true value of the land from the bona fide settler looking for good land, the holders of depreciation certificates, thinking that the land was of poor quality, were inclined to sell their claims at low prices, either to brokers dealing in certificates or to the speculators themselves. Nicholson acquired many of these certificates and used them as claims to secure additional lands. Nicholson watched closely the transactions in bounty lands and requested from the Land Office the names of widows and children of soldiers who had received certificates for lands. He was in the advantageous position to administer the distribution of lands to veterans with one hand, and with the other to buy their claims cheaply. He would appear at the Land Office on different occasions to claim donation rights entrusted to him by the widows of veterans. He even speculated in a fund that had been established for these widows by the Presbyterian Church of Philadelphia and bought lands with Widow Fund Certificates.

In addition to securing these donation and depreciation certificates himself, he had a host of individuals buying them for him. Captain John Henderson of the ship *South Carolina* as early as 1782 told Nicholson that marines under his command would be willing to part with their depreciation certificates cheaply. In 1786, he bought several from a broker, John Carr, and William Beatty, a clerk in Nicholson's office, secured many for his superior.

Other agents also secured many claims for him. Alexander Power, one of his agents in the donation and depreciation tracts, obtained 859 acres worth of claims on one occasion and on another told Nicholson that 45 donation warrants signed by General Henry Knox could be his at $8.50 for each 100-acre warrant. Power and other agents made trips all over the state buying up soldier claims and making certain that they were not buying certificates already sold. Nicholson insisted that Power and other agents, like Ennion Williams and Francis Kirkpatrick, make the soldiers sign oaths affirming that their claims had not been sold to others. And if the soldiers later claimed they had been cheated by Nicholson and brought suit against him, it was a simple process to bribe the county judges that would hear the cases. Nicholson's comptroller-general's office was the agency through which the salaries of county judges were paid. One might suspect that they would favor his position in any litigation brought by the soldiers.[11]

Nicholson had such a reputation for buying donation and depreciation lands that brokers constantly were soliciting him to buy the claims they held. One wrote, "please to let me know if you will give 10 dollars [a] hundred [acres] for gauranteed [sic] Donation Lands." A few months later John Young wrote, "I have a few more Donation Lands offered—does Mr. Nicholson incline to purchase any more?" Even budding speculators went to the master for assistance. One wrote, "Dear Johny help me if you can. . . . I would wish for a Number of Soldiers names that have wages and land due them and would beg of directions how to proceed, other-ways it would be of no use."[12]

There were many in the state who objected to brokers and speculators such as Nicholson persuading soldiers or their heirs in need of money to part with their warrants. The *Pennsylvania Packet* on 12 March 1785 described the situation in this manner: "A tribe of speculators have haunted the poor soldiers at every place where they are called to settle their accounts, and have, by every artifice in their power seduced them to part with their certificates at one-eighth, or one-tenth of their value. . . ."[13] Duc de la Rochefoucault-Liancourt, when he toured Pennsylvania in the mid 1790s, observed that "men of fortune and influence . . . bought it [certificates] up and give it in payment for public lands at a profit of ten hundred and sometimes thirty hundred per cent. The *depreciation* and *donation lands* were fertile subjects for their speculation."[14] A writer in the *Pennsylvania Gazette* deplored the situation observed by Liancourt when he wanted to know, "what must be the feelings of the widow and orphan, when they find themselves thus defrauded of a great part of their little all, and that, not unlikely, the earnings of their late husbands and fathers, who died in the service of their country, by these pests of society who aught to be despised."[15]

Since there were those then who despised the speculators, we may wonder how Nicholson escaped detection for such a long period of time. The answer seems to lie in his affiliations with men in responsible positions; that is, those who controlled the Land Office and those who politically controlled the state. From his appointment as surveyor-general on 3 November 1789 until his dismissal in 1800, Daniel Brodhead, a military hero of Pennsylvania, had control of the Land Office. Nicholson and Brodhead used their respective offices for mutual benefit until the former took leave of his duties as comptroller-general in 1794. A further point of interest is that Thomas Mifflin appointed Brodhead to the surveyor-general's office. Brodhead had married the widow of Samuel Mifflin, the governor's brother, in 1778, and was therefore remotely linked to him through marriage. Nicholson used both men in building and expanding his speculations in land.

Brodhead was averse neither to granting Nicholson credit in his land dealings with the state nor to certifying that he had paid fees that had not been paid. Evidence points to the fact that Brodhead expected and received compensation for aiding Nicholson with his improper claims. According to the land law of 1783, soldiers entitled to land had to make a claim within two years after the war terminated. This time limit was extended, and the Land Office in 1792 was directed to draw lots for those persons who failed to apply and were entitled to land according to the list furnished by the comptroller-general. Nicholson would supply the names of presumably bona fide claimants, and since Brodhead was in charge of drawing lands for these individuals, it was unlikely that investigations would occur, or even that any questions would be asked, regarding the names appearing on the list. The comptroller-general wrote in his diary that on 6 September 1792 he gave Brodhead the cash for 3,000 acres of land in payment for services rendered. On another occasion, Brodhead knew of 4,000 to 5,000 acres that were available and told the speculator about them—a short note stated that 400 dollars were given Brodhead for his information "in a day."[16]

Not only was Brodhead acting collusively with Nicholson, but he also was engaging in the same practices for personal aggrandizement, while using some of Nicholson's pseudonyms. For example, both used the name William Barker to secure lands in Beaver County, and both took out warrants for lands using the name of Joseph Williams.[17]

Brodhead altered warrants for Nicholson by postdating them so that his would take precedence over rival speculators, and he allowed special privileges in regard to patents so that his titles would be secure. In addition, he permitted Nicholson to switch his warrants from one district to another in order to obtain better quality lands. Also, under the Act of April 9, 1781, which established the Land Office, the surveyor-general was empowered to appoint deputy surveyors in any county and section of the state. Brodhead named Samuel Nicholson, Daniel Leet, Ennion Williams, and others whose loyalty could be counted upon to best serve their superior and Nicholson. Nicholson even worked to have his partner in some of his land companies, General William Irvine, appointed as a deputy surveyor believing "it would be mutually convenient."[18]

A very close relationship existed between Brodhead and Nicholson, each borrowed heavily from the other when in need. On one occasion Nicholson wrote: "To ask you to add 200 dollars to what I owe seems extraordinary but my demand for it is such that if you have it I think you'll lend it [to] me—and I will repay it and more before the end of the week."[19]

Brodhead was amply rewarded for the services he performed for his clandestine associate. Land claimed by Nicholson was given to Brodhead for services rendered. One payment to the surveyor-general consisted of 8,000 acres along Pine Creek (Clinton County) in the depreciation lands. At a later date he gave Brodhead lands along Sandy Creek, two miles from the Allegheny River, which Nicholson assured him "hath long been destined for you." In addition to land, Nicholson also conveyed soldiers' certificates to Brodhead and gave him sums of money to help pay for lands that he hoped to acquire. On the anticipation of one such gift, Brodhead wrote, "what you are about to give with that I have in [the] Bank wil be sufficient to discharge the whole claim and very little remains to be paid to the Land Office for my lands."[20]

But on several occasions, Brodhead wrote notes of desperation when he feared his illicit activities in behalf of himself and Nicholson would be discovered. In June 1794 he wrote, "I am called on . . . to pay a certain Sum of money into the Treasury tomorrow and if you cannot asist [sic] me I shall make a poor figure." In March 1795 "public accusers" were pressing him, and the surveyor-general lamented that "it only remains for me to make a great sacrifice on account of my personal regard for you unless you can afford me immediate aid."[21]

Practices such as these continued until February 1796 when Samuel Bryan, register-general of Pennsylvania, called on Brodhead to present his books for examination. The letters between Nicholson and Brodhead now assumed tones of desperation. Brodhead wrote:

> I have so frequently stated to you my embarrassment that it would be needless to repeat it here, and my wish is to know whether you have done, or can with certainty do, in the course of this week, anything to relieve me, begging at the same time that no hopes may be given which cannot be realized, as I am determined to make sacrifice of my property rather than incur the least degree of censure.[22]

But Nicholson's affairs were in such a bad state by 1796 that he could render little relief for Brodhead. In fact, his speculative empire was crumbling into many fragments. He replied to Brodhead:

> Be assured my affairs are not in the situation to permit my fulfilling my wish and my promise of securing you for the money for which I am indebted to your friendship. Would to God I could come with money to your aid. It would gratify my feelings to send you some but it may at no distant day be in my power to prove you that I want not the inclination.[23]

To prove to the surveyor-general that he did not lack the inclination, he let Brodhead draw a mortgage on some of his property, but since other creditors were pressing Nicholson more persistently than Brodhead, he could offer him little substantial relief. Brodhead, despite Nicholson's lack of support, was able to remain in office until newly-elected governor Thomas McKean summarily dismissed him in 1800.

Nicholson secured favors from the Land Office by other devious means. The lack of adequate compensation tempted some Land

Office employees to grant favors. One employee who aided Nicholson was John Barron, a clerk, who, in return for bribes in the form of money and land, would inform Nicholson of any good lands that could be obtained from individuals for pittances. On one occasion, Barron provided information on 20,000 acres in Berks county. "I have been told that it is really worth touching," wrote Barron. At a later date, Nicholson was informed that a "Mr. Jacob Richardson has the disposal of 12,000 [acres] in . . . warrants paid for—which he wished to dispose of—I have taken the liberty of introducing him to you." Even at the height of the yellow fever epidemic in Philadelphia in 1793, while Nicholson was safely at his country estate, Angelica Farm near Reading, Barron was writing from Philadelphia that it was Colonel John Meyers who had the 20,000 acres in Berks County for sale and asked Nicholson if he wanted them. The compensation that Barron received for his services was usually choice lands. For approving fictitious land claims, or for informing Nicholson of individuals who would sell their claims for a small sum, Barron on several occasions was given douceurs of 200 acres.[24]

Nicholson also persuaded Barron to process warrants for him after hours, and, at the speculator's request, to backdate them several months prior to the actual issuance, because, if a dispute arose over ownership of land, the Board of Property would grant the claim to the holders of warrants with the earlier dates. In 1792 Nicholson received 168 warrants from the governor and took them to the Land Office where John Barron waited after hours to process them for him. Thus three of Nicholson's cohorts, Mifflin, Brodhead, and Barron, were involved in the same operation in the comptroller's behalf. In the same year, Barron backdated warrants for Nicholson covering lands along the Susquehanna, and in January 1794 took out warrants for Nicholson in his own name and backdated them to 15 November 1793. He also sent Nicholson warrants that had not been paid for. And if some disputed warrants happened to slip by Barron, Mifflin and Brodhead as members of the Board of Property could support Nicholson. It was true that the defeated party could appeal the board's decisions to a regular court of law, but the Pennsylvania courts relied heavily on the board's decisions.

Not content with these services, Nicholson was audacious enough to borrow sums of money from Barron. Although not hesitant to ask for loans from individuals, he was extremely reluctant to return the sum when called upon. Letters from creditors habitually contained a note of yearning and desperation. Barron wrote, "Can you possibly let me have the ballance [sic] of the money I lent you as I am very much pushed." To one of his pleas Nicholson replied, "it is painful for me not to be able to do more."[25] But Nicholson did many favors for Barron in return for his services. For example, he endorsed notes of Barron's and persuaded Robert Morris to do the same.

Practices such as those involving Barron were halted when the General Assembly of Pennsylvania passed an act in 1795 providing for dismissal and a fine of $100 for any clerk found guilty of taking fees or granting favors. Later, after both were out of public office, Nicholson made Barron an agent of his North American Land Company. However, Barron suffered a fate similar to Brodhead's. He became deeply in debt and tried to rely on Nicholson for relief, but, as with Brodhead, Nicholson could offer small solace. Barron was in such desperate straits by 1799 that he was hiding from the sheriff and meeting clandestinely with Nicholson. By then both were trying to escape the clutches of the law.

In addition to these means of securing lands, Nicholson also made use of a very close relationship with the first governor of Pennsylvania, Thomas Mifflin, who served from 1790 to 1799. Counting his two years as president of the Supreme Executive Council, his service as chief executive is the longest in the history of the state. This was probably the main reason for Nicholson's long tenure in the comptroller's office. Furthermore, since Mifflin had also appointed Nicholson escheator-general and his brother Samuel deputy escheator-general, more opportunities for speculation were provided. In fact, even after Nicholson resigned his comptroller's job following his impeachment trial—and the governor did not request his resignation—Mifflin kept him at his post as escheator-general. But on 27 October 1795 Nicholson wrote the governor: "The increasing duties of the office of Escheater-General requires more time to attend properly thereto than it is in my power to give it. After returning you my thanks for the Confidence manifested in the appointment I have to offer you my resignation. . . ."[26] Then he wrote to his brother, "you are no longer Dept. Escheater genl. I have resigned and as your appointment flows from me you are out of course."[27]

In Nicholson's correspondence, there is evidence of numerous gifts of money being sent by him to Mifflin in return for favors. Charles Biddle in his *Autobiography* commented on Mifflin's propensity to exchange monetary favors when he wrote, "In money matters few men were more careless than Governor Mifflin. If he had what he wanted for to-day, he thought not of tomorrow. If he had a sum by him that he knew he would be called upon for the next day, he could not refuse it to any of his friends who called to borrow. By this unfortunate weakness he was continually kept in want."[28] Although Mifflin, Nicholson, Brodhead, and others were committing illegal acts, they were victims caught in their own speculative operations. Even such altruistic, political, and patriotic servants as George Washington and Benjamin Franklin contracted the contagious fever, although not always resorting to the same means. Washington, who complained in 1779 about ". . . speculators, various tribes of money makers, and stock jobbers of all denominations . . . ," had already been heavily involved in speculating in western lands.[29]

Pennsylvania land laws in the 1790s were designed to benefit the small land owner by prohibiting grants above 500 acres, but this prohibition could be thwarted if a speculator like Nicholson could secure a special order from the governor. Since Mifflin and Nicholson had a close association, the laws' restrictions presented only minor problems. On one occasion Mifflin wrote, "Mr. Nicholson has not a single friend in the world [that] would do more to serve him than I would."[30] Nicholson once selected fictitious names for 250 applications in depreciation and donation lands and shared these with the governor; on another occasion he secured 800 depreciation certificates and wrote, "I take 400 [and] the Governor 400." He later instructed Theophilus Cazenove, an associate in one of his land companies, to leave warrants covering 120,000 acres for the governor to sign. In return for this, Mifflin was to receive 40,000 acres, but his name was not to appear on any incriminating documents. Mifflin also signed warrants covering 30,000 acres in Northumberland County for Nicholson so that the speculator could have priority over rival Samuel Wallis.

Nicholson was constantly pressing Mifflin for this kind of service, and in one instance the comptroller's agent, Samuel Baird, trailed the governor all over the state. The governor complained that he could not sign because of the gout—it had made his hand sore. When still pressed, Mifflin exclaimed, "By god I cannot write. I have never been able to write a single note. . . ." He told Baird to tell Nicholson that he would sign them as soon as his hand healed. He not only signed these but others as well so that Nicholson could have his warrants validated before the 1 January 1795 deadline, a deadline imposed by a land law which stated that persons holding unsatisfied warrants could not obtain credit for them after the above date.[31]

Nicholson also found ways of using the governor to aid him in circumventing the land laws passed by the General Assembly in 1792 and 1794. The act of 1792 was designed to check speculators and to encourage actual settlement, but in reality it proved to be a speculative boon. Warrants were to be issued for 400 acres only, but Nicholson had already found ways to circumvent that restriction. In addition, the warrants when issued did not vest title "unless the grantee has, prior to the date of such a warrant, made, or cause to be made . . . within the space of two years . . . an actual settlement thereon."[32] In default of settlement, the state could issue new warrants to actual settlers. The loophole was that the settlement feature of the law could be waived if there were Indian uprisings which prevented the individual from making the settlement. All you had to do to certify this was secure a "prevention certificate" from a Justice of the Peace. The Indians of Western Pennsylvania did participate in the general uprising after the Revolution and continued to do so until General Anthony Wayne's victory at Fallen Timbers in 1794, and speculators of Pennsylvania used this situation to further their own ends. It was an easy task to bribe one of the justices into certifying that you had been "prevented" from making settlements, because despite the speculators' use of the situation, the danger was real and significant. A typical certificate would read as follows:

> Jacob Puderbaugh personally appeared before me, one of the justices of peace for the said County [Bedford] and being duly affirmed according to law saith that Jacob Neff in the course of the late War was driven from the plantation in Woodbury township, Bedford County, for which he now applies for a patten. Was drove through fear of Indians and the place left without any inhabitants affirmed this first day of July, 1795 before me.
>
> Andrew Dixon[33]

Nicholson could not only bribe these officials easily, but speculators, like himself, often sponsored the candidacy of compliant officials by recommending them to the governor. One of the justices was Ennion Williams, who was Nicholson's land agent in Westmoreland County and who worked for his land companies.[34] The governor, since he was deeply involved in Nicholson's affairs, would not question such practices. The comptroller would secure his patents and either hold the lands or sell them. Timothy Dwight, in his *Travels*, stated that in the United States, "several patents were often placed successively on the same tracts. That patents were often sold again and again in other states . . . , when the purchaser went to look for his land, he found it already occupied . . . and himself the purchaser of a mere bit of paper."[35]

It has been stated that Thomas Mifflin did not become suspicious of the practice because he "was easy going." Now it was true that

Mifflin at times did not think too clearly. One contemporary, Thomas Levis, commented that Mifflin "frequently came into council in such a *see saw* situation or intoxicated state that they were obliged to break up Council . . . [and] things were conducted there in such a manner that except when important business required his vote he 'seldom attended.' "[36] Oliver Wolcott, who succeeded Alexander Hamilton as Secretary of the Treasury of the United States, observed, "The governor is a habitual drunkard. Everyday, and not unfrequently in the forenoon, he is unable to articulate distinctly. The efficient powers of the government are exercised by Judge [Thomas] McKean and [Alexander] Dallas."[37] Despite Mifflin's tendency to overindulge, I feel that Mifflin probably was sober often enough to know what he was doing in his dealings with Nicholson, and that it was not his "easy going" nature that prompted him to overlook the comptroller-general's practices. The evidence reveals that Mifflin was amply rewarded for favors extended to Nicholson, and the governor found it easy to turn a blind eye toward Nicholson's questionable activities.

In addition to persuading justices to issue the prevention certificates that nullified the settlement and improvement features of the land laws, Nicholson often went to the governor to secure his aid in obtaining protection for settlers who wanted to establish homes on his frontier lands. Some Indians came to Philadelphia to air their grievances in 1790, and Nicholson wrote to Mifflin that the state as well as individuals had sustained losses because the area north of the Ohio and west of the Allegheny had not been settled due to Indian uprisings. He informed him of four men who were forced off their land in the depreciation district and lost all their improvements. They were put there "at a considerable expense and loss to my brother and myself," he continued, and he wanted the governor to bring this matter before the Indians to try to prevent further disturbances. In October 1790 he wrote that Indians were causing the state huge losses because they were keeping the western areas unpopulated. Again he asked for a more vigorous Indian containment policy. He might have added that Indian disturbance played havoc with land speculation schemes.

One of the practices that enabled these schemes to prevail was that speculators bought state lands on credit. The Land Law of April 1794 was passed with the purpose of collecting the money due on millions of acres of land. The act stated that all applications for land in the Land Office, if not paid by 15 June 1794, would be void. To beat the deadline, Nicholson filed for 202,400 acres in the New

Purchase, which was the title to lands in Northwestern Pennsylvania obtained from the Indians at Fort Stanwix in 1784. The counties that were involved in this purchase are Tioga, Potter, McKean, Warren, Crawford, Venango, Forest, Clarion, Elk, Jefferson, Cameron, Butler, Lawrence, Mercer, and parts of Allegheny, Beaver, and Erie. Nicholson offered a check to cover the price of the Land Office fees, but the check was no good. When he tried to offer money to the receiver-general, it was refused. The reason for the refusal could have been that as comptroller-general Nicholson had been impeached on 2 April 1794 and his activities were under investigation. The receiver-general could have feared political repercussions. But the speculator circumvented the law by simply transferring his applications in other names to different deputy or district surveyors' land offices where Brodhead and Mifflin could offer aid.

The actual settlers who were presumed to benefit from these laws protested vigorously against the use of the land offices by the speculators. Petitions were often delivered to the General Assembly in the settlers' behalf. A William Todd brought one of these from Westmoreland County praying that the land office "may be opened to all citizens in equal terms,"[38] but this was not to take place until the incoming governor Thomas McKean reformed the Land Office in 1799.

In addition to the above favors, Nicholson was able to use his influence with Governor Mifflin to secure appointments for friends and associates who aided him. In 1790 he recommended that the governor use his influence to help secure the appointment of John Wade, a clerk of his, to "one of the 4 additional officers of the United States. . . . This appointment would make him go to the western world where he might be useful."[39] A man named Andrew Russell wanted an office in the new county that was created when York County was divided. He told Nicholson he was depending "upon your known friendship & influence with his Excellency" to secure the position for him. On another occasion, Nicholson influenced Mifflin to appoint John Morrison as magistrate in Cumberland County. After securing the appointment, Morrison wrote to Nicholson and asked him if he wanted him to make out applications for unpatented lands and in what names the applications should be made.[40]

Not only did the governor aid Nicholson in his speculations but he also loaned Nicholson money and endorsed his notes so that he could pay for lands. When he purchased lands from John Hall, Mifflin endorsed the notes used by Nicholson to make payment. The governor also loaned him money which was repaid in bonds. In

1793 Nicholson even persuaded Mifflin to aid his partner Robert Morris by accepting his notes in payment for state debt certificates and then letting him delay the payment of the notes.

For the services rendered, Mifflin asked Nicholson several times to secure lands for him. In his diary Nicholson noted, "the governor wants me to interest him in [the] location of lands—agree . . . to take out 5,400 acres."[41] Twice Nicholson lent Mifflin one thousand dollars, and for interesting other individuals in taking shares in one of the speculator's land companies, Nicholson gave the governor 2,000 pounds in "49 equal payments." Nicholson also endorsed notes for Mifflin and helped obtain appointments for Mifflin's relatives.[42]

In addition to rendering each other favors, the comptroller-general and the governor collaborated on some deals. They jointly owned land along French Creek, and Nicholson complained that the governor still owed his half of the cost. In another deal Nicholson bought from Mifflin his country estate of 900 acres called Angelica Farm near Reading; at the time Mifflin owed Nicholson $6,748.70 and the latter canceled the debt in partial payment for the farm.[43] Mifflin was also a stockholder in several of Nicholson's land companies including the Pennsylvania Population Company and the North American Land Company.

Even though Mifflin, Brodhead, and Barron were Nicholson's major allies as he laid the foundation for his speculative empire, they were by no means the only ones. He used David Dunbar, one of the clerks in his office, to good advantage. Dunbar often advised him of rival speculators' activities and also helped Nicholson scrutinize bounty land operations to see what soldiers' certificates might be available. Long after Dunbar left his post as a clerk in the comptroller's office, Nicholson was still giving him money and doing favors for him such as writing letters of recommendation to David Rittenhouse with whom Nicholson had an "intimate acquaintance." Later when Nicholson was tardy with money and favors, Dunbar wrote that several wealthy Philadelphians had tried to lure him away from Nicholson's employ but "knowing what dependence you have placed on me and having a knowledge of a deal of your private business . . . I rejected their proposals. . . ." Nicholson kept him on as clerk in his private affairs after both left public office, probably to insure that Dunbar would not reveal private information.[44]

Even after Nicholson left public office in 1794, he maintained close relations with state officials. John Hall, who was secretary of the Land Office in the late 1790s, doubled, it seems, as Nicholson's informant and land broker. One of Hall's duties was to hear parties in dispute over donation lands. If some of the claimants interfered with Nicholson's title, Nicholson used his influence with Hall to act as arbiter in disputes involving his own tracts. On 5 August 1796 he asked Hall to delay the hearings involving his lands until he returned to Philadelphia at the end of the month. Nicholson also used one of Hall's Land Office clerks, William McKissack. The speculator wrote, "I will thank you to let me have a copy of my list of warrants for patening [sic] & the quantity surveyed for each & say that it has been surveyed and returned & there are no caveats, but that the balance being paid of purchase money & that they may be patened. . . ."[45] In addition to these services, Hall also sold Nicholson numerous tracts of land in the State of Georgia, transactions which will be discussed in a later chapter.

Nicholson was also audacious enough to secure the services of the man who replaced him as comptroller-general, John Donaldson. Donaldson had been register-general before his appointment to the comptroller's job, and he often gave Nicholson access to his books and records. Donaldson also acted as a broker securing Pennsylvania Bank stock for the speculator, and he endorsed Nicholson's notes in return for Nicholson's endorsing his. In 1794 the state ordered Nicholson to turn over all certificates and record books held and kept by him while he served as comptroller-general to Donaldson, and Donaldson generously allowed Nicholson to delay and postpone the transfers. One can surmise that Nicholson needed time to alter any incriminating records. As of 12 March 1796, Nicholson still had not turned over all of his accounts and records to Donaldson, but he promised to close his accounts "next week about Thursday." This he did not do because in 1800 Nicholson was still receiving letters from Donaldson, in tones of desperation, pleading with Nicholson "to shed some light on mysterious accts. you kept while comptl General."[46]

Samuel Bryan, son of Nicholson's Radical political friend of the 1780s, George Bryan, sought Nicholson's support in being placed on the state payroll. In 1790 Nicholson was instrumental in having Bryan appointed secretary of the Pennsylvania Senate. Later, when Bryan had been appointed register-general, Cadwallader Evans, Bryan's and Nicholson's political enemy, proposed to abolish this office. Bryan asked Nicholson to use his influence with Mifflin to prevent the move. Nicholson wrote, ". . . I will do everything I can with the Governor but quere—had you not better wait till the Assembly are adjourned before you agitate the question—perhaps something might be gained by it. . . ." Bryan did retain the post and processed warrants for Nicholson while holding office.[45] But this was one officer that later caused Nicholson grief. It was Bryan, while serving as register-general, who requested surveyor-general Daniel Brodhead to submit his books for examination, and this caused traumas for both Brodhead and Nicholson.

Thus by the use of his offices and contacts with influential individuals, John Nicholson became one of the dominant Pennsylvanians in the age of speculation and the major claimant to land in the commonwealth. This was a far cry from John Nicholson, sergeant of the First Pennsylvania Regiment, entitled as a war bonus to 250 acres. However, Nicholson's house of cards, based on his overextended speculations, collapsed, and a host of creditors descended upon him. Mingled with them were political enemies who joined the baying pack seeking the opportunity to redress past grievances.

John Nicholson. Oil on canvas by Charles Willson Peale.
Courtesy of The Art Institute of Chicago.

Mrs. John Nicholson and Son. Oil on canvas by Charles Willson Peale. Courtesy of The Art Institute of Chicago.

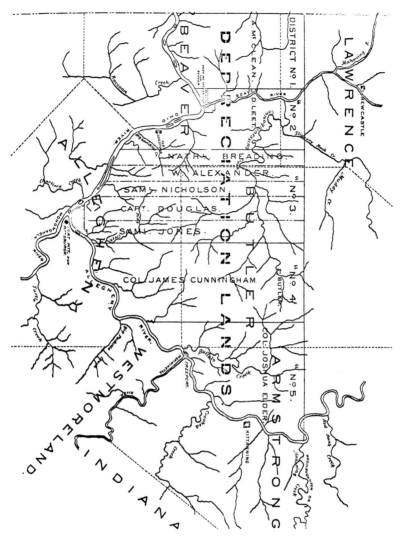

The Depreciation Lands of Pennsylvania. Pennsylvania Archives, 4th Series, vol. III, p. 92.

"Nicholson's Speculative Domain," adapted from "The Eastern United States of North America," a map used to illustrate Francois La Rochefoucault Liancourt, *Travels through the United States and Upper Canada in the Years 1795, 1796 and 1797* (London: T. Gillet, 1800), 2nd ed., vol. 1.

4
NICHOLSON AND PENNSYLVANIA POLITICS

Although revenue from land sales made the Commonwealth of Pennsylvania solvent in the 1790s and Governor Mifflin in 1792 exclaimed without flinching that "the operations of the land office . . . may be regarded with the most sanguine expectations of benefit and emolument,"[1] it was evident that Nicholson and his cohorts had made many enemies, and the comptroller soon began to feel their wrath.

Politics had much to do with Nicholson's ultimate ouster as a state official, especially since he had used his office for speculation and was therefore vulnerable. Nicholson was relentless in his quest for politicians who might be useful to him. However, by supporting some of these individuals and attacking others, he created a coalition of enemies. Evidence of the political opponents he created is present in the following letter written to him by his friend Alexander Wright:

> I often feel for you in your present situation, as the sphere you act in Sets you on a high and conspicuous emenence, [sic] exposed to all that storm which political resentments and malicious envy can pour upon you; but I trust sir, that an approving conscience, gives that peace, and tranquility of mind which your poor malignant enemys [sic] are strangers to. . . .[2]

Nicholson was a political opportunist and switched political parties easily. He moved from a radical revolutionary position to one of anti-federalism, and ultimately to federalism. His political views changed with the advantages that could be obtained from association with the group in power at the time.

The Radicals led by Joseph Reed had drafted the first state constitution in 1776, and this group, who believed in the democratic principles of the American Revolution, had political control when Nicholson was appointed an auditor. Therefore, he supported most members of the group as long as they held power and became an Anti-Federalist when conservative forces in Pennsylvania, led by

Robert Morris, Thomas Mifflin, and James Wilson, supported the new federal constitution.

As a Radical or Constitutionalist, Nicholson supported the Pennsylvania State Constitution of 1776 which followed the philosophy of the Declaration of Independence and provided for a unicameral legislature, with checks provided by the Council of Censors, a plural executive, known as the Supreme Executive Council, and frequent elections, all designed to protect natural rights. One of the chief formulators of the constitution of 1776, and Nicholson's best friend during his tenure as state official, was Dr. David Rittenhouse. Rittenhouse was Nicholson's neighbor in Philadelphia, which helped to foster a close personal relationship, and as state treasurer he had to collaborate often with Nicholson on matters dealing with state finance. With Joseph Reed elected to the presidency of the Supreme Executive Council and George Bryan to the vice-presidency in 1778, they, along with Rittenhouse, would be Nicholson's closest political allies in his early years in state office. Although Radicals were divided in their support of such measures as the Divesting Act, the depreciation and donation land acts, and the acts providing for the confiscation of tory estates, these bills did pass, and Nicholson was quick to realize how they could be used for personal advantage.

There are many evidences of the close association between Rittenhouse and Nicholson. In the elections of 1781 for seats in the assembly, the Constitutionalists lost some support, and the Republican or conservative faction, who believed in representative government without an excess of democracy, used their increased strength to try to curb some of Rittenhouse's power in the Treasury Office.[3] This resulted in the creation of the comptroller-general's office and, consequently, Nicholson's appointment to that post. Under the act creating this office, Rittenhouse, as treasurer, was instructed not to pay any public monies without a warrant signed by the president and vice-president of the council and recorded in the comptroller-general's office. Furthermore, the accounts of all the officers of the state, including Rittenhouse, were subject to the comptroller's jurisdiction and could not be closed until he audited them. This move did not provide the desired results for the Republicans because Nicholson's audits of Rittenhouse's accounts revealed little error, and the comptroller defended the treasurer when questions were raised.

Rittenhouse and Nicholson were jointly responsible for carrying out the law dealing with depreciation certificates. Nicholson, as auditor and later comptroller-general, established the tables of depreciation and certified persons eligible to receive the certificates. Rittenhouse handled cases which did not exactly fit the prescribed scales for establishing losses and also provided for the payments. In February 1781 Nicholson sent a report to William Moore, president of the Supreme Executive Council, which revealed the state of depreciation accounts. Nicholson's report substantiated the one submitted by Rittenhouse. Nicholson and Rittenhouse also held similar attitudes toward Robert Morris, superintendent of finance, and opposed his attempts to centralize the financial operations of the Confederation government. (Rittenhouse even refused to accept the position of receiver of taxes and monies for Pennsylvania when Morris offered him the post.)

Morris also wanted to establish a national bank that would help bring order out of the nation's chaotic financial situation. Nicholson was not adverse to banks, but he wanted one that would be under state control. Nicholson participated, along with Morris, in creating the Bank of Pennsylvania in 1780 for the purpose of persuading men of means to support the Revolutionary cause. It was, in Robert Morris's words, "in fact nothing more than a patriotic subscription of continental money . . . for the purpose of purchasing provisions for a starving army." But when Morris established the Bank of North America in order to help centralize finances, Nicholson opposed the move. Congress chartered the Bank of North America in March 1781 to restore the nation's credit and to stabilize its currency, and the state of Pennsylvania granted it a charter in April 1782. Thomas Willing became the bank's first president and Tench Francis its cashier. Not only did Morris solicit the aid of local capitalists but he also lured foreign investors to purchase stock in this bank.[4]

The Constitutionalists of Pennsylvania, whose major support came from agrarians and westerners, launched an attack to destroy the bank, which they regarded as a citadel of Republican wealth. Their case against the bank included the charges that it interfered with the state's right to issue money, that it refused to grant long term loans, and that foreigners held stock in it. William Findley, John Smilie, and other Radical leaders drafted an assembly report in 1785 recommending the repeal of its state charter and attacking the bank for its aristocratic and undemocratic nature.[5] Their attacks were launched partly because of the refusal of the bank to accept a new emission of unsecured paper money authorized by the state, and it was for this reason Nicholson opposed the Bank of North America.

As mentioned earlier, the Radical Assembly passed measures which resulted in state assumption of all debts due its citizens from the national government and the payment of interest on these debts from revenue, partly received from the sale of public lands and partly from an issuance of paper money. As Pennsylvania president John Dickinson suspected, many speculators had secured depreciated debt certificates held by soldiers and other citizens of Pennsylvania for a pittance and, under the above measure, would realize a rich profit. Nicholson speculated heavily in these certificates and consequently supported the Radical funding bills.

The measure providing for the paper money issue required that one-third of the total paper money issued (the total being 150,000 pounds or $400,000) be used for loans to individuals, with mortgages on real estate serving as security. This stipulation favored purchasers of state lands, like Nicholson. For example, Nicholson could borrow 100 pounds from the state using land he owned or claimed as collateral, take the money borrowed and buy securities at a third of their face value, turn these securities over to the state at par in exchange for public lands—such as the Depreciation Lands—then repay his original loan and emerge with a good profit. Not only Nicholson but Charles Pettit and Jonathan Sergeant, who helped devise and guide these measures through the assembly, held certificates in large numbers and stood to reap personal benefits.[6] The Republican merchants who supported the Bank of North America opposed the issuance of paper money to partially fund the debt assumption on the grounds that it would be detrimental to the commercial interests of the state, enabling debtors to repay in paper those loans that had been made to them in specie. The bank then refused to accept this paper money, complicating Nicholson's public and private affairs.

The Radicals in the assembly, led by individuals such as Jonathan Sergeant who exclaimed, "we are not bound by any terms made by Congress—Congress are our Creatures," were able to have the state charter repealed on 13 September 1785 by a vote of 47 to 12.[7] The bank continued to operate under its congressional charter and the states of New York and Massachusetts granted it charters, but the public's confidence in the bank was shaken and the value of its stock fell. So the friends of the bank, led by Robert Morris, James Wilson, Thomas Fitzsimmons, and Thomas Paine, launched a counterattack to regain the Pennsylvania charter.

Paine, in his defense of the Bank of North America, asserted that agitation against the bank was deliberate, diverting attention from Radical land speculators who were making twenty to thirty percent on paper money issued as a result of their funding schemes. In a statement that seemed to aptly summarize Nicholson's operations, Paine said:

> There are a set of men who go about making purchases upon credit & buying estates they have not wherewithall to pay for, & having done this, their next step is to fill the newspapers with paragraphs of the scarcity of money & the necessity of a paper emission, then to have a legal tender under the pretense of supporting its credit, & when out, to depreciate it as fast as they can, get a deal of it for a little price, & cheat their creditors, & this is the concise history of paper money schemes.[8]

An additional reason for Nicholson's opposition was also explained by Paine when he quoted George Emlen, a wealthy Philadelphian and frequent correspondent of Nicholson's, to the effect that his money was no longer as valuable as it had been before the bank was established and he would be able to buy "country produce for exportation cheaper" if the bank were destroyed.[9] Nicholson, as discussed in a later chapter, was also a major flour merchant and exporter, and he too wanted to buy country produce for exportation cheaper. Nicholson had agents in Pennsylvania establishing flour mills on his lands in the 1780s and 1790s, and the millers of Franklin County, where Nicholson's father lived, wanted him to serve as their factor in Baltimore as early as 1783. By 1794, Nicholson's counting house on Seventh Street near Race in Philadelphia was reputed to be as "public as the Bank of the United States."[10]

As a result of the Republican counterattack and the repudiation of the Radicals at the polls, the assembly granted the Bank of North America a new charter on 17 March 1787. Unlike the old charter, for which no length of time was specified, the new one was set for a period of fourteen years. But Nicholson and his friends could find some solace in the fact that Morris's bank was not used as the Bank of the United States by the new government under the Constitution of 1787. Alexander Hamilton explained, "The directors of this bank . . . have since acted under a new charter from the state of Pennsylvania, materially variant from the original one; and which so narrows the foundation of the institution as to render it an incompetent basis for the extensive purposes of a national bank. . . ."[11] Nicholson, ever adaptable, took additional comfort from the Bank of North America's existence by borrowing heavily from it to help finance his speculative endeavors in the 1790s.

In addition to his assaults on the Republican-supported bank,

Nicholson found irregularities in the official conduct of Samuel Miles, a member of the opposition party, and it was this affair that later led to the first attempt to impeach the comptroller. Miles was a leading Republican and a member of the Council of Censors. On 29 January 1783 Nicholson issued a report that revealed errors in Miles's accounts. Nicholson found that Miles, while an officer in the Continental Army, had not observed proper procedures in purchasing supplies and that he had conveyed public monies to some of his favorites.

To prove his assertions Nicholson requested and received Miles's accounts from Register of the United States Treasury Joseph Nourse. A committee of the assembly, chaired by Sharp Delany, a leading Republican, was established to investigate the charges. Delany requested the comptroller to convey to the committee his evidence. Nicholson complied by sending the material obtained from Nourse and an incriminating letter sent to Nicholson by Richard Dallam, an officer who had served in Colonel Miles's regiment. Dallam substantiated Nicholson's charges, verifying that Miles had procured supplies illegally and had given public monies to his friends.[12]

Henry Hill, a Republican assemblyman from Philadelphia County, wrote Nicholson saying that he had made a great mistake in attacking Colonel Miles. Hill said that he had been connected with Miles for over thirty years—in the Revolution, in business, and in politics—and that he never had found anything that would blemish Miles's honor. Furthermore, he accused Nicholson of taking council "from some disguised Enemy who regardless of your youth & inexperience exposed you to dangers which nothing could make himself encounter," and concluded by saying that Nicholson should have consulted him before investigating Miles.[13] Nicholson replied that "in my official conduct I have sometimes touched this man's friend, sometimes that man's friend, and very often my own friend. The representation of Col. Miles affair is not singlular, the Assembly have had similar reports from me in similar cases. . . ." He also stated that Hill's insinuation that he had taken the counsel of others was erroneous and that he hoped to keep Hill's friendship "but I wish much more to preserve a conscience that will not reproach me thro life and torment me at death."[14]

Regardless of the evidence presented, the Republican-dominated committee exonerated Miles of the charges, and the House passed a resolution to that effect. Nicholson received some consolation from the fact that Miles resigned his seat on the council, but Miles's political friends vowed to remove Nicholson from office. The move would have been so blatantly political at that time that they postponed their efforts; however, his opponents continued their attacks on Nicholson throughout the 1780s and finally gained satisfaction in 1794.

Primarily due to their opposition to the Bank of North America and to their paper money schemes, Nicholson and his Constitutionalist friends began to lose strength in the assembly elections of 1786 and slipped even more in 1787. Then the Republicans of Pennsylvania, led by Robert Morris and James Wilson, tied themselves to the Constitutional Convention of 1787 in Philadelphia—a move which the Pennsylvania Constitutionalists opposed. Nicholson was a leader of the opponents of the Federal Constitution in Pennsylvania because he feared its centralizing tendencies and because he had become the virtual financial dictator of Pennsylvania under the Articles of Confederation government. Nicholson and his friends also feared that ratification of the Federal Constitution would strengthen the Republican forces in Pennsylvania, probably resulting in a call to draft a new state constitution, something the conservatives had desired for years. Any new constitution for the state, Nicholson feared, would curtail his powers, and so he opposed the United States Constitution with vigor.

Meanwhile Nicholson was coming under the increased attacks of his political enemies. Richard Wells, a Philadelphia merchant, charged that when the ship *Anna* was seized for smuggling by the state, Nicholson pocketed part of the auction price when the ship was sold. He thereafter qualified his charges by saying that even if Nicholson had deposited in the treasury the full price received for the ship, the comptroller still made a ten percent profit by currency manipulation. Wells also charged that the comptroller obtained cash payment of his salary from Treasurer Rittenhouse without going through the customary procedure of securing a writ of procurement. This case dragged on for over a year, and Nicholson's friends charged that Wells was a "front" for the comptroller's political enemies who were plotting to remove him from office. Samuel Baird wrote that he saw in public print that a set of men were determined to give Nicholson trouble and "that they are urged along by some who have long envied you your office and flatter themselves they could enjoy the salary as well as another...."[15]

In 1787 the Republican-dominated assembly called on both Nicholson and Rittenhouse to submit reports of their accounts and to adhere strictly to legislative appropriations. Nicholson and Rittenhouse defended each other before the assembly, but their positions grew more difficult when the Republicans increased their majority with their victories in the 1788 election. Richard Peters, who became the new speaker of the House, opposed both Nicholson and Rittenhouse. The Legislature issued a call for a convention to "review, alter and amend the state constitution," despite the fact that the existing constitution could only be altered by the Council of Censors. This move, if successful, would serve to undermine the power of both Rittenhouse and Nicholson and so the latter did all in his power to block its amendment.[16]

The legislature also sought to sap Nicholson's power by reforming state finances. A committee report detailed Nicholson's immense powers and recommended that an officer be appointed to "methodize, state and keep the accounts of Pennsylvania." The office of register-general was created and Nicholson was required to submit his accounts to this officer for inspection. Also, that part of the act of 1785 which gave Nicholson a seven-year term was repealed. Nicholson gained some consolation from the fact that Thomas Mifflin and his friends on the Executive Council were able to have the comptroller exonerated of the charges leveled by Wells. When Nicholson's friends in Northumberland County heard that the assembly had appointed a man to oversee his accounts, they wrote "that these are steps ataking [sic] in order after some time to give you a finishing stroke."[17]

But Nicholson was not finished yet. His friend John Simpson told him that the great majority of people in Northumberland County were against the calling of a state constitutional convention but that they were sleeping, "for which reason matters may be carried against us." Nicholson sought to arouse them from their slumber by sending petitions for them to sign indicating their disapproval of the assembly's actions.[18] Nicholson then wrote a series of articles for Dunlap's *The Pennsylvania Packet* in July 1789 signed "a citizen of Pennsylvania." In one he stated that

> no form of government ever met with greater marks of approbation of the People than the Constitution of Penn[a]. A certain aristocratic Party joined with those who were unfriendly to the late Revolution, have been ever attempting to destroy it but . . . the people have Manifested their determination to Support the Constitution in such a manner as to deter them from proceeding with their designs . . . the present attempt against our government will end in the Same Manner.

In another, Nicholson said that a gentleman of reputation had toured most of the states and ". . . observed no States where the government was so energetic . . . so free, where property was so secure and debts so readily recovered as in Pennsylvania."[19] But Nicholson's efforts were not enough, for the Republicans continued to dominate the assembly, acquired control of the Executive Council, and, as a result of the October elections, dominated the state constitutional convention.

On 8 November 1789 Rittenhouse resigned as state treasurer, leaving Nicholson as the only leading Constitutionalist still in public office, and, therefore, next on the list for attack and removal. As stated earlier, Christian Febiger was selected to replace Rittenhouse, and Nicholson and Febiger clashed over the latter's claims that Rittenhouse had mishandled the treasurer's office. Thereafter, the council passed a resolution reprimanding Nicholson for his actions and a motion was entertained to dismiss him from office. Earlier Nicholson had informed Simpson of his success in persuading the council to undertake a full investigation of his accounts, which he said should frustrate those seeking his destruction. His friend prophetically told him to be on guard, because even if he succeeded this time, his opponents would try again. "Ambition is not easily gratified."[20]

Samuel Miles, Nicholson's old antagonist, had returned to his seat on the Executive Council as a result of the Republican victories, and remembering Nicholson's previous attacks, which resulted in his resignation from council in 1784, he headed the committee of the council which investigated Nicholson's accounts. He and his committee reported on 6 April 1790 that the comptroller-general had paid three pensioners more than they should have received, and on 9 April that he had altered the orders of the council in making payments of pensions. The council unanimously resolved on 14 April 1790 to disapprove of his actions and held him responsible for all overpayments.

At a meeting of the Supreme Executive Council on 15 April 1790 Samuel Miles made a motion that Nicholson be removed from his post, but his motion failed to pass, with Thomas Mifflin, president of the council, naturally voting against the proposal. At the 21 April meeting some of the real reasons for the attacks on Nicholson were aired when George Ross, vice-president of the council, accused the comptroller of writing letters encouraging people to take up arms to prevent the 1776 Constitution from being revised, ". . . thereby endeavoring as much as in him lay, to cause a civil war, and to indulge the country in blood."[21]

But Nicholson had not escaped yet, as charges were leveled in the Pennsylvania House that he used his office for acquiring personal lands and for embezzling 70,000 pounds of state money. He was also accused of "defacing and altering sundry warrants on the treasury for forms not warranted by certificates. . . ."[22] In addition, the Wells charges were brought to the fore again by Nicholson's enemies. Samuel Bryan, a Nicholson supporter, told him that the brother-in-law of one of the proprietors of the ship *Anna* was leading the attack and that the chief justice of the Pennsylvania Supreme Court, Thomas McKean, was also involved. Nicholson published a defense of his activities while comptroller-general in Eleazer Oswald's *Independent Gazetter* and in a pamphlet entitled "An Address to the People of Pennsylvania." Oswald was threatened because he published Nicholson's defense, and Nicholson had McKean and John Taylor, the man who threatened Oswald, bound over to the court for "attacks made on him [Nicholson] and not proved."[23]

During the inquiry, a member of the House from Northampton County, Charles Ihril, threatened Nicholson with bodily harm and two "mercenary lawyers" waylaid him on the way to his office and abused and insulted him. But according to Nicholson's friend, "you defended so well that they lost Credit in their scandelous [sic] undertaking." His friend advised him to carry pocket arms at all times. Manuel Eyre of Philadelphia County, "a Villain and only made of Catspaw," was a leader of the attack on Nicholson, and he and the others prevented Nicholson from presenting a complete rebuttal to their charges. Nicholson wrote a letter to President George Washington giving his side of the story as he wanted to stand justified in the president's eyes. Evidently, Nicholson's enemies were even trying to secure Washington's help in bringing Nicholson down. As the proceedings dragged on, it became evident that the comptroller's enemies in the House could not prove the charges against Nicholson but were only degrading themselves. Even Federalist Thomas Scott of Pennsylvania and several other members of the Federal Congress meeting in New York who were following the proceedings observed that Nicholson's abilities were superior to those of his enemies in the House, that he was growing in popular esteem because of the attacks, and that he was political enough to have his accounts inspected "but still in such a way that no person can go through them but yourself."[24] Nicholson survived this move to dismiss him from office but worked under trying conditions for the next four years. During this time many of the functions of his office were given to the register-general, and in 1791 Nicholson relinquished part of his salary because of the decreased work load.

After the Republican victories in rechartering the Bank of North

America, ratifying the United States Constitution, and drafting a new Pennsylvania Constitution in 1790, many Constitutionalists switched political affiliations and joined the Republican camp. One of these was Thomas Mifflin, whose political allegiance had always been suspect and who, like Nicholson, seemed to make political alliances according to his personal needs. Mifflin served as presiding officer at the Constitutional Convention which drafted the Pennsylvania Constitution of 1790.

Nicholson also eventually made accommodations, especially when he realized that he could not prevent the new state constitution from being ratified and that Mifflin would probably be the Republican candidate for governor under the Constitution of 1790. Nicholson's associations with Mifflin have already been discussed, but it should be noted at this point that even while Mifflin was serving as the Republican president of the Supreme Executive Council from 1788 to 1790, the comptroller was still receiving numerous favors from him.[25] In any event, there were no general party organizations in Pennsylvania by 1790; everything was in flux.

Under the Constitution of 1790, supreme executive authority was vested in a popularly-elected governor who held the veto power and large appointive privileges and who had a three-year term with the possibility of re-election to a term for nine out of any twelve years. These provisions could serve Nicholson well if Mifflin were in the governor's chair, and the evidence suggests that Nicholson worked hard to have him elected. Part of the reason for his efforts were explained in a letter from his friend, John Irwin of Westmoreland County, when Irwin wrote, "I flatter myself that the . . . arrangements of our New Government will Silence the power of that Junto who have to [sic] long viewed you as an object of their Revenge. It is my opinion that Mifflin will Run so unanimous in all the Western Counties for Governor that he will not miss a Dozen of Votes."[26] Nicholson, needing this ally, tried to insure that he did not miss a dozen of votes.

In addition to sending campaign materials to his friends, Nicholson also wrote political pieces in support of Mifflin and had John Simpson and others disseminate them in Northumberland County. Simpson reported in September 1790 that Mifflin would win easily in his area and so would Samuel Maclay, a Republican assemblyman from Northumberland who had defended Nicholson when he had been under attack earlier in 1790. Nicholson also used his influence to obtain support for Mifflin from his friends in Carlisle, and one of his lieutenants reported that the political committee there would support Mifflin and that he would probably carry all of the Carlisle area and Mifflin County.[27] Nicholson's efforts were not in vain as Mifflin won the governor's post in a landslide victory over Arthur St. Clair, and Nicholson triumphantly attended Mifflin's inauguration. With Mifflin in the governor's chair, Nicholson was still in an excellent position to receive governmental favors, and he would influence the governor to secure positions for his friends and to promote his own fortune.

Nicholson's case would seem to substantiate the point that "it so happened that the Anti-Federalists of 1787 contained many men, a nucleus as it were, of the group that later became anti-Hamilton or anti-administration, but not anti-government."[28] The comptroller, and many of his political and business associates in Pennsylvania, did not like the credit restraints imposed by Hamilton's Bank of the United States and by the Bank of North America, both dominated by Federalists. In 1793 Nicholson wrote his friend George Meade that he could not get enough credit or discounts done at either of the above banks because of the restraints imposed by the conservative directors of the institutions and exclaimed, ". . . for gods sake let us have our own a bank a going and we shall be able to get some accommodations."[29] He was as good as his word; he became one of the principal promoters of the Bank of Pennsylvania which obtained a state charter in 1793. The individuals associated with Nicholson in this venture were Anti-Federalist merchants like John Barclay, John Stanwick, Samuel Howell, Clement Biddle, Edward Fox, and John Ross, or spokesmen for the western farmers like Albert Gallatin. This act establishing the bank provided clues as to additional motives for Nicholson's support of the institution.

The state, in chartering the bank, required that it serve as the official deposit agency for the state funds; the state was to subscribe to one-third or 2,500 shares of the stock and the legislature was to appoint six of the twenty-five directors, the rest to be elected by the stockholders. In addition, the charter required that the bank lend the state $500,000 at interest not to exceed six percent for the purpose of establishing a loan office for the assistance of farmers. In 1793 the loan office was established; applications were made to county treasurers with mortgages on real estate serving as security. The bank, as the official deposit agency for state funds, would facilitate Nicholson's handling of state finances in the comptroller's office. Also, by becoming one of the major stockholders, he could help to determine the bank's policies, including its credit policies, and to staff the board of directors with individuals friendly to his interests.

Since he was a major land speculator in the state, the fact that the bank was required to lend the state money for the purpose of assisting farmers, who used real estate as security, could also be turned to his advantage. This feature would facilitate the movement of settlers out to the frontier where they could purchase his lands, and he could also secure loans from the fund using his own real estate as security.

On 14 June 1793, an election was held to select the directors for the bank who would represent the public stockholders. Among those chosen were the following business associates and friends of Nicholson: Walter Stewart, Godfrey Haga, John Ross, Samuel Howell, Charles Pettit. John Barclay, another friend, was elected president. Nicholson was one of the first subscribers to purchase stock in the bank, but it is impossible to determine just how much of it he held, because he had others purchasing some of it for him. This was probably a deliberate move on his part to keep others from knowing how much control he had in the institution. On 31 May 1793 he had his broker, Andrew Summers, purchase 100 shares for him, and on 1 June, 30 more. John Oldden procured 75 shares for him in April. By December 1794 Nicholson had taken another 100 shares in his own name.[30]

Additional evidence that Nicholson was a major stockholder was provided by a notice in the Nicholson manuscripts announcing that a meeting of the stockholders was to be held on 5 August 1793 and that a committee was established to report such "bye laws, & regulations as they shall deem necessary." Nicholson's name headed the list of committeemen, which included John Swanwick, Jared Ingersoll, Clement Biddle, John Fry, and Jonathan Sergeant.[31]

Although Nicholson was a major stockholder in the bank, he secured most of his stocks using notes as security for payment. On 19 June 1793 the directors wanted to make a payment of $300,000 due the state and wrote to Nicholson that his share had not been paid and that he was causing the payment to be delayed. Nicholson replied that "you may be assured no operation either of the reputation or interest of the bank shall suffer by me."[32] Not only was Nicholson securing stock with credit but he also was securing bank shares for Governor Mifflin in exchange for various canal company shares. The governor supported the bank, held stock secured for him by Nicholson and others, and probably hoped that the requirement that the bank help the state loan money to western farmers would aid him in his political campaigns. Since Nicholson was a close friend and advisor to the governor, he probably made him aware of the political effect of such a bank. But by 7 July 1793 Nicholson still had not paid for all of his shares, as he still owed $21,333.33 for his subscriptions.

Nicholson was so constantly in debt to the bank which he had helped establish that Jonathan Mifflin, the cashier, warned him that a notice was being sent by the directors that all notes held by the bank and not paid within twelve days from 4 December 1793 would be put in suit. Mifflin was the governor's cousin and a friend of Nicholson's; he told Nicholson when he overdrew his account, and altered the records to give Nicholson time to make up deficiencies. Young Mifflin, in offering assistance to Nicholson, got himself into difficulty. He wrote, "if the notes are not paid this afternoon it will be a Circumstance of the most serious importance to me, and may end in the loss of Character. I trust as my Friend you will guard my Reputation." And on 30 December 1794, the cashier lamented that "one Day more closes the year when the Balance of every account . . . must be carried forward to the New Books. I just give you this hint, trusting that the Friendship which induced my Conduct towards you will be sufficient on your side to prevent my being brought into a Dilema [sic] which I view with constant anxiety."[33]

Another individual to whom Nicholson brought anxieties was John Barclay, the bank's president. Barclay loaned Nicholson money to help cover some of his debts to the bank and endorsed some of his notes. In 1796, Chauncey Goodrich wrote to Senator Oliver Wolcott of Connecticut that the president and the cashier of the Bank of Pennsylvania had embezzled money which resulted in their dismissals. He also said that Governor Mifflin had taken $15,000 through the cashier "who was his son-in-law."[34] Nicholson's lawyer, James Gibson, informed his client that Barclay had withdrawn a total of $150,000 of the bank's funds to put in his own account. Nicholson replied, "I shall be sorry if J. Barclay's Conduct shall implicate Jonas Mifflin or any other Person . . . but be that as it may I know how capable Public Suspicion is to raise the report without foundation."[35] Nicholson had undoubtedly contributed to the plight of Barclay and Mifflin. Barclay in 1797 was still trying to salvage his reputation and pleaded with Nicholson to repay the money that he had been loaned. But Nicholson was having difficulties of his own trying to preserve his good name and could not help Barclay.

A major Nicholson crisis of the early 1790s occurred when his political enemies made their greatest effort to destroy his reputation and to remove him from state office. As comptroller-general Nicholson had created a host of enemies, not the least of whom was Christian Febiger, who had replaced Nicholson's friend David Rittenhouse as treasurer of the state in 1789. It was Febiger who investigated Nicholson's records and brought the charges that led to impeachment proceedings in 1793.

Lands purchased from Pennsylvania could be paid for at the receiver-general's office in depreciation certificates for the commutation and arrearage of pay, in quarter-master's and forage-master's certificates, and in new loan certificates instead of gold and silver. Nicholson and other speculators overextended themselves in trying to wrest these certificates from veterans of the Revolution. Nicholson acquired trunks full of continental paper money, which was accepted in the Pennsylvania Land Office, at least $600,000 in "40 for 1 Virginia Money," secured on another occasion 1,000 pounds of unassumable Pennsylvania debt, acquired "New Jersey Paper Money," and speculated in New York state certificates.[36] One contemporary aptly described the situation in verse:

> Then ask them for whom in summers heat they glow?
> For whom they shiver in the winters snow?
> For whom, if naked, scout from hill to dale,
> Whilst thirst and hunger cruelly assail?
> For us the Speculators answer, sure,
> For us the soldiers all their toils endure;
> For us the state shall special statues frame,
> Let soldiers, yeomen, be content with fame.[37]

But once the new federal Constitution was ratified, the state, anticipating that the central government would be assuming the debts held by the citizens of Pennsylvania and owed by the federal government, passed a law on 27 March 1789 repealing the act of 1786 and providing for the return of continental certificates to the holders of state new loan certificates. A four-year grace period was granted for the exchanges to take place. Thereafter many sent applications and petitions to have their certificates exchanged, but not Nicholson. The Pennsylvania law of 1786 enabled citizens of the state to exchange their national certificates, such as continental certificates, for state certificates, called new loan certificates. This was done because the Articles of Confederation government could not meet its obligations and thus the Commonwealth of Pennsylvania assumed the responsibility of reimbursing her own citizens with the new loan certificates. It was assumed in 1789 that the new government under the United States Constitution would be able to assume its own debt, which it did under Hamilton's Assumption Plan on 4 August 1790. Thus the Pennsylvania law of 1789, made public by Nicholson on 1 June in the

53

Pennsylvania Packet, provided for the reexchanging of certificates. According to Treasurer Febiger's interpretation of the act of 1789, new loan certificates were no longer an assumable debt of the state but merely receipts for continental paper certificates of the United States, hence they could not be subscribed to a loan proposed by the new Congress of the United States. Nicholson, as has already been stated, disliked Febiger and wrote ". . . was it not for the interference of official Business you are the last Man with whom I should seek a Correspondence." Nicholson accused Febiger of hurting his public character and image, as well as those of his friend Dr. David Rittenhouse.[38] A friend wrote that he had long known Febiger was no friend of Nicholson's and predicted that Nicholson would triumph over this "little body" as he had over the "great bodies."[39]

On 4 January 1793 Febiger sent a letter to the speaker of the Pennsylvania House of Representatives which accused Nicholson of speculating in new loan certificates and declaring them to be an assumable debt of the state. He also informed the governor, the secretary of the commonwealth, and the register-general of Nicholson's activities. He advised them that Nicholson and other speculators, including Robert Morris, had made a net profit of twenty-five percent. When Nicholson heard of Febiger's move, he wrote to John Moore of Philadelphia and secured information that Febiger used his office to speculate in depreciated certificates.

Later Jared Ingersoll, attorney-general for the state, reported that $63,075.37 worth of new loan certificates had been subscribed and redeemed by the state after the Act of 1789 had been passed and that "$60,220.41 . . . were subscribed in the name . . . of John Nicholson."[40] The comptroller then wrote letters to the House of Representatives and Senate stating that he had done nothing illegal and that Febiger was an enemy out to slander Nicholson's name just as he had slandered Dr. Rittenhouse's name. He further stated that everyone had had the same opportunity to buy these certificates and that the state owed him and all of the others for whom Nicholson had taken out new loan subscriptions, including Dr. Rittenhouse, Judge Alexander Addison, and, interestingly, Jonathan Mifflin.[41] Another reason for Nicholson's purchases of the new loan certificates, and his declaration that they were an assumable debt of the state and ultimately the national government, was that they had risen in value from four shillings and six pence in March 1788 to ten shillings by December 1789, after the Federal Government had begun to make payments on them in October 1789.

After Febiger's report was sent to the House, an investigation committee was established to examine Nicholson's accounts. One of those selected to serve on the committee was Albert Gallatin, a new force in Pennsylvania politics and in the nation, and a member of the Ways and Means Committee. Gallatin was, at this stage in his career, a spokesman for bona fide western settlers who were engaged in a continuous struggle for lands with large speculators such as Morris, Nicholson, and Wilson. Although Gallatin and Nicholson cooperated in establishing the Bank of Pennsylvania because it was mutually convenient, they were not good friends. Gallatin, in his first legislative session, had made the comment that "the State finances, governed by expediency and improvisation had steadily grown more chaotic." This would not endear him to Nicholson who had played the major role in handling state finances since 1782; the comptroller later wrote of Gallatin, "that troublesome fellow hath been endeavoring to raise difficulties."[42] The two other members of the committee, Benjamin Morgan and Cadwallader Evans, were also Nicholson's political opponents.

As a result of evidence acquired by Gallatin's committee, the House voted to impeach Nicholson and passed a resolution on 5 April 1793 directing Jared Ingersoll, the state's attorney-general, to confront Nicholson with the charges and to initiate a suit against him for the recovery of the amount of new loan certificates he had redeemed and paid for out of the state treasury. Ingersoll listed the major charges as follows:

1. The New Loan Certificates were not assumable [by the State].
2. They were not redeemable.
3. That the defendant knowing that they were neither assumable, nor redeemable, from interested motives, acting as Comptroller-General to derive a benefit to himself to the injury of the state, certified them to be assumable and redeemable in some instances; and in others procured them to be assumed, and certified they were redeemable.

The charges were published in the Philadelphia papers and later Nicholson asked that he be given space to refute the allegations.[43]

Many members of the House and Senate, like Robert Hare and John Lardner, wanted to request that the governor immediately dismiss Nicholson, but Albert Gallatin blocked the move because of the existing negotiations between the federal government and the state regarding finances; even Gallatin recognized that "there was no man in the Commonwealth so capable of doing that business as Mr. Nicholson. . . ."[44]

Pennsylvania Speculator and Patriot: John Nicholson

Nicholson wrote to Senators Jonathan Hoge and John Edie requesting that the Senate take up his trial immediately because he feared a loss of public respect with a delay. (This attitude is not characteristic of a man who thinks he is guilty.) But the Investigating Committee delayed the proceedings because, as Gallatin said, ". . . the business we are to report on is so complex and extensive that it will take up the whole of the [summer] recess to do it even in an imperfect manner." Nicholson also wrote Matthew Clarkson, mayor of Philadelphia, that the investigating committee was raking "not only Jails but every vile place where they could get some person to say anything against me." One of Nicholson's defense counsels, Nathaniel Cabot Higginson, believed that the committee delayed to try to find some proof of the allegations that Nicholson had used his office illegally and stated that they "have used every effort during the recess, after trying by every means to discover official frauds, yet they have been unable to fasten on a single instance of the sort, among the numerous documents and the voluminous records of that department. . . ."[45]

It would have been very difficult, if not impossible, to hold the trial during the summer and fall of 1793 in any event because a yellow fever epidemic hit Philadelphia. Dr. Benjamin Rush, who tried to combat the disease, warned all of his friends to leave the city, and Nicholson, a close friend, took his advice and went to his country estate near Reading. This farm had been purchased from Governor Mifflin, and there is ample evidence that Mifflin, during this time of strife, was still firmly on Nicholson's side. One of Nicholson's correspondents wrote, "the governor desired me to caution you to keep to the Farm as much as possible & not to have any communication or as little as you can with those from Philadelphia as there is danger of the disorder being communicated."[46] After approximately 4,000 people had died, the fever abated in late October 1793.

Despite Mifflin's warning about communicating with people during the epidemic, Nicholson used this time in preparing his defense and in trying to secure adequate counsel. Because of the charges of malfeasance in office and the power of his antagonists, he knew that only the best of defense attorneys would succeed. Aside from the principal charges mentioned above, Nicholson's misuse of his office in other ways would certainly be pointed out by Jared Ingersoll and others. For instance, in 1785 Nicholson acted as a "shill," appearing in person at an auction sale of state lands to bid for the purpose of raising the price. Using state funds, he purchased sixteen lots and then presumptuously asked the Supreme Executive Council to inform him if he should consider these lands his personal property. The council promptly ordered that they revert to the Comonwealth.[47]

One of the best qualified and reputable lawyers of the age was Aaron Burr, soon to become Jefferson's vice-president but then on the Board of Directors of the Pennsylvania Population Company, a land corporation founded by Nicholson. The two were friends as evidenced by the fact that they borrowed from each other on several occasions and by the fact that Nicholson tried to help secure the vice-presidential nomination for Burr in the election of 1792. Burr wrote in 1794, "herewith will be paid you two thousand five hundred and fifty dollars to be applied to the Discharge of my larger note." In fact, Burr had been so hard-pressed for funds in 1791 that he had had to forfeit one hundred shares of the Population Company stock, and by 1793, he still owed the company $1,971.30. Since Burr was in his debt, the speculator sent him an account of what had occurred and asked him to serve as a defense lawyer. Nicholson said, "there [was] never a person so well fortified as I am with testimony to support my cause and when I examine it I consider the hand of providence concerned in my having the proof of every fact I wish to establish. . . ." Nevertheless, Burr must have suspected Nicholson's "divine" contacts, because he declined to serve as his counsel but did offer to act as consultant.[48]

If there was one characteristic that John Nicholson did not lack, it was perseverance. Edmund Randolph, the attorney-general of the United States, was known to be heavily in debt. Nicholson was one of his creditors and approached Randolph with a proposition. In exchange for stock in two of Nicholson's land companies, he was asked to serve in Nicholson's defense. Since the attorney-general then received only $1,500 annually as a salary, it was accepted that a private law practice could be maintained while holding such a government position. The prosecution also contacted Randolph and asked him to help present their case against Nicholson, but Randolph refused them. During the summer of 1793, Randolph was serving as Nicholson's counsellor in his case before the Supreme Court of Pennsylvania; this involved the state's attempt to recover money Nicholson had received for the new loan certificates, in a case divorced from the impeachment proceedings. But Randolph, although he did become deeply involved in Nicholson's speculative activities, declined to serve as counsel during the impeachment trial due to his official position. He apologized saying, "I greatly regret that I do not feel myself at liberty to give an opinion upon the subject you hinted to me.... It would seem improper in me to yield to your wishes on this occasion."[49]

But before the trial began on Wednesday, 25 February 1794 before the Pennsylvania State Senate, Nicholson was able to secure three very able attorneys and two junior counsellors. It was interesting to note that most of Nicholson's advocates were ardent Federalists, the party of the largest landowners—William Bradford, William Lewis, and Edward Tilghman all held extensive lands. Bradford, for whom Bradford County, Pennsylvania, is named, had been attorney-general of Pennsylvania in the 1780s and in 1791 was appointed as one of the judges of the Supreme Court of the state. On 28 January 1794 he succeeded Randolph as attorney-general of the United States. William Lewis explained why he took the case when he said, "I have not approved of his politics, Sir, but his well known kindness and benevolence of disposition are virtues which command my respect, and I cannot but feel for the degraded honor of Pennsylvania, when I find these *amiable virtues converted into a crime.*"[50] Another counsellor who served Nicholson well was Nathaniel Cabot Higginson, the youngest of the five lawyers. He was instrumental in obtaining Alexander Hamilton to appear as a witness in behalf of Nicholson, because Higginson's father was a good friend of the secretary of the treasury.

The trial before the Senate lasted twenty-three days, and Nicholson wanted all of the testimony recorded and published to vindicate himself with the public and show that his enemies attacked him not from "mistaken zeal but from black malevolence...." Consequently, Nicholson helped to finance Edmund Hogan's account of the trial, which was a subscription volume. In fact, Hogan ran advertisements in Philadelphia papers asking people to subscribe so that he could enlighten the citizens about Nicholson's conduct as a public official, because this was the first impeachment trial of a public official since the ratification of the Constitution of the United States.[51]

To prove that Hogan's account was not entirely objective, one need only read Nicholson's correspondence which contains some interesting letters between the two. During the trial Benjamin Morgan, one of the prosecutors, let Hogan see his notes because Hogan was supposed to be an impartial observer. Hogan then let Nicholson know exactly what Morgan was going to present on the following day, advising Nicholson that Morgan was going to use oral testimony and that the defendant should object to all that was not in writing. Hogan concluded his note with, "Mr. Hogan requests that you would not reveal this to any person living (not even your own Council) because he will want in future to apply to them for their notes & he does not want to appear to any person any other than [a] disinterested Agent in the Business." Hogan later kept asking Nicholson for money and favors.[52]

During the trial, Jared Ingersoll and the other state attorneys tried to prove that Nicholson had violated the law of March 1789 by declaring new loan certificates to be assumable and redeemable debts of the state and for subscribing $63,073.37 worth after this law had been passed, $60,220.41 of which had been "subscribed in the name of . . . John Nicholson." It is easy to imagine that Governor Mifflin had some uneasy moments during this trial because he had utilized the defendant in securing some of these for himself and for his cousin, Jonathan Mifflin. In fact, one of the charges against Nicholson was that he had deceived the governor and register-general of the state in declaring these assumable. Tilghman, Nicholson's lawyer, proved that in all of Nicholson's letters to these officers, he had always maintained that the new loan certificates were subscribable and redeemable and, furthermore, that the governor never told Nicholson that they were not subscribable to the loan of the United States. Alexander Hamilton also testified that Nicholson always thought that the new loan certificates were legitimate debts of the state and nation.

William Lewis, Federalist and political opponent of Nicholson, concluded Nicholson's defense by charging that Nicholson was attacked primarily for political reasons. He said more than thirty million pounds had passed through his hands, he had been subjected to thorough investigations, and "though monthly weighed in the balance, he was never found wanting. . . ."[53]

Jacob Hiltzheimer, a speculator at the hearings and a member of the House who had voted to impeach Nicholson, remarked that "one of the Councils for Nicholson spoke nearly three hours, with much force, but argument without fact seldom prevails."[54] However, speeches and evidence presented must have influenced the senators because on 5 April 1794 when the votes were cast—with the stipulation that a two-thirds vote of guilty on any *one* of the seven charges would make Nicholson guilty of all of them—a majority of senators voting guilty could not be obtained on any of the charges. Perhaps the senators, in voting for acquittal, agreed with the Investigating Committee's report submitted by Gallatin to the House which said that "if all the duties of the Comptroller have not been equally well performed, the fault perhaps laid most with the Legislature, who had increased both his duties and his powers, farther than any man was able to perform, and farther than any man should have been entrusted with."[55]

But the House was not content. Cadwallader Evans proposed a resolution calling on the governor to remove Nicholson from office because he had lost the confidence of the citizens of the state. One can imagine the governor's dilemma at this turn of events. Nicholson had earlier written him, in a letter marked "private," that he had taken precautions so that Mifflin would not be implicated in the proceedings. Mifflin must have felt relieved when he was able to report that "Mr. Nicholson has superseded the necessity of a removal by resigning the office of Comptroller-General, which resignation, I accepted on Tuesday last." He actually resigned on Friday, 11 April 1794.[56] Nicholson probably thought that if he remained in the comptroller's office his activities would be so closely scrutinized that any appreciable gains would be prevented. In any event, there was no point in exposing the governor, since he could be of further use, and Nicholson still retained the position of escheater-general.

While in office, Nicholson handled thirty million dollars of state funds and the distribution of millions of acres of land. Although he had helped the state to become solvent, he also had used his office and his official contacts for personal gain. On 21 April 1794, the House resolved to direct the attorney-general to bring suit against Nicholson for monies unaccounted for while serving as comptroller-general. The Commonwealth of Pennsylvania placed a lien of $180,-000 on his property in 1796 to assure payment of $100,000 due the state for money he had "received in the exercise of his office." In addition, a suit was decided on 18 December 1795 against Nicholson for $11,222.50, another in September 1795 for $15,209.22 for balances due on continental certificates, and two others in 1797 totaling $73,000 for stocks and funded debt shortages. Nicholson, thinking that Providence had deserted him, wrote a note to himself in his diary: "I feel I have not assigned a proper portion of this for devotional exercises—to attend more thereto in the future."[57]

5
NICHOLSON AND THE NATIONAL POLITICAL SCENE

Nicholson's vow to resume his religious devotions was belated, for while he faced difficulties in state politics, he was also entangled in the national political arena. As an Anti-Federalist he opposed the United States Constitution because of the threat that it represented to his power and that of his confreres in Pennsylvania. In aligning himself against the new national charter, he made political alliances with those in the western parts of the state. One of his allies wrote,

> I am very confident that on the West side of the Susquehanna in this State there is at least nine out of every ten that would at the risk of their lives and property be as willing to oppose the new constitution as they were the British. . . . There is some of your neighbors in Philadelphia which if they should have occassion [sic] to travel toward the western end of this state I think it would be prudent in them to make their wills before they leve [sic] home.[1]

Another Anti-Federalist writing from Carlisle informed Nicholson that "the new constitution has a great many cordial enemies in this place. . . ." He asked Nicholson for more advice on how further to oppose the Constitution. Later another supporter wrote from Sunbury wanting to know what amendments Nicholson would propose to the Constitution since Virginia had "warmly recommended Amendments. . . ."[2] Nicholson did want to amend the document and was the major promoter in Pennsylvania in trying to persuade others to start a movement for a new national constitutional convention, but his efforts failed.

Nicholson nevertheless continued his opposition to many of the policies proposed under the new Constitution, among them Alexander Hamilton's Report on Public Credit presented to Congress on 14 January 1790. In this report Hamilton recommended full payment of the foreign debt and its interest, payment of both principle and interest of the domestic debt at par, and the assumption of the state revolutionary debts on equal terms with Federal securities. On the first recommendation, there was little dispute, but Nicholson, James Madison, and many others had questions about Hamilton's other proposals.

In his report, Hamilton called for the funding of the debt by the issuance of a new loan and the issue of federal stock in exchange for old securities brought in as subscriptions. Hamilton provided several options to the public creditors. They could receive two-thirds of the value of their subscription in six percent stock and one-third in western lands at the rate of twenty cents per acre; they could take the full value of their subscription in four percent stock and receive $15.80 in western lands for every $100 subscribed; or, if they did not want lands, they could take all stock: for every $100 subscribed, $66 two-thirds in six percent stock and $26.88 in deferred six percent stock which would begin to draw interest after a ten-year period. If a creditor were willing to subscribe half in specie and half in old securities, he would receive stock bearing an immediate interest of five percent.[3]

Nicholson used his office to become a major speculator in state certificates—especially new loan certificates of Pennsylvania—which carried a flat six percent interest rate and which also could be used to pay for state lands. Hamilton proposed to assume all state securities on equal terms with national securities, and Nicholson, content with his situation in Pennsylvania, stood to lose by this plan. It has been pointed out that of the $63,075.37 worth of new loan certificates redeemed by the state after 1789, "$60,220.41 . . . were subscribed in the name . . . of John Nicholson." Even before 1789 Nicholson was probably the major speculator in these state securities. Among the petitions filed to exchange new loan certificates after the Pennsylvania law of March 1789, the following represented some of the largest amounts: Mordecai Lewis, $293,360—the largest amount on record; Matthew McConnell, $87,272; Blair McClenachan, $74,434; and Andrew Summers, $46,230. Lewis, McConnell, and Summers were security brokers in Philadelphia and many of the petitions they filed in their names actually represented the holdings of someone else. Nicholson secured new loan certificates in large amounts from these three individuals. After hearing of Nicholson's protest against Hamilton's plan, McConnell wrote him that "Mr. Hamilton's plan is much misrepresented and little understood, you will however be pleased with it, and he allows a full equivalent to six percent but in various ways. . . ."[4] However, Nicholson was fully aware of what Hamilton proposed and still preferred the six percent offered by the state.

Despite the opposition of Nicholson and other Pennsylvanians, Hamilton's proposal was passed with minor revisions. For example, creditors who refused to take any of Hamilton's options could keep their old securities and receive four percent interest, but the interest would be paid only after all of the other creditors had been paid. Pennsylvania later made compensation to her citizens by offering to make good, up to six percent, the lower rate of interest they received on deferred and four percent federal stock. Nicholson probably played a role in having this measure passed, and directly after its passage on 10 April 1792 he redeemed the $60,220.41 worth of new loan certificates that he still held. In fact, Albert Gallatin used the same arguments advanced by Nicholson in pushing the law through the Pennsylvania legislature. There is no evidence that Nicholson opposed federal assumption out of fear of the discovery of the illegal use of his office in acquiring new loan certificates, for he made no effort to hide his purchases and always maintained that he had done nothing illegal.

An additional reason for opposition to Hamilton's assumption scheme was due to the fact that Hamilton made no provision for discriminating between the original holders of public securities and the speculators who stood to reap a rich reward. James Madison urged that the original holders be paid the full six percent interest promised them by the Articles of Confederation Congress. During the debate on this proposal, Thomas Fitzsimmons of Pennsylvania supported Hamilton's plan, which was based on a four percent interest payment. Nicholson wrote to one of his supporters in Congress, Thomas Hartley, and told him to support Madison as Hamilton's plan would be a breach of faith with the creditors. When Fitzsimmons maintained that the lower rate would actually induce more people to acquire and retain the securities and not dispose of them to speculators, Nicholson countered by asking Hartley to ask Fitzsimmons to test it. He said, "let us pay all creditors at Madison's 6% rate and then offer new securities at the 4% figure and see how many creditors would buy them," using the existing revenues of the government to pay the current holders of certificates, many of whom were original holders, at the six percent rate. Nicholson said that the original holders should be paid first and then, in a revealing statement, suggested that if there were not enough revenues, "let's tap a sinking fund that the government has—Namely—western lands." He said these should be sold not merely for twenty cents an acre (as Hamilton suggested in one of the options available to federal creditors) but for whatever they could bring. He could have added that this would enhance the value of his lands in the process. He concluded by saying that his ideas would not only bring in a great revenue but would also populate the nation, which of course would also aid his land operations.[5]

Land speculators like Nicholson were threatened with serious loss if the government securities, state and national, with which they were buying lands rose appreciably in value. This was why Nicholson was anxious for the federal government to use land and not securities as the sinking fund. It has been stated that land speculators at the Philadelphia Constitutional Convention of 1787 did not know that the continental debt would be funded at par. If they had, then they never would have speculated in western lands with the idea of paying for them in depreciated continental certificates. When Nicholson was advised of Hamilton's proposals, he wrote his brother Samuel telling him to take out 30,000 acres for him before "Continental Certificates be shut out." Nicholson had agents all over Pennsylvania securing continental certificates so that he could use them in payment for lands. In comparison, two speculators, Oliver Phelps and Nathaniel Gorham of Massachussetts, had contracted to buy immense tracts in western New York State with depreciated certificates and could not make the payments for all of the land when the certificates suddenly quadrupled in value. Hamilton tried to appease speculators like Nicholson with the idea that the increase in the supply of money and the increased circulation which his programs would bring would raise land values as well. He said "the beneficial tendency of a funded debt in this respect has been manifested by the most decisive experience in Great Britain."[6] But Nicholson was not impressed by his argument.

In a letter to Congressman Hartley, Nicholson suggested that the central government "apportion a tract for the payment of the depreciation of certificates. Under proper regulation the act of injustice would not embarass the public funds nor add to the burdens of taxes."[7] Evidently, Nicholson was trying to get the federal government to duplicate the conditions that worked so well for him in Pennsylvania, even to the extent of establishing a depreciation tract. Additional evidence that this was his intent was found in a letter written to James Madison in which he said, "the *practicability* of effecting a Separate provision for original holders I am well convinced of. I have carried into effect a similar plan in Penn.ᵃ adopted by the Legislature with respect to the depreciation debt and with a few alterations it might be done with great exactness and very little difficulty. . . ."[8] To publicize his ideas, he had them presented in *Freeman's Journal.* He also had other informants and supporters in Congress, like Daniel Hiester and William Maclay, voice his opinions and support Madison's proposal.[9] However, in spite of Nicholson's efforts, the Assumption Bill proposed by Hamilton passed the House with minor revisions by a 36 to 13 margin. Nicholson, again displaying his adaptability, proposed that the original holders of certificates be paid six percent interest and the speculators four percent.

If Madison's proposal of paying a flat six percent rate to the original holders had passed, it might have blocked the assumption of state debts which both he and Nicholson opposed. Nicholson summarized his reasons for opposition to federal assumption in a letter to Senator William Maclay. (Maclay and Robert Morris were Pennsylvania's first two senators under the Constitution.) He wrote that it would be "injurious to Pennsylvania" and would "reward delinquency and punish the forward States for their exertions whereas the contrary policy should ever prevail." Furthermore, he wrote that Hamilton's plan to assume twenty-five million dollars in state debts would require a yearly revenue of one and one-half million dollars just to pay the annual interest. "The *Fanaticism* [in support of] . . . the new government which has prevailed will decline in proportion as the people feel the pressure of taxes laid on them by it. . . ." One might add at this point that the most prevalent form of taxation was that placed on real estate. Any increases here would be detrimental to Nicholson's land speculations. He further maintained that

it will disatisfy [sic] the States such as Penna. & several others [including Virginia] who have large balances due them to be contributing their share annually of 1½ Million . . . to see it given out to others who have less due them and they getting little or none of it. Those states who have contributed least to the common cause will get more in proportion while the states who exerted themselves the most & redeemed most of their debts will be penalized.

In another revealing section, Nicholson wrote that the only way the United States could take these debts equitably would be by *bidding higher* for them and "giving them better funds than they presently rest upon." He explained that Pennsylvania funded the debt better than the United States proposed to do—and, he might have added,

65

gave him a better return on his securities than he could get if the debts were assumed by the central government under Hamilton's program.[10] Senator Maclay was influenced by Nicholson's ideas and opposed the Assumption Bill on the same grounds. Maclay published articles against the measure because he thought the Pennsylvania land office would be ruined by assumption. He felt that land sales would drop due to the increase in the value of the certificates assumed by the federal government.

One of Maclay's and Madison's major fears in regard to Hamilton's Assumption Bill was that speculators would become wealthy. The logic that Hamilton's supporters used in defense of the speculators might have been used in Nicholson's case as well. One wrote, "The holders of such certificates are called speculators, and what then? Is not every member of the community a speculator? Is it not as just and as honorable to speculate in certificates as in houses, lands, articles of merchandise, etc.?" Nicholson, of course, speculated in all of these. And Hamilton, himself, defended the speculators when he said, "It is a strange perversion of ideas and as novel as it is extraordinary, that men should be deemed corrupt and criminal for becoming proprietors in the funds of their country."[11]

Senator Maclay commented on 18 January 1790 that "Hawkins of North Carolina, said as he came up he passed two expresses with very large sums of money on their way to North Carolina for the purposes of speculation in certificates. . . . Nobody doubts but all commotion originated from the Treasury. . . ." He also revealed that Robert Morris was heavily involved in the speculations since he had been a close consultant of Hamilton's: "Dr. [Jonathan, Senator from New Jersey] Elmer told me that Mr. Morris must be deep in it for his partner, a Mr. [William] Constable, of this place, had one contract for forty thousand dollars worth. . . ."[12] In fact, by 1790 only one-quarter of the holders of government bonds were original purchasers, the rest had acquired theirs at from one-half to one-tenth of their face value.

Southern congressmen were especially angry over the state of affairs because northern speculators like Morris and Duer (the assistant secretary of the U.S. Treasury) had sent their agents into their states to gobble up securities before Hamilton's plans were made public. However, Morris and Duer were not the only ones speculating in securities with the hopes of realizing a bonanza once the funding and assumption bills were passed. Nicholson, shrewd operator that he was, had a habit of taking into account likely contingencies. Thus while he was supporting Madison, he was also buying securities. The view has been advanced that "delay and indecision in Congress worked in favor of the speculators who snapped up securities at bargain prices while the congressmen debated." The eight-month delay on Hamilton's proposals and Madison's opposition helped to establish the idea, especially in the South, that the funding-assumption bill would be defeated. Therefore, many southerners sold their securities cheaply.[13] These observations helped to explain Nicholson's activities. On the one hand, he was writing to various congressmen, including Madison, which had the effect of prolonging the debate, and on the other hand, probably sensing the inevitable passage of Hamilton's programs, he was sending agents out to buy securities. Maclay recorded in his journal that General Daniel Hiester was supplying Morris with money in order to buy securities. As has already been related, Hiester was a primary informant and friend of Nicholson's in Congress and the money given to Morris to buy securities could have been Nicholson's. By 1790–91 the latter had become associated with Morris in business ventures.

Unless Nicholson was being very hypocritical or lying, he must not have been a participant in the initial excursions into the South, for he wrote to Senator Maclay on 29 January 1790 that large sums of money had made their way from Pennsylvania to North Carolina to invest in the latter state's debt. He said the result "will be a nation overrun by Speculators." Nicholson's friend Dr. Benjamin Rush wrote to Thomas Fitzsimmons, "your funding system is to me a monster, calculated to sow the seeds of every vice and calamity in our country. . . . We must finally perish under the weight of Mr. Hamilton's 'public blessing' which you have imposed on our country."[14]

Nevertheless, once Hamilton's Funding Act became law on 4 August 1790 with $18,200,000 in state debts ultimately assumed and converted into federal securities, Nicholson took full advantage of the opportunities it offered. In 1791 he sent his agent, Alexander Power, to North Carolina, South Carolina, and Georgia to buy securities. John Young, a Philadelphia broker, wrote and asked Nicholson if he wanted to buy "$600,000 worth of 40 for 1 Virginia. . . ." Nicholson formed a partnership with George Meade, another speculator, and the two sent public securities to Europe to sell when prices increased. Their agents in London were the firms of Barrell and Servante and George Barclay and Company, the latter a European brokerage firm used by many major speculators. The company sold securities not only in England but throughout Europe.

And in March 1792 Nicholson and Meade sent Barclay $130,000 worth of public securities.

But by July 1792 the bottom had fallen out of the security market due to overspeculation. Many were ruined in what has been called the Duer Panic. Barclay wrote to Nicholson, "the many unfortunate Failures which have taken place on your side in consequence of Speculations in the public funds have materially injured Public Confidence and lowered the price of Stocks."[15] Nicholson asked Barclay to try to peddle his securities in Holland, but Barclay replied the prices offered there did not encourage him to sell.

The remainder of 1792 brought no relief as the Dutch still were not buying; nevertheless, Nicholson was able to survive the panic and, as is the case with major capitalists in many panics in United States history, became wealthier as a result. While hard pressed investors were selling securities for whatever price they could get, Nicholson, William Bingham, and the other major speculators were buying them at the depressed prices. Nicholson had a contact in the Treasury Office. He was William Barton, an assistant to Commissioner of Revenue Tench Coxe. Barton probably aided Nicholson in his security speculations as Nicholson gave him money many times. In May 1792 Nicholson purchased $68,000 worth of three percent securities and sent them to George Barclay and Company with instructions not to sell until the market rose. In December 1792 Barclay sold $10,000 worth and between January and March of 1793 the other $58,000 worth. Throughout 1793 and 1794 Nicholson was buying and selling stock in great quantities through Philadelphia broker Andrew Summers. In 1797 he wrote to Oliver Wolcott, then secretary of the Treasury, for payment for "a number of trunks of old Continental money—deposited on or before May 1, 1795." He even used stocks as collateral for his land ventures.[16]

The final part of the Hamiltonian program in which Nicholson had an interest was the Bank of the United States. He was a major formulator of the Bank of Pennsylvania because he thought the Bank of the United States too restrictive in advancing credit. Nevertheless, he was one of the original subscribers to stock in the Bank of the United States and continued to buy and sell the stock throughout the 1790s. Evidently Nicholson felt that the more banks there were, the more opportunity to borrow funds to use in his business ventures there would be. By 1794 he owed money to all three of the banks of Philadelphia: the Bank of North America, the Bank of the United States, and the Bank of Pennsylvania. In fact, his creditors were so confused by Nicholson's accounts that they were sending Nicholson's notes to the wrong banks for collection. Throughout the 1790s bank presidents and cashiers wrote notes to Nicholson pleading with him to take care of notes deposited in their banks with insufficient funds to discharge them.

Hamilton's financial policies along with contemporary events in Europe helped to stimulate the development of the two-party system in the United States. In September 1792 a republic was established in France, in January 1793 Louis XVI was guillotined, and in February a coalition of monarchs was formed to eradicate democracy and republicanism in France. American public and political opinion was divided over these events, with the newly-created Democratic-Republican Party, which Nicholson supported, generally favoring France and the Federalist Party supporting Britain and the coalition. On 6 April 1793 political divisions were widened by the arrival in Charleston Harbor of Edmond Genet, French minister to the United States. Hamilton, fearful lest the enthusiasm for Genet shown by the Republicans lead the United States into supporting France in the European wars, was able to help persuade Washington to issue the Proclamation of Neutrality on 22 April 1793. Meanwhile, Genet was making a triumphant trip northward to the capital and Nicholson and the Democratic-Republicans were making elaborate plans to give him a royal welcome. Nicholson, David Rittenhouse, Alexander Dallas, Dr. Hutchinson, and other leading Republicans met the minister at the dock and escorted him into the city.

A meeting was held the evening of 19 May 1793 at the State House and Nicholson was appointed to a committee to draft a formal address congratulating Genet on his arrival in America. They praised Genet as a Republican and as a representative of their best ally, France. A banquet was held in his honor at Oeller's Hotel where toasts by Governor Mifflin and others were exchanged and cannons were fired outside. Genet was also invited to a dinner with the Society of Cincinnati but refused because Count de Noailles, a French aristocrat (and future business associate of Nicholson's), would be in attendance. Genet lost some popularity by not disseminating money to white refugees who had fled from black uprisings in Haiti in 1791 and 1792. Many French aristocrats in Philadelphia wanted funds from Genet so that they could return to France and tell their story to the French government. Later the Emigrant Aid Society was established to help the French refugees in Philadelphia and Nicholson served as an officer and was unanimously elected president of the society in 1795. In 1793 he personally contributed $1,000 for the relief of the refugees.

Pennsylvania Speculator and Patriot: John Nicholson

On 30 May 1793, soon after Genet's arrival in Philadelphia, the Democratic Society of Pennsylvania was organized, and its charter, which stressed support for civil rights, liberty, and freedom, was published in the newspapers.[17] The constitution of the society was drafted by Alexander Dallas, and he and other old Anti-Federalists, like Nicholson, asked other states to form similar societies to promote liberty. David Rittenhouse was elected president of the society. The constitution stressed support for democratic France in her struggles against the monarchial coalition, and Henry Wansey, an English traveler, said that men holding aristocratic principles of any kind were not welcome in the villages of America.[18]

Alexander Dallas may have given the major reason for Nicholson's membership in the society when he said that such organizations, products of a revolutionary democracy, "instead of wishing, deprecated change; for the change they most feared was that retrograde one into which the supposed monarchial theories and habits of certain eminent statesmen might gradually glide." So the societies opposed Hamilton's financial programs which were changing the status quo in the direction of centralized control.[19]

Two events later split the Democratic-Republican societies, and, as a result, John Nicholson became a Federalist. These were the Whiskey Rebellion, which broke out in western Pennsylvania in the fall of 1794, and the Jay Treaty of 1795. At first Nicholson did not discourage friends who were organizing protests against Hamilton's Excise Tax, passed on 3 March 1791, a tax on the manufacturers of whiskey which injured western Pennsylvania farmers. A friend from Pittsburgh informed him of some of the first protest meetings that were held in 1791 and Nicholson did nothing to stop the protests. The complaints and discontent grew until the summer of 1794 when the Scotch-Irish farmers, most of whom were Democratic-Republicans, took up arms to prevent enforcement of the law. President George Washington delivered an address to Congress in November 1794 declaring that the revolt in western Pennsylvania had "been fomented by combinations of men" who had circulated charges against the government. He mentioned "certain self-created societies" that had "concertedly condemned the excise."[20] The Democratic press answered charges such as this by stating that the Federalists deliberately provoked the situation to show the power of the central government.

Nicholson was disturbed by the western insurrection because he and other large land owners in the area regarded it as a threat to their property. Nicholson had organized the Pennsylvania Population Company in 1792 and some of the lands of the company were in the area where the rebellion was taking place. Nicholson also probably agreed with the Federalist, Fisher Ames, who feared that the popular societies might bring on what occurred in France where property was taken for public purposes.[21] He and other conservative members of the Philadelphia Society, such as Alexander Dallas, were able to persuade the organization to go on record opposing the violent methods of protest against the government. Nicholson, John Swanwick, and others later left the Philadelphia Society because, despite the repudiation by the society of the Whiskey Rebellion, the public associated the violence with the democratic societies and Nicholson probably thought that continued participation in the society would injure his land sales and other promotional schemes.

Nicholson had agents in the state reporting to him on the progress of the rebellion. William Budden, a revenue agent and land agent of Nicholson's, reported from the former Nicholson stronghold at Carlisle in September 1794, that the rebels had erected a "whiskey pole" in the center of town and that the federal agents had arrested eight men who had done it. He reported that he and the other agents were waiting for the arrival of Governor Thomas Mifflin, who also opposed the rebels, before proceeding further. He concluded his report with, "we expect some little bustle shortly, but are well satisfied that we must be victorious."[22] Samuel Baird, another Nicholson agent, reported in October that President Washington had arrived at Carlisle and had appointed Governor Henry Lee of Virginia as Commander-in-Chief of the forces sent to suppress the revolt and Thomas Mifflin as one of the Major-Generals. Finally, Budden reported that the president would be arriving at Bedford, Pennsylvania, on 18 November 1794 and that they would probably march on Pittsburgh to end the rebellion and eliminate the "opposers of government."[23] Nicholson must have sighed with relief when the rebellion was crushed in mid-November 1794. Now he could resume his land operations and settlers could move onto his holdings.

The British caused Nicholson additional anxieties by inciting Indian disturbances in frontier regions to disrupt land operations. They also injured his export trade with their operations on the high seas. For example, Captain Benjamin Feltknapp, in command of Nicholson's ship the *Mihitable*, was stopped on the high seas and his cargo of flour confiscated because it was destined for France. He and his ship were taken to Halifax and then to Bermuda. Nicholson tried for over a year, without success, to obtain payment from the British for the flour and damages. Furthermore, British practices were hurting his land sales in Europe; Nicholson's agents in London reported that American land company shares and lands were not selling well because of the fear by some that a war between Britain and the United States might develop.

As a result of these problems, Nicholson was anxious for the United States to come to an agreement with the British that would end such disturbances. Someone suggested that the United States Government reimburse the despoiled merchants like Nicholson for their losses as the result of British practices and the *General Advertiser* editorially commented that this was insulting because it would make the innocent pay for the guilty. The editor asked, "are the United States so abundant in resources that they can lavish millions out of their resources rather than to redress them?"[24] Evidently, the administration's response was negative since John Jay was dispatched to London to seek an agreement which would resolve the difficulties between the two governments. In the meantime, Samuel Bayard was appointed agent of claims and appeals in regard to the British seizures and sent to London. Bayard also was a Nicholson agent helping to sell lands and land company shares from London.

A committee of merchants in Philadelphia was established to coordinate efforts of protest against British policies and to communicate with Nicholson's associate, Secretary of State Edmund Randolph, concerning claims and court proceedings then under way in the British islands of Bermuda, the Bahamas, and so on. Nicholson was probably a member of the committee and certainly was in contact with Randolph about these proceedings. Nicholson was particularly disturbed by British confiscation and detainment of his flour shipments to France, because by this time he was deeply engaged in the Federal City project and was depending on the funds received from the cargoes to meet his obligations there. When he heard that the *Mihitable* had been carried off to Halifax, he lamented to his partner Robert Morris, "this is a blow added to one other blast—in short we are in a strong gale of misfortune." The "other blast" was their failure to negotiate a loan in Holland because of the European War, again partly caused by Britain.[25] Thus Nicholson, anxious for an accord to be reached with the British, hailed Jay's mission.

The Jay Treaty was signed 19 November 1794 and was submitted by President Washington to the Senate for ratification on 8 June 1795.

After much debate, the treaty was ratified on 24 June. On 25 July a mass-meeting of Pennsylvania Republicans was held in the State House yard. Blair McClenachan, a Philadelphia merchant and speculator, exclaimed, "what a damned treaty! I make a motion that every good citizen in this assembly kick this damned treaty to hell!" A petition was drafted to send to the president protesting the fact that the treaty still did not settle the western post controversy. The British merely promised to evacuate these posts but retained the right to cross the border for purposes of fur trading. It restricted American trade in the West Indies, but little was said of the impressments and confiscations, and for ten years Britain and the United States were to treat each other on a most favored nation basis.[26]

Nicholson was not pleased with everything in the treaty, declaring it an inhibition against United States trade with the West Indies and an inhibition against his trade there, and if these restrictions remained, "Mr. Jay paid too dearly for the Treaty & things were better before the Treaty was signed." He concluded by wishing that the treaty would be modified.[27] But as the protests grew, Nicholson and many others feared that the House might not vote the appropriations to put the Treaty into effect and that a general rupture with Britain would take place. Nicholson said if war erupted with Britain, the sale of stocks in his land companies in Europe would be ruined. In August 1795 he was still expressing his fears in this regard, but by October he was adopting a more hopeful posture. He told a European agent,

> Stocks are rather low & flat, Clamours and Murmurs are heard not in whispers as before, but thro the Newspaper Channel, sharpened with black malignity against the President for his Conduct on acct. of the Treaty—it hath resounded from Massachusetts to Georgia—but now things are growing calm and the people who are disturbed with the calmours begin to see the treaty is not so bad.

He predicted that when the House voted the appropriations and the British delivered the western posts "the clamour will die down."[28] Nicholson's prophecy came true because the House voted the appropriations on 30 April 1796 and war with Britain was averted.

Since the Federalist Party had come to represent the large land owners and entrepreneurs and, through the suppression of the Whiskey Rebellion and the acceptance of the Jay Treaty, had shown its inclination to protect property and to avoid a war with Britain—a war that would have been disastrous for Nicholson—he moved from a Democratic-Republican political posture to support the Federalists. By 1796, however, Nicholson had become so entangled in land speculation and other economic schemes that he no longer could devote much time to the political arena. His first stop on the road to a speculative quagmire was a land corporation known as the Pennsylvania Population Company.

6
NICHOLSON'S
ROLE IN THE
PENNSYLVANIA
POPULATION
COMPANY

In the period from 1790 to 1795, Nicholson was becoming hopelessly entangled in a mire of land deals, land companies, and other speculative ventures. When one enterprise failed, he would begin another, deluded by the hope that a miracle would wrest him from the morass. He provides an example that refutes the traditional myth that debtors are poor people. Like a majority of his speculative confreres, he dealt for the most part on credit, and in the beginning bankers advanced him loans frequently. A poor man would not have had the opportunity to become so involved. Prince Talleyrand, when he visited the United States in 1794, observed this phenomenon and wrote, "There is a trait of character common to all merchants of this place—they are generally borrowers. I do not know if there is a single one whose operations do not exceed his capital and credit." For this reason it was impossible to ascertain the extent of Nicholson's fortune or even when he first acquired it. Like George Washington and others of this era, Nicholson was "land rich but money poor." He borrowed using his land as collateral and hoped that the future growth of the nation would enable him to pay his debts and reap great profits. Through the use of credit, his office, and private transactions, Nicholson massed considerable landholdings by 1794. To meet the expenses of tax payments and of promoting sales, he became entangled in many incorporated as well as unincorporated land companies, which eventually helped to cause his ruin.

His first stop on the road to disaster was the Pennsylvania Population Company, which was incorporated on 4 May 1792. Pennsylvania was a fertile field for speculative endeavors in the 1790s. The population was increasing every year; for example, in 1787 it was estimated at 360,000, and by 1791 it had grown to 434,713. Thus, speculators had an increasing number of settlers to purchase their lands. Prince

Pennsylvania Speculator and Patriot: John Nicholson

Talleyrand, who later invested in lands in Pennsylvania, calculated that if a speculator bought lands in the state at four dollars per acre in 1794, he could expect to sell those lands twelve years later at thirteen and one-third dollars per acre and realize a profit of 233 percent.[1] Little wonder then that Nicholson was so enthusiastic about this avenue of investment.

The lands which formed the basis for the Population Company's operations were chiefly Nicholson's and were located primarily in the Erie Triangle. The boundary line between the states of New York and Pennsylvania had been drawn at the forty-second parallel in 1788–89 by James Clinton and Simon DeWitt of New York and David and Andrew Ellicott of Pennsylvania, the latter both friends of Nicholson's. As a result of the Fort Harmar Treaty of 9 January 1789, the Iroquois Nation sold the Erie Triangle to the United States, which in turn sold it to the state of Pennsylvania. Joseph Brant, the Mohawk chief, denounced the sale by Cornplanter and Little Billy at Canandaigua, New York, in October 1794, because they acted without authority and received the paltry sum of $4,000. This led to Indian resistance which helped in thwarting the operations of the Population Company and brought pleas for assistance from Nicholson to Governor Mifflin.

Another major reason for purchasing the triangle was brought forward by General William Irvine (another friend of Nicholson's and a stockholder in the Population Company), who saw the need for Pennsylvania to secure an outlet on the Great Lakes. Governor Mifflin obligingly appointed John Nicholson to handle the financial transactions for the state; he negotiated the purchase in 1792, with Joseph Nourse acting on behalf of the national government. The Erie Triangle consisted of 202,187 acres and cost the state $151,640.25 or seventy-five cents per acre.[2]

In what was probably the best example of Nicholson's use of his office for personal gain, he brashly pre-empted the entire area, with the exception of some tracts retained by the state for future public use, as soon as the land was offered for sale. Nicholson's ability to do this, since under the act of 1792 only 400 acres could be granted on a warrant to any one person, was due to his influence with Governor Mifflin and to the fact that the governor was later to own at least 400 shares in the Population Company out of a total of 2,500 shares. Furthermore, Daniel Brodhead in the surveyor-general's office made himself useful by asking no questions when fictitious names were used in the land offices to cover this large purchase. Nicholson confessed that since only 400 acres could be taken out, "the necessity resulted of using borrowed names as was usual in the Land Office in cases where one person takes out more than the quantity aforesaid. . . ."[3] Nicholson simply dispersed the various warrants among different district surveyors' offices using borrowed names, with Brodhead and Mifflin providing a protective shield.

On 3 April 1792, Nicholson took out 390 warrants of 400 acres each to cover the Erie Triangle, excluding the 46,187 acres retained by the state. On 15 April 1792, just two weeks later, one of the major stockholders in Nicholson's Population Company, Theophilus Cazenove, who represented Dutch financiers, made a call on Governor Mifflin and agreed to take 200 of the governor's shares in the company. He also received names which could be used on warrants from Mifflin and turned these over to Nicholson. Some of the more interesting names appearing on the list of warranties submitted by Nicholson to cover the purchase included John Donaldson, the register-general of the state, who was supposed to be watching Nicholson's activities, Hannah Nicholson, John's wife, Joseph Nourse, register-general of the United States who negotiated the sale of the Erie tract with Nicholson, Jonathan Mifflin, the governor's cousin, Charles Pettit, one of the leading merchants and Republicans in the state, John Nixon, president of the Bank of North America, and Edmund Randolph, attorney-general of the United States. Nicholson not only used their names on warrants for the Erie Tract, but he also applied these and other names to 250 additional warrants to cover 100,000 acres of land near Beaver and Shenango creeks where another settlement of the company was planned. On 18 May 1792, after the company was formally launched and all the subscriptions for stock filled, Nicholson made application for 500 more warrants to cover 200,000 additional acres west and north of the Allegheny and Ohio rivers in the Donation District, including land along French Creek. In 1793 Nicholson was still sending blank conveyances to his friends in the Land Office to be filled in with his name to cover these purchases. Edward Robinson, one of the Land Office clerks, was given seventy-five of these to be backdated to 1 May 1792. Nicholson conveyed 490 acres of Population Company lands to Robinson for "favors rendered."[4] Even after the surveys were made on this land, Nicholson's secretary was roaming Philadelphia trying to secure enough names to fill the deed polls.

Thomas McKean, the man who succeeded Mifflin as governor in 1799, charged that Nicholson and his company, in order to have the warrants approved under the act of 1792, bribed the deputy surveyors. One of these deputies received $6,000, and Theophilus Cazenove admitted that to meet the competition of the actual settlers, the directors of the company judged it necessary to make some "extraordinary gratifications to the deputy surveyors."[5] Nicholson was able to make a partial payment for these lands by using bills of credit (presumably acceptable by Brodhead) and depreciation certificates. In relation to the latter, which were obtained from former soldiers for a paltry sum, an observer, Pelatiah Webster, wrote, "like flies about a sore or crows around a carcass, these vermin have no design to heal the sore, or restore life, but to feed themselves."[6]

A total of 483,000 acres were turned over to the Pennsylvania Population Company, including the 202,813 acres of the Erie Tract and 297,813 acres in that portion of the state bounded by the Ohio and Allegheny rivers and Conewango Creek. On 11 May 1792, the company was officially organized and an election of officers held in the courtroom of the State House in Philadelphia. Nicholson was elected to the presidency by a unanimous vote of 1,430, with some of the stockholders voting by proxy, and served as president until 1798. Tench Francis was elected treasurer and the first board of managers included Theophilus Cazenove, representing his Dutch financiers, General William Irvine, a commissioner of the United States, George Meade, Philadelphia merchant and broker, Daniel Leet, a member of the Pennsylvania House of Representatives, John Hoge, a member of the Pennsylvania Senate, and Walter Stewart, a former general of the army. The election was held after 1,000 shares had been subscribed, and because all of the subscriptions had been taken by 18 May 1792, Nicholson and the managers applied for the additional 200,000 acres mentioned above. A total of 2,500 shares were placed on the market with each share representing 200 acres. Nicholson and the others also agreed that whoever should turn over to the company a donation tract of 200 acres would in return be entitled to one share of stock in the company. Nicholson used this stipulation to good advantage as he had secured rights, through his position as comptroller-general, to several tracts in the donation district and secured additional rights through broker John Young of Philadelphia.

Initially, Nicholson was the largest shareholder in the company, subscribing 535 shares—347 to be paid for in money and 188 in donation lands. Eventually, he acquired 860 shares, but by 13 January 1796, this had dwindled to 14 because of his need to raise ready cash to appease his creditors. In fact, Nicholson never transferred the 200 donation tracts to the company as promised in payment for part of his shares. He shrewdly conveyed unfulfilled soldiers' certificates which did not give title to a single acre. As late as 1797 the

78

managers of the company were still asking Nicholson where the titles were to 40,000 acres of donation lands.

In addition to Nicholson, the other large shareholders included Robert Morris, 100 (subscribed for him by Nicholson), James Wilson, 100, Aaron Burr, 524 (also subscribed by Nicholson), and Theophilus Cazenove, 1,000. Theophilus Cazenove was the major agent for the Holland Land Company which operated in northern Pennsylvania and western New York. He took out subscriptions for the following Dutch capitalists: Peter Stadnitski, Peter and Christian Van Eghen, Isaac Tinlake, and T. Vallenhover. It was Cazenove who introduced Prince Talleyrand to American land speculation and speculators. The prince said, "M. Cazenove was a man of a rather enlightened, though slow, mind and of a timid and almost careless nature. But his qualities and his defects made him very useful to me." Nicholson could have said the same thing of Cazenove because he was able to persuade the Dutch representative to make the first payments on the lands of the company on 6 June 1792.[7] In addition to this service, Nicholson used Cazenove's brother, John Henry Cazenove, who operated a financial house in London, in his land and stock affairs. Nicholson even used the Dutch minister to the United States, Van Berekel, to help sell company lands.

Aaron Burr, a major force in New York politics and later vice-president of the United States, was also valuable to Nicholson. He used Burr's reputation to entice other New England and New York speculators like George Eddy and James Wadsworth to take shares in his company. Burr and Nicholson also endorsed each other's notes, and later, when Burr got into financial difficulties, he asked Nicholson to sell some of his shares in the company for him. By this time Burr's financial reputation could bring nothing but, "I have faithfully tried to raise a Loan on Poppulation [sic] Shares, but Find it impossible Mr. Burr Notes the Discounters have nothing to do with. They have at present so great a choice of paper that Nothing but what they call prime will be looked at."[8]

As for Robert Morris and James Wilson, they both had national reputations that could be used in promoting the company. Morris was regarded as a hero by some because of his financial contribution to the Revolution and his services in framing the Constitution of the United States. As has been stated, Nicholson did not regard him as such and opposed most of his efforts, but Nicholson, always putting profits above politics, knew that Morris could be very useful as a business partner. He had the same attitude in regard to James Wilson, another member of the Pennsylvania delegation to the Constitutional Convention and later one of the ablest lawyers and judges in the United States. Wilson was a rival speculator in Pennsylvania lands and a debtor of Nicholson's, so Nicholson probably felt that he could partly eliminate a rival and possibly collect the money due him by having Wilson as a stockholder.

The promoters formed the company with altruistic platitudes stating, "Whereas the forming [of] settlements on the Western Boundary of Pennsylvania will establish a barrier to the frontiers and enable the settlement of the other lands to be made in safety, and will promote and expedite the population of the same, and therefore promise to great public utility . . . the subscribers hereto agree . . . [to form the Pennsylvania Population Company]." The noble assertions were for public consumption, for there was no doubt that the actual motivation for the formation of the company was speculation. All six of the original managers—Cazenove, Irvine, Meade, Leet, Hoge, and Stewart—were land speculators as were most of the stockholders. And no decade was more conducive to this type of activity than the 1790s. The profit motive was clearly evident in the stipulations that the company was to hold the lands in common with title vested in trustees, that the president and managers were to dispose of the lands "for common account—and the proceeds to be divided, pro rata, among the stockholders," and that the company was to exist for fifteen years, at which time the assets of the company were to be divided among the shareholders.

Since the land law of 1792 stated that warrants taken out for lands would not vest title "unless the grantee has, prior to the date of such warrant, made, or cause to be made . . . within the space of two years . . . an actual settlement thereon," the managers had to conduct a campaign to attract settlers. Furthermore, actual settlement was defined in the law as "clearing, fencing and cultivating at least two acres for every hundred acres contained in one survey . . . and residing, or causing a family to reside thereon for the space of five years. . . ."[9]

Since the company estimated that it would have to pay for the lands at the rate of $80 per 400-acre tract within two years or face forfeiture, except in cases where Indian uprisings impeded settlement, the managers were all the more anxious to attract settlers. Therefore, Nicholson and his associates thought that the most attractive offer that could be made would be to give free land to the first families that would come to the Population Company tracts and hope that once these established homesteads other relatives and friends would follow. Accordingly, an offer was made whereby the first 50 families to settle on any of the company's lands would receive 150 acres, gratis. The next 100 families would be given 100 acres, and thereafter, individuals would be required to purchase the land. The first 30,000 acres, including some of the Donation Lands, sold for $1.00 an acre, and by 1795 the company's lands were selling for the stipulated price of $2.50 per acre. No more than 300 acres was to be sold to any one person. But even with these liberal terms the company was never able to attract enough settlers to make it successful.

As an added inducement to those who could not immediately secure the funds, the company provided a credit feature when it placed the initial 30,000 acres on the market. A settler was permitted to pay one-third of the purchase price within the first two years without interest, one-third the following year with interest, and the balance the fourth year with two years interest. The company also offered to help furnish supplies on easy terms. The settler was required by the company to establish a settlement within two years, to build a house, and to clear ten acres of land. These requirements would enable Nicholson and the others to fulfill the terms of the land law of 1792.

To publicize the lands, 2,000 copies of the Plan of Association were printed and distributed in a brochure, which also included the act of the Pennsylvania Legislature which permitted aliens to own lands in the state. Inclusion of the latter would facilitate sales to European investors. George Barclay and Company of London received some of these circulars and was given 100 shares in the company.

The managers were reluctant to sell more than 300 acres to any one individual because they feared that rival speculators would gain a base of operations in the Population Company's domain. Ironically, Andrew Ellicott, who because he was surveyor of the Erie Triangle knew the quality of the land, once offered to buy 4,000 acres from the company but was refused, "it being obviously intended as a matter of speculation rather than actual settlement. . . ." Later, after Ellicott helped to survey and establish the town of Presque Isle (Erie), both he and General William Irvine were given 4,000 acres on Lake Erie for services rendered.[10]

Not only did Nicholson use the services of Ellicott and Irvine but he also was able to acquire the services of Thomas Rees, a state surveyor, to serve as agent for the company in the Erie Tract. William Power served as the agent for lands along French Creek, and Ebenezer Denny, and later John Hoge, carried on the same responsibilities for the lands along Beaver Creek—now the Beaver Falls area of

Pennsylvania. Rees and the others not only did the surveys but also advised Nicholson of additional lands to buy and of rival speculator activities.

Neither Rees nor anyone else had much success in bringing settlers onto the company's lands. In fact, by 1795, only four families were permanently settled in all of what is now Erie Country. This extreme sparsity of settlement stemmed from the fact that Nicholson had begun his company at an inopportune time. Indian hostilities flared because Joseph Brant and his Indian allies objected to the land-grabbing treaties of Fort Stanwix and Fort Harmar and did not stop until General Anthony Wayne's victory at Fallen Timbers in 1794. One grievance that the Indians had was that the Population Company only paid them $250 for their claim to lands on the northwestern boundary of Pennsylvania near Lake Erie. Later Nicholson tried to placate Cornplanter by sending him $1,200 worth of presents so that some surveys could be finished in safety.

Nicholson naturally was quite disturbed about the situation in northwestern Pennsylvania and solicited the aid of Governor Mifflin. He complained to the governor that the military forces in the area were inadequate to protect settlers on the company's lands. "We wished not to take out families to be massacred by the Indians," wrote Nicholson, and he requested that troops from other parts of the state be sent.[11]

Coupled with the request for troops was a request by Nicholson and others for forts and towns to be established by the state. This would afford additional protection for the company's operations. Alexander J. Dallas, secretary of the commonwealth, replied to Nicholson that the governor would take steps to protect Pennsylvania citizens. Consequently, on 8 April 1793 an act was passed by the legislature for laying out a town at Presque Isle, "in order to facilitate and promote the progress of settlement within the Commonwealth, and to afford additional security to the frontiers thereof."[12] Nicholson and other speculators then offered to build roads to the town from French Creek. Upon receiving these proposals, the legislature, obviously influenced by Morris, Nicholson, Wilson, and Mifflin, with his speeches on behalf of internal improvements, appropriated 1,000 pounds for the construction of roads. Under the act of 11 April 1793, the governor was empowered to contract with private individuals or companies for road construction, and, very conveniently, Nicholson acquired a contract to build a road from French Creek to Lake Erie. Mifflin commissioned William Irvine and Andrew Ellicott to conduct the surveys for the town at Presque Isle and sent the following order to Major Ebenezer Denny, an agent of the company: "The Legislature having made provision for surveying and opening the roads, one from Reading and the other from French Creek to Presque Isle . . . therefore you should deem it your duty to grant all the aid and protection to the respective commissioners and contractors employed in surveying. . . ."[13] But Irvine and Ellicott could not do their surveys, nor could Nicholson construct his road because, as explained in a letter to Aaron Burr, "altho much was contemplated and desired here with respect to Lake Erie the executions of all hath been suspended for the issue of the Indian Treaty in which I fear little good will result to the United States."[14] Nicholson, Ellicott, and Mifflin all blamed the British for causing the Indian difficulties on the Pennsylvania frontiers that were delaying the company's operations. Mifflin was determined to proceed with the town and internal improvements early in 1794, with Nicholson and other major speculators probably lending him support. But President Washington asked the governor not to send the 1,000 troops as he had planned until a new treaty could be drafted with the Indians. "A Pennsylvanian" in the *General Advertiser* urged the governor to abide by the President's wishes, "because the *private* interest of a few men is to be promoted by this settlement must the great interests of the *nation* be sacrificed to their clamours?" He urged the governor not to be terrified by the speculators but to do his duty and avoid sacrificing himself "for sake of securing a *local* and *partial* popularity."[15]

The governor delayed the operations but complained to the president about federal interference in a state matter. The situation was eased when General Wayne defeated the Indians at Fallen Timbers on 20 August 1794. Then a treaty was negotiated at Canandaigua, New York, between the Six Nations and the United States Government on 11 November 1794. Nicholson sent Thomas Rees, agent of the company, to the parlay and Rees reported that "the Indians there gave up Presque Isle County entirely & don't ever claim to claim any part of it because they said they already sold it. . . ."[16]

As a result of the treaty, the government lifted the suspension of operations in Pennsylvania. The Pennsylvania Assembly then passed an act authorizing the establishment of the towns of Franklin, Warren, Waterford, and Presque Isle. All the sites for these towns were on Population Company lands.

But towns on company lands were of little value unless settlers had access to them. Therefore, Nicholson became one of the major promoters of internal improvements in the state and solicited

Mifflin's aid in pushing these projects. Most of Nicholson's activities in this regard will be discussed later but there was one project which directly affected the Population Company. This was Nicholson's effort to improve the navigation on French Creek. He was able to persuade Governor Mifflin to appoint a commission to explore the possibilities of improving not only this waterway but also all of the major rivers and streams that ran through Population Company lands. An improvement committee for western Pennsylvania was formed and Nicholson and other speculators like William Bingham served on it. Isaac Weld helped to explain Nicholson's interests, as well as the interests of others like him, in these projects when he wrote that "if the lands in one part . . . are superior to those in another in fertility; if they are in the neighborhood of a navigable river, or situated conveniently to a good market; if they are cheap and rising in value, thither the American will gladly emigrate. . . ."[17]

Realizing the importance of Weld's observations, Nicholson did all that he could to make his lands accessible and attractive, but getting settlers to come into northwestern Pennsylvania proved to be an arduous task. Many promotional schemes were used both at home and abroad to get individuals to settle on company lands. Nicholson and Morris employed agents in Europe to try to sell Population Company shares and lands. One such agent was Gouverneur Morris, the stylist of the United States Constitution and later minister to France. He wrote many notes to the speculators concerning the diffiiculties of the task and of the techniques that he utilized to entice emigrants to come to the company's holdings. Lands were just not selling, though Morris even "caused an offer to be held out to the Priests but they, whether they believed in Efficacy of their own Prayers or found it most convenient to seem to believe, I know not, but they declined also on the Score of Indigence."[18]

It is a cliché of American foreign policy that Europe's distress has meant America's success, but in the case of Nicholson and his fellow speculators, Europe's distress meant their own duress. All of Nicholson's agents like William Cammond, Enoch Edwards, and James Gibson, reported that because of the wars of the French Revolution, the land market was depressed in Europe as funds were being channeled into the war effort. A typical answer to one of Nicholson's queries about foreign land sales was made by Griffith Evans, another agent of his, when Evans wrote from Amsterdam that "The Capitalists here have their funds tied up in loans to their government. This includes the Willinks and Cromilyns. Willink told me the Hamburg market is just as bad. The European market will be poor until peace is restored to the continent." Part of the agents' difficulties stemmed from the fact that Nicholson was trying to sell Population Company shares at $600 each in this depressed market. Coupled with this was the fact that European investors who were buying land were securing forfeited aristocratic estates in France. Griffith Evans reported "speculations in National [French] and other property cuts out every thing & renders our pursuits very hopeless indeed."[19]

An interesting case in point was that of James Monroe, minister to France from 1794 to 1796 and future president of the United States. Monroe was a friend of Nicholson's and many of the letters that Nicholson sent to his agents in France were forwarded through Monroe. Monroe helped Nicholson in his land promotions until he, himself, began to speculate in the French property. On 26 August 1795 Edwards wrote that "Mr. Monroe is not a Friend to our Land Speculations in this Country nor does he like to be the vehicle thro which Settlers be sent there." He advised Nicholson that

> Mr. Monroe has purchased (of the owner) twenty three acres of Land within the Walls of Paris with a very elegant House & great Improvements for less than two thousand pounds & which cost above forty thousand pounds in good Times—I don't know but there are forty thousand as good Bargains as that for Sale—besides forfeited Property—in short the Americans, English, Dutch & all the world are buying here very largely.[20]

Nicholson replied that he was not sending any more of his agents' letters through Monroe nor would he ask the minister to promote his land companies. Not only was Nicholson having problems with Monroe, but the British consul at Philadelphia, Phineas Bond, was warning his countrymen not to invest in the wild lands of America, even though Bond himself was speculating in these lands in several deals with Nicholson.

But despite the difficulties, Nicholson did all in his power to lure settlers to the Population Company lands. He was especially active with immigrant groups. In these promotions he was probably trying to fulfill Thomas Jefferson's goal when the latter wrote in 1782, "the present desire of America is to produce rapid population by as great importations of foreigners as possible."[21] The population of the United States, Pennsylvania in particular, swelled in the 1790s and early 1800s. From 1783 to 1790 there was a fifty percent increase in the population of the state, bringing the total to more than 430,000.

Pennsylvania Speculator and Patriot: John Nicholson

In the years from 1790 to 1800, 168,000 more were added to Pennsylvania's population. Immigrants, and especially French immigrants, accounted for some of this increase and so to capitalize on this influx, the "Pennsylvania Society for the Information and Assistance of Emigrants and Persons Emigrating from Foreign Countries" was formed on 29 September 1794. Nicholson became the president of the organization and even helped to draft the birthday greeting the organization sent to President George Washington. The society provided food, shelter, medical care, legal and financial aid, and, above all, advice on land and settlements. Nicholson was especially active in aiding French immigrants and persuaded some of them to go to the lands of another company of his, the Asylum Company.

Nicholson and his company continued their attempts to entice settlers to their lands in northwestern Pennsylvania after the Indian dangers abated. On 19 May 1795 the agents were instructed to sell the lands of the company at one dollar per acre, to be paid one-third in cash, one-third in one year, and the remaining third in two years. The buyer had to build on the land within two years and clear at least ten acres in order for the company to meet the requirements of the Pennsylvania law of 1792. Alternate tracts of land were to be reserved for future company use. In addition, the company would help settlers open roads to their lands as long as the expense did not exceed $400. The company also granted 400 acres to ministers who would come and establish congregations on its lands. Nicholson brought English farmers to the Population Company lands and sent Pennsylvania Dutch farmers into the northwest to show American settlers improved agricultural techniques. He provided other necessities as well by importing experienced gunsmiths and cabinet makers.

However, all of these efforts brought few results. The company could not attract enough buyers, so in 1797 it started to give lands away. To induce settlers advertisements were circulated offering 100 acres free in each 400-acre tract, and another 100 acres adjoining the first at one dollar an acre, with seven years to pay for them. There was no compulsion for the settler to purchase the rest of the tract but he could for one dollar per acre on the same credit terms. The Company also offered employment for men who would come and clear company lands at the rate of twelve dollars per month plus five dollars for expenses.

Part of the difficulties of the company derived from the fact that the people who were coming onto the company's lands were not paying for them but squatting. A typical instruction to the company's agents stated that "an important part of your trust will be to prevent intrusions on the Land of the Company by persons not settling under them [Articles of Agreements]. . . ."[22] The Population Company was having difficulty fulfilling the stipulation of the land law of 1792 which required improvements and families on the lands within two years; the company's failure would result in the lands reverting to the state and becoming subject to resale. The actual settlers in the western part of the state were well aware of the improvement required under the Pennsylvania land laws and knew that if they could prove that they had settled and improved the land, it would be offered to them at reduced rates.

The settlers formed squatter clubs and were represented in the legislature by Albert Gallatin, John Smilie, William Findley, and others. They pressed hard for the enforcement of the Pennsylvania Land Law of 23 April 1794, which stated that no warrants would be issued for lands unless persons could prove that settlement and improvements had been made, and also provided that application for lands on file in the land office, if not paid by 15 June 1794, would be void. Knowing that this law was going to be passed, and in order to thwart the efforts of the settlers and their representatives, Nicholson brashly applied for 202,400 acres in the New Purchase—land obtained from the Six Nations in the Fort Stanwix Treaty of 1768—on 21 April 1794 paying for them with a check. Later, when these lands were not delivered to him, he applied to Attorney-General Ingersoll to force the issue.

Nevertheless, as soon as the Indian danger subsided in 1795, squatters invaded in increasing numbers. All of the agents of the company complained about the intrusions and asked for help. Nicholson answered one of his agents with "they will serve me more than themselves." He meant that they would improve the land and then his agents would move them off. Liancourt observed that the speculators "sue for the ejectment of the poor families who took possession on the faith of the law."[23] Aiding the speculators, and especially Nicholson, in this process of ejectment was the Board of Property which, with Brodhead and Mifflin serving as members, was very friendly to him in the 1790s. The board gave the Population Company more time to make settlement if the company could present "prevention certificates" from local justices of the peace certifying that the Indian hostilities of 1792–93 had prevented actual settlements from being made. Since Nicholson and other speculators in his company were responsible for the appointment of many of these justices, these certificates were not difficult to obtain.

In 1796 the board certified that the Population Company had rightful title to its lands under the Pennsylvania Land Law of April 3, 1792. To reinforce the board's decision, Nicholson and the Board of Managers of the company solicited the opinions of some of the leading lawyers of Philadelphia, including Jared Ingersoll, Edward Tilghman, William Lewis, William Rawle, and Moses Levy, and they agreed with the Board of Property. The Population Company, Nicholson's North American Land Company, and the Holland Land Company, each of which held lands in northern Pennsylvania, split in thirds the cost of a pamphlet which contained these opinions. This pamphlet was then distributed to settlers. However, the settlers recognized the biased opinions of the board and of these lawyers, many of whom held stock in the land companies. Thomas Collins, another agent for the Population Company, warned that the people would not look kindly on the company appeals to the Board of Property because they feared that speculators controlled it and its decisions.

The settlers received legal help of their own. William Power reported to Nicholson ". . . the Intruders are getting support from some Character of Influence at Fort Pitt."[24] The man to whom Power was referring was Hugh Henry Brackenridge, the most prominent lawyer in western Pennsylvania, and Nicholson tried to woo him into the company's employ, but Brackenridge wanted the company to give him $5,000 as a retainer. Furthermore, he audaciously asked the company to pay him a sizable salary. Nicholson and the Company were financially embarrassed at that point and could not meet his demands. So Brackenridge started to support the settlers and countered the other lawyers' arguments with the contentions that those who had settled on the lands and made improvements thereon should prevail and that the company had taken out warrants fraudulently. Brackenridge later did accept an offer to serve as legal counsel for the company.

To counter the efforts of the actual settlers and their supporters, the company secured the services of Judah Colt, one of the major land agents for Alexander Macomb in the Adirondack region of the state of New York. Colt had come into the triangle with his brother Samuel on a mission to pacify the Indians in 1795–96. He met Thomas Rees, the company's agent, and purchased some land from him. But he wanted to purchase more so in March 1796 he set out for Philadelphia to appear before the board of the Population Company to have his purchase confirmed and to ask for permission to buy 30,000 acres more at the east end of the triangle at one dollar per acre. Nicholson and the others declined to sell him such a large tract. Aaron Burr suggested that Colt become an agent for the company. Nicholson, Morris, and Cazenove then wrote to Morris's son Thomas, his father's agent in New York, inquiring about the character of Colt. Evidently his response satisfied them, because Colt was made the general agent for the company in the Erie Triangle at $1,500 yearly salary plus ten percent of the profits from his sales. Furthermore, he was elected to be a manager of the company to replace Tench Francis who resigned.[25]

Colt's instructions were written by Nicholson and Cazenove and they required that he give each settler on company land a twelve-month credit in the company store in proportion to their improvements at the rate of fifteen dollars per acre for the first two acres cleared and fifteen dollars for the construction of a house. In addition he was to build grist mills and saw mills at the company's expense and to build roads and hire workmen to clear land. Nicholson shrewdly instructed him to have settlers build so that their houses would stand on the point where boundaries of four tracts intersected and to divide their improvements equally among the four tracts so that their improvements and settlements would satisfy the land laws for all four tracts. They then sent Colt out to the squatters with this admonition, "May Judah Colt, agent for the Population Company, drive the intruders before him as Samson did the Philistines."[26] Colt may have had Divine sanction, but just to be certain, he employed from forty to one hundred men to help fight the squatters. Occasionally, he did resort to force in order to combat those who were destroying company property and to enforce ejectment notices.

But Colt and the company preferred to use non-violent means in regard to intruders. The latter instructed all of its agents to avoid open ruptures; they were to give squatters formal legal notice in the presence of a witness, present the company's title to the tract and then make an offer for the squatter to buy the tract on easy terms. If this failed, then ejectment was to follow.[27]

The company, however, tried a different approach with another intruder, the McNair brothers—Robert, David, and Dunning—of Pittsburgh. The McNair brothers claimed 240 tracts, totaling 96,000 acres, of Pennsylvania Population Company lands. The McNairs were destroying company improvements and harassing surveying crews, so the company decided to compromise. The McNairs were to supervise the settlement of the disputed tracts in the Erie Triangle which were to be held in common, with the company partially financing the operations. Ultimately, the company had to pay $23,000 in expenses. Profits from land sales were to be evenly divided between the McNairs and the company. The company benefited from this arrangement because the McNairs were assuming the settlement and improvement requirements of the Pennsylvania land laws. The McNairs eventually became indebted to the company and were forced to sell their holdings.

But expedients such as these were of little value in promoting the company's fortunes. Land sales were poor despite instructions to the agents to build houses, make improvements, and then "give such houses and improvements [to settlers] as an encouragement to get the lands settled."[28] But despite all of their efforts, by 1796 only 113 sales of 26,000 acres had been made, and by 1798 only 248 settlers had complied with their contracts in the Erie Triangle. Judah Colt's total expenditures for the period from 1796 to 1799 were $113,595.34; his income from sales was only $31,995. Settlers preferred to squat on lands rather than to pay for them even on the very liberal terms offered by the company. Judah Colt, in an exasperated moment, exclaimed, in a masterly understatement, "the obstinacy of adverse settlers renders my employment in some respects unpleasant."[29]

Nicholson and his associates also had an unpleasant experience with the Pennsylvania Population Company. Since income from land sales was slight and taxes on unsold lands remained to be paid, the managers were hard pressed to sustain solvency. Nicholson, because of difficulties in this and other ventures, was especially desperate. He offered to buy Robert Morris's shares in the company, giving as his reason, "I want to make the same use of them that you do, that is to raise ready money on them. . . ."[30] Morris did sell his shares for $20,000, but it had to be a credit arrangement. By 1796 Nicholson was heavily in debt to the company, as he had not paid for the assessments on shares that had been levied to keep the company in operation. One of the managers, John Field, blamed Nicholson for mismanagement, and Nicholson countered by ridiculing Field. It was a fact that Nicholson was so involved with other land schemes and enterprises by 1796 that he was not devoting as much time as he should have to the Population Company, but it was decided to continue the enterprise.

Nicholson sold many of his shares in the company by 1797 in order to try to raise cash to pay his innumerable debts. In this period he wrote, "I have been endeavoring to save the shares in the Population Company from fine & forfeiture. I hope I can get an advance to pay the contributions."[31] But he could escape neither fine nor forfeiture and his associates, on one occasion, thought that he had absconded. He later dejectedly informed them, "Were I circumstanced as I formerly have been I should add . . . that the sum should be paid by me within the time stipulated, but my situation is not unknown to most of you. I am without the command of money."[32] The only recourse he had was to give notes, with his remaining Population Company shares in the hands of a trustee as security for payment. In 1798, Nicholson was forced to relinquish the presidency of the company he had founded and was succeeded by John Field. The managers, upon Nicholson's failure to honor his notes, held a sheriff's sale of 400,000 acres of his lands in the Donation Tract and later held another sale of his Erie lands. Finally, on 1 January 1812, twelve years after Nicholson's death, the secretary of the company declared his fourteen remaining shares forfeited.

After the Republican administration of Thomas McKean attained control of the state in December 1799, the land policy of Pennsylvania underwent a transformation. The Board of Property then became dominated by Republicans and reversed its earlier policies—it now favored the actual settlers in their disputes with the companies. Thereafter, many court battles ensued over contested land, which cost the company both money and buyers for its lands. As a result, when a decision was reached to liquidate in 1812, the company even had to borrow $500 to conduct an auction sale. The company received $70,739 from the sale, debts to be paid totaled $44,715.94; the remainder was divided among the stockholders, and on 1 June 1815 the company closed its books. Judge William Griffith of New Jersey and J. B. Wallace, a Philadelphia attorney, purchased some of the company's lands, but clear titles to most of its holdings required long litigation. After 1812 many of the lands of the company were sold to actual settlers. Later, in conjunction with a lien the Commonwealth of Pennsylvania had placed on Nicholson's lands, a dispute developed. The Nicholson Commissioners, who had been appointed by the state to collect monies due the state, were to sell the lands the state claimed belonged to Nicholson's heirs at auction in Pittsburgh in 1842. This land had been sold by the Population Company and individual proprietors long before and the lands were no longer the property of the Nicholson family. Harm J. Huidekoper, a former secretary-treasurer of the company, wrote a pamphlet in 1842 in which he defended the right of the 40,000 settlers who had purchased the lands and were then residing on them. In it he stated, "for nearly forty years a special Board of Commissioners has existed, charged with the duty of finding out, and selling, the property of John Nicholson and none of these has ever pretended, that any of the lands [of the Population Company] were subject to the State Lien."[33] The state must have agreed with him because the sale was not held, and the Nicholson Court and state lien were abolished shortly thereafter.

7
ASYLUM FOR FOREIGNERS, BUT NOT FOR NICHOLSON

"Were I to characterize the United States, it should be by the appellation of the *land of speculation,*" an English traveler once wrote, and Nicholson helped to justify the characterization.[1] The Pennsylvania Population Company was only one of the many enterprises in which Nicholson had an interest. One wonders how any one individual could keep pace with the schedule Nicholson maintained. His memberships included everything from the American Philosophical Society to the Diligent Fire Company. Yet these activities were peripheral to his main concerns, the formation of land companies and the pursuit of other speculative schemes.

One of the most interesting of these additional projects was an enterprise in partnership with Morris to profit from the effects of the French Revolution. During the Reign of Terror, thousands of the French nobility fled their homeland to escape the guillotine. Coupled with this was the fact that the revolution spread to the French colony of Santo Domingo in 1791. Thousands of French refugees also had to leave this domicile and most seemed to seek a refuge in Philadelphia.

Oliver Wolcott observed that "the wretched remains of the whites are daily falling in here, [Philadelphia] and into the Chesapeak, most of whom are, in a deplorable state of poverty, and for whose subsistence immediate provision will be necessary."[2] Nicholson, always eager to aid prospective customers, served as president of the society established to help them. The state also appropriated $5,000 for their relief. But not all Americans looked upon the refugees in the same way that Nicholson did. Many blamed the émigré for bringing yellow fever to Philadelphia from the West Indies in 1793. Nicholson, then safely at Angelica Farm, eating garlic as a preventative, agreed with his friend Dr. Rush that it was caused by the marsh covered with water that surrounded the city. Thomas Jefferson, upon hearing that aristocratic French refugees were coming

Pennsylvania Speculator and Patriot: John Nicholson

to Philadelphia, said, "I would wish we could distribute our 400 among the Indians, who would teach them lessons of liberty and equality."[3] More than 10,000 French refugees came to the United States. In Philadelphia they congregated around Walnut Street between Third and Fourth streets, and established their own community, complete with cafes, clubs, newspapers, bookshops, and so on, many of these with Nicholson's aid. Liberals used the bookstore of Moreau de St. Mery at Front and Walnut streets as their headquarters, and Nicholson also helped finance this establishment.[4]

But Nicholson had other uses for refugees as well, and in 1793 he offered each family 200 acres of his lands free. The money collected so far for their relief he proposed be used as a fund to transport them to his lands and to provide them with three month's provisions.[5] Nicholson probably felt that once these poor refugees were on the frontier, more lucrative cash-paying customers would follow. They would also help him to satisfy the improvement and residency requirements of the land law of 1792. But the Committee for the Relief of the Sufferers of Cape Francois rejected his offer and so Nicholson drafted other plans to take advantage of the great influx of foreigners during the 1790s.

Many of the émigrés who came to America wanted to establish French colonies here and some participated in such ill-fated ventures as the Scioto Company's settlement of Gallipolis in Ohio. The most successful of the French colonies was the one established in Pennsylvania with the help of Robert Morris and John Nicholson. Probably one of the reasons why the French came to Nicholson for help was because he had a reputation as the man who made more money at land speculation "than any other man in Pennsylvania."[6] Also Nicholson spoke French and this would facilitate operations. One of the two original French promoters of the colony in Pennsylvania was General Louis de Noailles, a veteran of Rochambeau's army which had helped in the American Revolution. When the French moved out of Newport, Rhode Island, to join Washington on the Hudson, Noailles marched on foot all the way in order to set an example of endurance for his men. After the Revolution he returned to France and, as a member of the National Constituent Assembly, on 4 August 1789 proposed the acts which abolished feudalism in France. Later the revolutionary government condemned him to death, so he fled to England in 1792 and made his way to Philadelphia in 1793.[7] He had been the dancing partner of Marie Antoinette at various balls and was worried about her safety. The *General Advertiser*, in announcing his arrival, said that he came with 1,500,000 *livres*! Nicholson probably took note of this.[8] In July 1794 Noailles's wife and her mother and grandmother were guillotined. During his stay in Philadelphia, he resided at the home of William Bingham, and Samuel Breck recalled that "every day at the coffeehouse, or exchange, where the merchants met, that ex-nobleman was the busiest of the busy, holding his bank-book in one hand and a broker or merchant by the button with the other, while he drove his bargains as earnestly as any regular-bred son of a countinghouse."[9]

The second of the French colonizers was Antoine Omer Talon. When the French Revolution broke out in 1789, Talon was serving as governor of the Chatelet and criminal prosecutor. He later became chief justice of the Criminal Court of France and chief of the king's secret service; in 1792 he attempted to smuggle the king safely out of France. When his plot was discovered, he was forced to make his escape to England concealed in a wine cask. He joined Noailles in Philadelphia in 1793.[10] Alexander Graydon in his *Memoirs* described Talon in this manner:

> I have seldom seen a gentleman with whose manners I was more pleased. Though he spoke little English, and I less French, yet from the knowledge we had of each others language, we contrived to make ourselves mutually understood. On one of his visits to Harrisburg he was attended by not less than ten or a dozen gentlemen, all adventurers in the new establishment [Asylum] from which they had just returned on their way to Philadelphia. . . . Talon had been adverse to the Revolution in France in all of its stages and modifications. He was the person on account of whose courteous reception George Washington had been roundly taken to task by the Citizen Genet.[11]

Noailles and Talon sent emissaries in the persons of Charles Felix Bui Boulogne and Adam Hoops to explore possible sites for the proposed colony in 1793. Hoops had been a former officer who had served under General Sullivan in his expedition against the Indians in 1779, a surveyor for Morris of lands he purchased from Phelps and Gorham in New York, and later, founder of Olean, New York.

Boulogne was familiar with land speculations and colonization schemes as he had been associated with the Scioto debacle. He contacted Nicholson about buying lands for the proposed colony, and Nicholson offered him 60,000 acres at one dollar per acre payable one-half in cash and the remainder in two installments. After consulting with his fellow colonizers, Boulogne informed Nicholson that the promoters needed more land than that proposed, so the speculator offered him 160,000 to 320,000 acres on the same terms, located between the Delaware River and the east branch of the Susquehanna. Boulogne and Hoops made a trip to inspect these and Robert Morris's lands in that area, and Nicholson wrote river trader Mathias Hollenback, whose fur trading business Nicholson had helped finance, to offer them assistance. Boulogne and Hoops were shown locations along the upper Susquehanna. The emissaries were instructed to select a site that was remote—for security purposes, close to water communications with the coast and interior, partly under cultivation, abundant in natural resources, and occupied with friendly Indians. The location that they selected was land owned by Morris and Nicholson in the present Bradford-Wyoming section of Pennsylvania. Noailles and Talon then negotiated with the speculators to purchase 200,000 acres in this area where they planned a colony to be located on the Susquehanna twelve miles downstream from the present town of Towanda.

When Boulogne and Hoops arrived at this site, they found some settlers already there. They were Yankees who held titles to the land from the State of Connecticut, purchased from the Susquehanna Company. Connecticut claimed the Wyoming Valley under the terms of its colonial charter. The Susquehanna Company had been in existence since 1753 establishing settlers in the valley. Under the Decree of Trenton of 1782, Pennsylvania was given title to the land and jurisdiction, but the decree did not deal with the question of the private title to the soil. Connecticut settlers were on the land and the Susquehanna Company continued to exist and to urge the settlers to remain on the land and contest Pennsylvania's claims. Pennsylvania land speculators and settlers then acquired title from Pennsylvania, and a law of the state legislature in 1790 reaffirmed the Decree of Trenton, rescinded the Connecticut titles to the area, and validated those of Pennsylvania.[12] Nicholson was buying lands in the Wyoming Valley in the 1780s, lands which later became part of the Asylum Company, and he wrote to one of his land agents that the Pennsylvania claims should take precedence over the intruders. His agent replied, "the first evident mark of the Decadence of the Roman Empire if I recollect right was a similar measure in favor of the Goths (allowing them to settle in their domains)."[13] Facilitating Nicholson in the acquisition of these lands was his position as comptroller-general. He made tours throughout the area collecting taxes, buying lands, and telling his wife not to worry as he was well armed against the Yankees. He then sent settlers into the Wilkes-Barre area to solidify his claims and established a store. In fact, by 1794, Nicholson through his brother-in-law and agent, Joseph Duncan, had a monopoly on the town lots and on the surrounding mountains in Wilkes-Barre, except for a few owned by the Hollenbacks and Timothy Pickering.

Because court litigations involving the rival claimants were in progress when Talon and Noailles decided to establish their colony, the Frenchmen insisted on securing both Pennsylvania and Connecticut titles to the Asylum tract. Consequently, Mathias Hollenback was charged with procuring the Connecticut claims and Robert Morris with securing the Pennsylvania titles. Morris thought the Frenchmen were paying too much for the Connecticut claims, and he preferred to threaten the intruders with ejectment if they would not sell rather than pay high prices. Hollenback paid from $133 to $800 for the lots at Asylum out of his own pocket expecting Morris and Nicholson to make compensation later. Hollenback could expect this from Nicholson as the two had worked together in the past when Nicholson had helped to outfit his trading expeditions along the Susquehanna in return for valuable information on desirable lands in the area and a share of the profits. Nevertheless, Hollenback was not paid for the advances he made, and in 1795, after Nicholson had taken almost complete control of the enterprise, he wrote to Nicholson and Morris and demanded payment, threatening to sue if he were not paid. Long after Nicholson died, Hollenback was still seeking payment.[14]

With the titles secured, the Frenchmen began their settlement on the Susquehanna, which they called Asylum, and supposedly a *Grand Maison* was prepared for the fallen queen, Marie Antoinette. Talon, after his arrival in December 1793, supervised the operations at Asylum while Noailles handled affairs in Philadelphia. Talon took pride in the building of the *Grand Maison*, a vast structure eighty-four feet long and three stories high with French windows and two great fireplaces. There is near unanimity among the historians of the colony as to the authenticity of the "Queen Legend." But, even though some altruism might have motivated Noailles and Talon, it seems that the rumor of the queen's impending presence might have been a device to attract settlers to the area. It seems unlikely that the republican Noailles and the royalist Talon would have united to bring Marie Antoinette to America. It is more credible to view the project as a land promotion scheme especially considering that no mention was made of the queen's house but only of the *Grand Maison*, which was Talon's residence for the duration of the project.[15] Talleyrand observed, when he visited the colony in 1794, that Talon was living in the house with women, a French cook, "and everything that could persuade purchasers that they are not arriving at a wild place."[16] If the mansion were indeed intended for the queen, these plans were thwarted on 16 October 1793 by the guillotine. Some Pennsylvanians in the vicinity of Asylum welcomed the news of the queen's demise. An innkeeper erected a sign on which was depicted a decapitated female, the head lying beside the bleeding trunk.

Initially Boulogne and then Montulle, an exiled army captain, were entrusted with the clearing of lands and the erection of the town buildings. The building materials were supplied by Hollenback and shipped up river from Wilkes-Barre in Durham boats—a four or five day journey. John Keating, an Irish refugee from Santo Domingo, also joined the colony and helped to survey rectangular street patterns, establishing the 413 town lots of one acre each, and to lay out the central market square with a broad avenue leading from it to the river landing. At its peak, the settlement had forty or fifty houses, inns, shops, a chapel, a theater, a blacksmith shop, and a bakery. The only thing it lacked were colonists and this was a major reason for Asylum becoming one of the first ghost towns in United States history. A major reason for its failure was explained by Talleyrand, whom Nicholson and Morris should have consulted before becoming involved in the project. In 1794 he said it was a mistake for American speculators to rely on French émigrés to buy and settle their lands because all Frenchmen long to return home and would, if and when a general amnesty were granted. "Do not count on that class of emigrants to clear the forests of America!," he warned. He also related that most Frenchmen with royalist sentiments, such as those who were expected to come to Asylum, were being welcomed by Catherine the Great of Russia who gave them lands gratis; also, their aristocratic prejudices would be placated there and not in republican America. As a result, there were only about forty inhabitants in Asylum when Talleyrand visited it in 1794.[17]

But Nicholson and Morris did not seek Talleyrand's advice and when Talon and Noailles ran out of money and could not make the payments due the speculators, the latter came forth with a proposal. Partly out of an interest in the welfare of the exiles and partly because a thriving settlement in northern Pennsylvania would increase the value of their holdings, the speculators agreed to form a land company with Noailles and Talon to try and save the project.

The capital for the Asylum Company consisted of one million acres—in what are now Sullivan, Lycoming, and Bradford counties—for which the speculators held warrants. Titles to the land were held by two trustees, Jared Ingersoll, the attorney-general of the state, and Matthew Clarkson, the mayor of Philadelphia; a Board of Managers was formed to supervise the sale of stock. Five thousand shares were offered of 200 acres each and the land was sold for two dollars an acre. Noailles and Talon each received shares totaling 6,000 acres. To induce sales, Nicholson and Morris added a guarantee of six percent interest on each $500 share, but as usual, the two had to borrow in an attempt to honor this pledge. The company also agreed that at the end of three years, in addition to paying six percent interest on shares, an option would be given that would enable the purchaser to sell his shares back to the company at the original price.

In regard to this offer, the speculators were probably hopeful that by making such a guarantee, settlers would flock to the Asylum tract, build settlements and transportation facilities, and thereby raise the value of adjacent lands held by Nicholson and Morris. Nicholson further pledged to guarantee one-third of the shares, and credit was extended to the refugees for five years, with a six percent interest charge in the third year. The speculators maintained a supply agency, Nicholson's store at Wilkes-Barre, where buyers could obtain needed articles on credit. Lest the price of a dollar an acre and the credit features appear generous, one should note that the speculators had secured this land for fifteen cents an acre but "much had been spent in promoting and surveying."[18]

From 1794 to 1796 Morris and especially Nicholson did everything in their power to make the company a success. They hired as agents for the company Charles Boulogne, Adam Hoops, James Duncan, and John Keating. Nicholson, always the shrewd operator, previously had sent trusted agent and friend Samuel Baird into the Asylum area ostensibly to survey some of Nicholson's lands nearby, but also to report to him on the activities of the Frenchmen. Baird wrote, "I have found little difficulty in covering my real views here from everyone, even Hoops, I think, has not the least suspicion of them." Baird did do some surveying and reported to Nicholson one of the hazards of his profession when he wrote, "you must excuse me from writing more as miraids [sic] of skunks and musquitoes [sic] are pestering me altho I am setting in the smoak [sic] of six fires made to drive them off."[19]

Boulogne was angry because the others were receiving salaries of

$1,000 to $1,200, whereas he, who could speak French and knew accounts, was only receiving $800. Nicholson, to maintain harmony, raised his salary to $1,000 and also gave him some shares in the company as compensation. Boulogne did not forget the favor and not only sold Asylum Company shares and lands but also served as Nicholson's agent in selling his lands located in Northumberland and Westmoreland counties, which were not part of the Asylum project. In 1796 Boulogne drowned in a stream near Asylum and his widow turned to Nicholson for assistance. It might be well to add at this point that Nicholson was besieged constantly by downtrodden individuals seeking help.[20]

Aside from trying to keep their agents content, Nicholson and Morris were interested in continuing the roads begun by Talon and adding new ones. They finished what is still known as the Old French Road from Asylum to Laddsburg, and Nicholson and Morris subscribed to a corporation to construct a road through the Wyoming Valley. In 1795, Nicholson, with the support of Dr. Joseph Priestley and others, started a road from Asylum to the west branch of the Susquehanna, and agent John Keating in 1796 asked Nicholson to use his influence with Governor Mifflin to have the proposed road from Northampton to Tioga pass through Asylum because "it will be of infinite advantage to the Settlement."[21] In addition to the roads, Nicholson also had plans to establish a college, school, and rural bank to attract settlers.

By April 1795 the company was floundering and so was Robert Morris. Nicholson offered to buy Morris's shares in the company and Morris agreed. Morris sold him shares amounting to $487,375.45. But Morris owed Nicholson money so when the deductions were made, Nicholson only paid $464,479.84 for the shares. As part of the deal, Nicholson agreed to transfer his titles to 80,830 acres in the county of Luzerne, between the Susquehanna and Delaware rivers, to James Donatianus Le Ray De Chaumont in 1797. Chaumont's father was Grand Master of the Waters and Forests in France and Honorary Intendant of the Invalides. Chaumont had purchased lands from Morris in New York and he later intended to use this and the tract transferred to him by Nicholson to establish a refugee colony similar to Asylum. All that remains to remind us of his efforts is a town called Le Raysville in Bradford County, Pennsylvania.[22]

Nicholson had already purchased most of the shares held by Talon and Noailles in the company and so by 1796 was almost the sole proprietor. Noailles retained fifty shares and Talon one hundred, but Nicholson had bought their others on the condition that both

Frenchmen serve as agents for the company. Nicholson was well aware of their contacts in Europe, and he needed these contacts if he hoped to salvage the company.

Nicholson then reorganized the enterprise and his scheme was described by Liancourt when he wrote,

> Mr. Robert Morris has entirely left it, and Mr. Nicholson, being now the only proprietor, has formed a bank of his million acres, divided into 5,000 shares containing 200 acres, the price of which is $2.50 per acre. . . . If the company shall proceed with judgment and prudence . . . there can hardly remain a doubt that the Asylum will speedily become a place of importance.[23]

Nicholson, as president of the concern, tried to make this dream come true by attempting various promotional and organizational schemes. The new board of managers consisted of John Ashley, William Crammond, James Gibson, and General Noailles. Town lots were to sell for twenty dollars each and the surrounding lots at five and seven pounds, ten shillings per acre. Nicholson also stipulated that the lands and lots could be paid for at one-half in cash and the remainder in three-years plus interest, but the buyer had to have a family reside on every 400 acres within two years of the purchase.[24]

Nicholson then dispatched Talon to Europe at an annual salary of $3,000, plus five percent commission, to sell Asylum Company shares and lands. Noailles also made a contract with Nicholson to sell lands, and agents Hoops, Keating, and Duncan were offered a commission according to the number of sales made, in addition to their basic $1,000 salaries. Talon went to Paris and Amsterdam in an attempt to sell Asylum shares and was surprised to find upon his arrival in Paris that he had also been given Population Company and North American Land Company shares to sell as well. The latter was another of Nicholson's enterprises which will be considered later. Evidently, Nicholson thought there was strength in numbers and variety. Talon was offering 300,000 acres of Asylum lands at two and one-half dollars per acre out of which he promised a two and one-half percent commission to a sub-agent he had hired. He did not have much success and later wanted to lower the selling price, but Nicholson stubbornly refused, saying that this would be cheating the stockholders. Talon traveled about in England, Germany, Holland, and France trying to sell land company shares and on one occasion wrote Nicholson that he had negotiated a deal for 300,000 acres at three dollars per acre. One month later, however, he reported that the sale could not be consummated and that prospects would remain poor as long as war raged in Europe.[25] The market was so depressed in Europe that Nicholson had another agent, Enoch Edwards, return the Asylum shares that he was trying to sell in Paris; he said that he probably could do better with them in Philadelphia.[26]

One of the difficulties, in addition to the wars raging in Europe, was that certain Europeans, like the French minister Fauchet, were warning Frenchmen against buying Nicholson and Morris land company shares. Nicholson and Morris sent rebuttals to Europe for their agents to publish in the European newspapers to counter these caveats. Another problem for the Asylum Company ironically developed from the fact that Nicholson had so many other companies in operation at the same time. The shares of his various companies were actually competing with each other in the European markets. Charles Cadignan, agent in London, informed Nicholson that he could not sell Asylum Company shares because the North American Land Company shares were more in demand.[27] Talleyrand summarized the company's plight in regard to buyers in explaining why he would not participate in the Asylum project. He wrote, "When one has a good scheme to propose it is not necessary to have three or four agents in England, as many in France, eight in Holland, and several in American ports to keep watch for arrivals."[28]

While Nicholson was trying to lure Europeans to come to the company's lands, he was also personally supervising some of the economic pursuits of the Asylum settlement in order to increase its prospect. He had acquired an early interest in the production of potash which was used in the making of soap, fertilizer, and glass. Potash revenues would not only help the settlers at Asylum, but Nicholson could use the material in his glass works which was located at the Falls of the Schuylkill, then about four miles from Philadelphia. He had earlier tried to secure state aid for the potash industry in Pennsylvania but with little success. The Asylum project was admirably suited for potash and pearl ash production because it usually developed in locations where money was scarce, transportation difficult, and an industry or product to bear the cost of transportation to market necessary. Salts of lye were secured from the ashes of burned wood, by-products of the clearing of forests and of the burning of fireplaces. Ashes of green wood and oak were preferred, and ashes five or six months old were better than new ashes for potash production. Generally 500–600 bushels of ashes produced one ton of potash. Pearl ash was potash purified by calcination—that is, potash was put into a kiln made of plaster of Paris and the intense heat converted the potash into pearl ash. This process took about one-half hour. Pearl ash was heavier and less likely to be deliquesced by the air than potash.

Samuel Hopkins had invented a new process for making potash and pearl ash, properly called calcinated alkaline salts, and had Dr. David Rittenhouse, Benjamin Rush, James Hutchinson, and others certify that by using his method white pearl ashes were produced instead of the old black types and without the loss of weight that usually accompanied the ordinary process of calcining. Hopkins published their testimony throughout the mid-1790s in the Philadelphia papers trying to entice entrepreneurs to join with him in a partnership or to buy the rights to his process.[29] Nicholson, always looking for new ways to make money, contacted Hopkins and they established potash works at Wilkes-Barre and Asylum supplying potash kettles to the settlers. Adam Hoops reported from Asylum that the pearl ash was "remarkably fine and of unusual whiteness."[30] However, Nicholson and others found that potash production often destroyed the kettles because of the intense heat required to melt the salts. Many then switched to produce pearl ash in kilns instead of potash. This resulted in the flooding of the market with pearl ash, with an accompanying drop in prices. Consequently, Nicholson purchased the rights to a process invented by Thomas Ryan whereby potash was produced in stone furnaces, thus avoiding the kettle destruction of the old process. Stone furnaces were erected at both Asylum and Wilkes-Barre. But potash and pearl ash enterprises did not contribute much to the Asylum Company's coffers and Nicholson's glass works averaged a yearly profit of only seventy-seven pounds.

Nicholson also supplied kettles for maple sugar production to the Asylum settlers in an attempt to make that project a paying proposition. He was producing maple sugar at Wilkes-Barre and in Susquehanna County before the Frenchmen came, and it was a simple matter to begin the process at Asylum. Nicholson had about 12,000 acres in the area bearing 3,000 maple trees; although the trees were scattered, he hoped that the five pounds of sugar obtained from the twenty-five gallons of sap of each tree would enable him to start a refinery. He hoped to tap 2,000 of the trees with the help of the Frenchmen. Francis Baily observed that "the season of sugar-making is a very busy time in those parts where trees are plenty; it furnishes employment for every branch of a family . . . it employs them night and day; for in the day they are busily employed in collecting the sap as it runs from the trees, and during the greater part of the night in boiling this sap down to its proper consistency."[31] Dr. Benjamin Rush estimated that the forests of America could produce 135,000 pounds of sugar per year, enough to supply all of the nation's domestic needs and provide a surplus for exportation.[32] Although a tree of ordinary size yielded from twenty to thirty gallons of sap per year and produced five pounds of sugar per season, William Winterbotham observed a Northumberland County farmer who obtained one pound of sugar from three gallons of sap.[33] Nicholson vainly hoped that the Asylum residents could do the same. However, the French at Asylum were not farmers. One lamented, "I did flatter myself that the farming business would enable me to support my family; but for all I exerted myself to the utmost, I could raise but small crops. I sunk money every day in the improvement of new land and impaired my health by a labour altogether too hard to a man not used to work from his infancy." He said he was giving up farming and wanted Nicholson to give him other employment.[34]

Although few permanent settlers were attracted to Asylum by Nicholson's activities and promotions, the settlement did receive many famous visitors, not the least of whom was the future king of France Louis Philippe. Louis Philippe spent more than three years in exile in America, and he and his two brothers traveled thousands of miles in the United States from Maine to New Orleans. When Nicholson heard that he was coming to America, he wrote Dr. Enoch Edwards, his agent in Paris, to contact him about purchasing Nicholson's lands, and after his arrival, wrote General Noailles to seek out Philippe about purchasing Asylum shares. But Philippe showed little interest in the Asylum project probably because most of the inhabitants were Legitimists and he was Orleanist.

Another French aristocrat who came but did not stay was François Alexandre la Rochefoucauld, Duc de Liancourt, former grand master of the king's wardrobe. He traveled throughout the United States and Canada and left a voluminous travel log. One of the characteristics that he observed about Americans (including individuals like Nicholson) was their desire to accumulate wealth, "which passion is not diminished even by the possession of the greatest fortune." He spent twelve days at Asylum in 1795 and made several poignant observations concerning the difficulties of the settlement which help to explain its failure. He pointed out that it would have been more successful if more ready cash had been available, if the artisans imported had been more prone to work and less to drunkenness, if the prices for necessities had been lower, and if the disputes over land titles could have been settled. When he departed on 2 June 1795, he predicted that the colony would either "rise or fall rapidly" and, unfortunately for Nicholson, the latter occurred.[35]

Prince de Talleyrand, another famous French traveler, also pointed out many of the difficulties in trying to establish a French colony in America. As previously mentioned, Talleyrand thought Pennsylvania was one of the best states for land speculation but that the Asylum project was doomed to failure because Frenchmen all longed to return home. There is a dispute among historians as to when he visited Asylum, but in any event, he was not interested in joining with Frenchmen to establish a colony in America (although both Talon and Noailles had served with him in the French Constituent Assembly) but rather in personal speculation in land for quick resale. Pennsylvania was attractive to foreign investment because it was the only state that permitted foreigners to buy and hold land. The state passed this law in February 1789 during Nicholson's tenure as comptroller-general and renewed it every three years during Mifflin's terms as governor until it was allowed to lapse in February 1797. Although Talleyrand declined to take an interest in Asylum, he desired to speculate in land deals with the great speculators of America, including Robert Morris, William Bingham, and John Nicholson. Talleyrand was introduced to American land speculation by Theophilus Cazenove and agreed to purchase 106,000 acres in Pennsylvania from Robert Morris in 1797. Morris obtained the part of these lands in the Northumberland area from Nicholson and hoped to use the funds from the sale to Talleyrand to try to salvage his and Nicholson's Federal City project (Washington, D.C.). However, the deal failed to be consummated.[36] He also proposed to Nicholson and Morris to exchange 270,000 pounds of India cotton for Washington lots. The speculators agreed but Talleyrand typically reneged on the deal.[37] Evidently, Talleyrand was following his own advice written in 1794,

> it is true that these lands increase in value by the sole effect of the passage of time but to benefit by this increase it would be necessary to be in a position to postpone resale for several years and most of them [speculators] are bound by engagements which make it necessary to resell soon, failing in which, they experience constant demands for money and are obliged . . . to have recourse to expedients which have soon exhausted their credit.[38]

Though he failed in persuading these members of the French aristocracy to invest in the Asylum venture, Nicholson sought to appeal to other Frenchmen and Europeans by financing and taking a partnership in a newspaper called the *Level of Europe and North America* (*Le Niveau de l'Europe et de l'Amérique du Nord*). Pierre Egron, formerly a magistrate in France who later lived in Santo Domingo, advertised in the Philadelphia papers that he was beginning his publication printed in English and French, and asked for support. The paper was to contain information on climate in America and Europe, prices of products in the various cities of Europe and America, ship arrivals and departures from Philadelphia, and the like. It was to be published as a weekly and sell for $8 per yearly subscription.[39] When Nicholson agreed to finance the publication, Egron exclaimed, "your understanding, your talents, have excited such esteem that the youngest of your children, with a just glory, will observe . . . [your fame] in the minds of their contemporaries!"[40] A prospectus of the *Level* was published which included probably the principal reason for Nicholson's participation; it stated, "among the principal advantages of the publication ought to be computed that of giving rise in Europe to a great number of speculations in the lands of the United States and of attracting many capitals to North America."[41] Despite this optimism, the *Level* brought little in the way of tangible results to Nicholson and the monies advanced to keep the publication in print probably could have been put to better use in paying creditors. Boissiere de la Tanguay, the man who had pleaded with the French Convention for the life of Louis XVI, was also associated with Nicholson in this venture, and he provided Nicholson with the following consolation, "Might all your vessels return home full of goods and money; Might all your lands sell well . . . because the benificence is as natural to you, as covetousness gouvern the greatest part of mankind. . . ."[42]

Unfortunately, Nicholson's fortunes did not improve. He tried to induce some interest by trying to lure Edmund Randolph, a man of influence, to purchase stock in the Asylum venture. Nicholson, as has already been discussed, was associated with Randolph in other activities during the 1790s, and he sent him the plan of association of the Asylum Company and asked him to become a trustee as well as a shareholder. When Jefferson resigned as secretary of state in 1793, he was asked by President Washington what he thought of his proposed successor, Randolph, who assumed his new duties on 2 January 1794. Jefferson wrote in August 1793, "I knew that the embarrassments in his private affairs had obliged him to use expedients which had injured him with the merchants and shopkeepers, and affected his character for independence . . . these embarrassments were serious, and not likely to cease soon."[43] Jefferson may have been referring to Randolph's association with Nicholson, for the secretary of state had many private entanglements with him. Randolph agreed to purchase $3,000 worth of stock in the company but had to rely on Nicholson for credit. He also consented to have his name used as a trustee in not only this but also in Nicholson's Territorial Land Company, as long as no impropriety was involved. In return for these services, Nicholson loaned money to Randolph, who was tardy in making payments. Nicholson wrote "any money you can give me today be the same more or less on acct. you may class as given to charitable uses—do let me have a check from you for some for I am in great distress." As of May 1795, Randolph had not paid for his stock purchases and Nicholson kept asking him for payment. "If you can help me to the 3000 dollars this morning you relieve me, if you give me any part you serve me so far."[44]

One of the chronic problems, among the many that besieged the company, was that of title disputes. Liancourt observed that a speedy adjustment of the differences between the Connecticut and Pennsylvania settlers over titles was essential for the success of Asylum, and Adam Hoops expressed the same sentiments.[45] Nicholson was appointed by Governor Mifflin to a committee to collect information regarding the entry of New Englanders into Pennsylvania. The governor had proclaimed that the Pennsylvania titles to the area were the only valid ones, but the Connecticut claimants were ignoring his proclamation. The disputes were chronic and partly involved the contention by the Connecticut claimants that Pennsylvania land jobbers were defrauding them. As a consequence, the whole board of managers of the Asylum Company threatened to resign in 1796 unless Nicholson did something.[46] Nicholson tried to solve the problem by buying the claims of the Connecticut settlers, but his agent, Joseph Duncan, told him some Yankees were forging title claims in order to fleece speculators like Nicholson. Then on 13 May 1795 in the case of *Vanhorne's Lessee* v. *Dorrance*, the Pennsylvania District Court ruled that the Pennsylvania law of 1790 validating the Pennsylvania titles to the area was a constitutional act. Upon hearing this, Nicholson said he was sorry for those who had paid a lot of money and settled under the Connecticut titles. He then bought the Connecticut right to the lands on which Asylum stood for 2,000 pounds. His brother-in-law, Joseph Duncan, who had many friends among the Connecticut settlers, aided Nicholson in this venture.[47]

Nicholson inaccurately predicted that sales would increase with the resolution of the title disputes. However, the disputes did not cease with the Vanhorne case, and in 1799 a compromise act was passed granting titles to the Connecticut settlers who had been in the Wyoming Valley before the Decree of Trenton of 1782. The Pennsylvania claimants received compensation for these lands. Dividends remained to be paid to the stockholders, and Nicholson grew desperate when he could not pay them. He wrote Morris, "I am almost wild for the want of 1410 Doll. which are yet lacking to make good the sum Necessary to pay the *Asylum dividends.* Will you let me have that sum out of the *Washington appropriations* and on my honor it shall be repaid before tomorrow night."[48] But by 1796 the Washington project was encountering as many difficulties as the Asylum venture, and no relief could be obtained from this source. Nicholson either had to sell his shares or use the shares he had in the company as collateral in an attempt to raise money. But at this stage, few would advance him cash. He was so desperate that he once offered to sell fifty shares in the company for $9,000 and at the end of sixty days, buy them back again for $10,000. He did not even receive his own dividends from the company because he was in debt to it. None of these efforts were able to salvage either the company or Nicholson. Talleyrand's prophecy in regard to French colonizers came true. Isaac Weld observed that

> The French settlers here seem however, to have no great inclination or ability to cultivate the earth, and the greater part of them have let their lands at a small yearly rent to Americans and amuse themselves with driving deer, fishing and fowling; they hate Americans, and the Americans in the neighborhood hate and accuse them of being an idle dissipated set. The manner of the two peoples are so different that it is impossible that they should ever agree.[49]

Even Liancourt, who was sympathetic to the colony and wanted it to succeed, commented that "one of the greatest impediments to the prosperity of the settlement will probably arise from the prejudices of some Frenchmen against the Americans . . . some of them vauntingly declare that they will never learn the language of the country, or enter into conversation with an American."[50]

The colonizers did not remain at Asylum long enough to become acclimated to the environment or culture, for Napoleon's star was on the horizon in France, and when he became emperor in 1802, a general amesty was declared. As early as 1799 the émigrés began to desert the colony at Asylum and return to their homeland as

Talleyrand had predicted. By 1802, very few remained. Nicholson by 1797 was well on the road to bankruptcy, and he deeded such patents as he had remaining to the trustees to satisfy debts owed the company. Some of the lands were sold at sheriff's sales for taxes and others were sold by courts to settle state liens.

In 1801, the Asylum Company was reorganized by William Crammond, James Gibson, John Ashley, and the rest of the managers ". . . in consequence of the inability of . . . the late John Nicholson to perform . . . covenants . . . arising from pecuniary embarassments [sic] & judgments. . . ."[51] The company existed for an additional fifteen years, but after Napoleon's decree, these individuals had no settlers with which to support the enterprise. On 1 September 1808 new trustees for the company were appointed, Archibald McCall, John Ashley, and Thomas Ashley, but the company never became a financial success. Lands were sold to Charles Homet and Bartholemew Laporte but these sales were not enough to improve the company's fortunes. The company officially closed its books in 1819 but the final 20,000 acres of the company's lands were not sold until 4 March 1843 when William Jessup of Montrose bought them.[52]

As for the two originators of the plan, Noailles did not return to France; he accepted a commission in the French Army under General Rochambeau in the Santo Domingo theater. He died in Havana of wounds received in a battle with the British. Talon did return to France and died at Grez, on 18 August 1811, completely insane. All that remains of the efforts of these men to build a great city on the banks of the Susquehanna is a small settlement known as Frenchtown, names such as Asylum Township and Laporte, a museum, and a bronze plate marking the site.

Asylum was but one of Nicholson's attempts in Pennsylvania to establish a haven for European refugees, and to make a profit in the process. Some Englishmen were experiencing difficulties at home because of their position favoring the French Revolution and sought an "Asylum" of their own. Two such individuals were Dr. Joseph Priestley, world renowned scientist and theologian—discoverer of oxygen and later founder of the Unitarian religion in Pennsylvania—and his son-in-law, Dr. Thomas Cooper, later an ardent Republican in America and one of the editors sent to prison under the Alien and Sedition Acts of 1798 for attacking the Federalist Adams's administration. These two Englishmen were being subjected to violent attacks in their native Birmingham for their liberal views. For example, on one occasion, in 1791, Priestley's house was destroyed by a mob. As a result, they sought a refuge where they could speak and practice their political and religious beliefs without fear of recrimination.

Thomas Cooper and Joseph Priestley Jr. were sent to America in 1793 to explore possible sites for settlement. Dr. Enoch Edwards, Nicholson's land agent in Europe and a doctor and scientist who had been a student of Dr. Benjamin Rush, was also a friend of Priestley and Cooper. He informed Nicholson of their mission and asked the latter to treat them kindly and supply them with information on lands, and in return, Cooper would explain to Nicholson all about the cotton business, as Nicholson was also interested in establishing textile manufactures in Pennsylvania. On 17 August 1793, Edwards advised Nicholson that he was talking to Dr. Priestley and his son about the purchase of Nicholson's Angelica Farm near Reading, a 900-acre estate, that Priestley was "exceedingly captivated with," and that Priestley would continue his investigation of the matter with Nicholson when he came to Philadelphia. Edwards told Nicholson to be sure and show it to him before "the Roads frighten him."[53]

Cooper and Priestley Jr. arrived in Philadelphia with letters of introduction to Nicholson from Edwards and others to John Adams, vice-president of the United States, given to them by Joseph Barnes, another Nicholson agent in England. Nicholson wrote to his agents and friends in the Pennsylvania hinterland about their arrival, told them of their purpose, and asked them to supply Cooper and Priestley with information about the country, especially about Nicholson's lands on the east and west banks of the Susquehanna near Northumberland and Sunbury. Nicholson informed another friend that Dr. Priestley had decided not to take Angelica Farm until he had explored all of the possible sites for the settlement, so Nicholson told his friend to show the travelers the land around Northumberland.[54]

On 14 December 1793 Cooper and Priestley Jr. left Philadelphia for their journey up the Susquehanna as far north as Loyalsock Creek. Cooper was completely captivated by Nicholson's lands in the area and wrote,

you look down upon the Susquehanna, about three or four miles off; a river about half a mile broad, running at the foot of bold and steep mountains, through a valley, not much above three miles broad in that part, rich, beautiful and variegated. At the distance of about four miles on the bank of the river, you catch the town of Sunbury, and on the opposite side of the river, about two miles farther, Northumberland. These are towns of about two or three hundred houses each delightfully situated near the Susquehanna.[55]

Priestley was also enthusiastic and wrote, "As an instance of the rapid advance of land, we were informed that the unoccupied land in this town [Northumberland] were offered to sale, two years ago, for two thousand pounds. This year the owner refused ten thousand pounds."[56] Cooper and Priestley then negotiated a deal with Nicholson and Morris, who also had lands in the area, to purchase 300,000 acres fifty miles from Northumberland near Loyalsock Creek. Cooper tried to organize a company, sell stock, and then complete the deal by making the payments for the land to the speculators. Priestley said the settlement was not to be confined to any one class of people but "it was set on foot to be as it were a rallying point for the English, who were at that time emigrating to America in great numbers. . . ."[57] Some Englishmen were reluctant to subscribe and come to this spot, so Thomas Cooper wrote *Some Information Respecting America* in 1794 to induce migrations. Nicholson supplied him with some information about the lands which Cooper included in this glowing report on America's prospects.

On 31 January 1794, Cooper and Priestley left for England with the agreement, made with Nicholson and Morris, to show to their other associates. While there, they tried to entice all sorts of their countrymen to take part in the enterprise. One of the more interesting Englishmen whom the Priestleys and Cooper hoped to attract was the poet Samuel Taylor Coleridge. He and some other writers, like Robert Southey, were looking for a place of peace and solitude where they could live utopian lives, a place which Coleridge dubbed Pantisocracy. The settlement they envisioned was similar to the literary utopia established by the American transcendentalists of a later era, Brook Farm. When Coleridge was asked by Joseph Priestley to come to America, the poet envisioned "trying the experiment of perfectability on the banks of the Susquehanna." The writers did not take part in the English settlement but the prospect did inspire Coleridge to write *Monody on the Death of Chatterton*, part of which reads,

> Yet will I love to follow the sweet dream
> Where the Susquehannah pours his untamed stream;
> And on some hill, whose forest-frowning side
> Waves o'er the murmurs of his calmer tide,
> Will raise a solemn, cenotaph to thee,

Pennsylvania Speculator and Patriot: John Nicholson

Sweet harper of time-shrouded minstrelsy!
And there, soothed sadly by the dirgeful wind
Muse on the sore ills I had left behind.[58]

The English promoters, although unable to attract writers like
Coleridge, returned to America in April 1794 and asked Nicholson to
show them the patents for the land, the exact locations of the 300,000
acres, and the like. Cooper hoped that this Northumberland settlement would act as a lure for English immigrants because "it is the
only *English* settlement I know of in America." He also pointed out
the internal improvement projects then under way in the state, the
favorable climate and the rich soil to be found in the area.[59] Dr.
Priestley was impressed by his reports and did come to America
on 4 June 1795. He made a triumphant tour from New York to
Philadelphia, wined and dined by officials along the way, and then
up to Northumberland, where he planned to reside until the settlement was finished.

The Englishmen began their settlement, which the French visitor
Liancourt called the worst-built town he had ever seen, but they
could not attract enough settlers to the place nor enough subscribers
to their company. Consequently, they decided to abandon the project. Henry Wansey, one of the Englishmen who contracted to take
part in the colony, said that "disagreements among the parties" led
to its collapse.[60] The best explanation was probably given by Joseph
Priestley Jr. when he wrote,

> Fortunately for the original proposers, the scheme was abandoned.
> It might and would have answered in a pecuniary point of view, as
> the land now sells at double and treble the price then asked for it,
> without the advantage which that settlement would have given
> rise to; but the . . . Englishmen . . . unless previously accustomed
> to a life of labour, are so ill-qualified to commence cultivation in
> a wilderness, that the projectors would most probably have been
> subjected to still more unfounded abuse than they have been,
> for their well meant endeavors to promote the interests of their
> countrymen.[61]

This, of course, was the major reason for the failure of the Asylum
project as well. It seemed that Nicholson and Morris should have
been more selective in the type of individuals they lured to their
lands. But perhaps any buyer, no matter how ill-equipped to take
up life in the American wilderness, looked promising to men in
their financial conditions.

112

Nicholson and Morris took back the forfeited lands when the payments were not received, but not after waiting to see if the company could yet salvage its fortunes—this even though "we did not consider ourselves well treated by some of the subscribers." Nicholson did sell to Priestley and his family land on which they built their their country estate, and later, when the Priestleys wanted more of his land around Loyalsock Creek, Nicholson informed them that he had no more left to sell (he wished that he did, because he needed the money). Thomas Cooper also stayed in the Northumberland area and purchased 100 acres from Nicholson. The land that was not sold to the Englishmen became part of the North American Land Company, a land scheme undertaken by Nicholson, Morris, and James Greenleaf. Although Nicholson must have been disappointed in the failure of the English project, he remained on friendly terms with the Priestleys, despite some title disputes over lands he had sold them. Dr. Priestley was very anxious to learn about Nicholson's glass factory at the Falls of the Schuylkill and often went with Nicholson to watch glass blowing.[62]

As evidenced by the above, Nicholson had little success in trying to establish refugee colonies in Pennsylvania. They did not prove to be the "asylums" Nicholson sought in his attempts to gain relief from his financial morass. His next excursion, to the banks of the Potomac, would be even more discouraging.

8
NICHOLSON'S ROLE IN THE DEVELOPMENT OF THE NATIONAL CAPITAL

Although a touch of altruism may have been a partial motivation for the attempts to establish asylums for refugees, nothing but a desire for profits led Nicholson to the next stumbling block on his speculative path. When Alexander Hamilton was seeking support for a national bank and his debt assumption plan, Thomas Jefferson gave it in exchange for the location of the national capital on the Potomac River.[1] Thus a new sphere was opened within which speculators could display their talents. John Nicholson was not one to miss such an opportunity, and when a scheme was presented to monopolize building lots in the proposed Federal City, he was eager to participate and formed a partnership with James Greenleaf and Robert Morris.

In 1793 James Greenleaf was a twenty-six-year-old speculator from a New England Huguenot family which later collaterally included the poet Whittier. He had already amassed a fortune in the mercantile business as a partner of James Watson, a well-known capitalist of Hartford and New York. His shipping business required that he go to Holland in 1786, and there he made friends with several Dutch bankers. In 1793, he was appointed the American Consul to Holland and was able to make financial connections with Dutch banking establishments. Greenleaf speculated in anything that seemed likely to offer financial rewards and, as one might expect, was a major speculator in the public debt of the United States. When he tried to entice his brother-in-law Noah Webster to indulge, Webster refused, replying in words Greenleaf, Morris, and Nicholson should have heeded, ". . . I believe it best for man to grow slowly, the trees which are long acquiring their full growth are firm wood, and durable. Those of rapid growth make poor timber."[2] Greenleaf, while in Holland, had married Antonia Cornelia Albertine Schotten, a Dutch baroness, and this probably further enhanced his contacts with Dutch financiers. These contacts enabled him to negotiate several loans for use in his mercantile business with Daniel Crommelin and Sons, Dutch bankers, and later he would attempt to interest the Dutchmen in the Washington venture. Upon receiving news of the proposed capital on the Potomac, Greenleaf became interested in this first of America's boom towns and contacted Robert Morris about the possibility of a partnership. Morris, in turn, induced Nicholson to take part in the scheme, and in the end, Nicholson became the manager of the whole project. The perceptive Liancourt remarked, "In America where, more than any other country in the world, a desire for wealth is the prevailing passion, there are few schemes which are not made the means of extensive speculation, and that of erecting of Federal City presented irresistible temptations, which were in fact not neglected."[3] Morris was so enthusiastic about the prospects that he exclaimed, "Washington building lots will continue rising in price for one hundred years to come!"[4] Nicholson later echoed these sentiments when he said, "all other places have risen by slow degrees, this will astonish the world by its rapidity, the people are all ready and only wait for houses to rush in."[5]

Under the Federal Residency Act of 16 July 1790, the exact site for the new capital was not designated. It authorized the president to select a site not exceeding ten square miles on the Potomac River, somewhere between the mouths of the eastern branch, known as the Anacostia River, and the Conegocheague, a distance of eighty miles. The president was further empowered to appoint three commissioners who were to survey and define the district, supervise the sales of lots, and provide for the public buildings to house the government. In January 1791 Washington appointed Daniel Carroll, Thomas Johnson, and David Stuart to serve as the first commissioners. In March 1791 Andrew Ellicott was appointed to survey the sites and, shortly thereafter, he was joined by Pierre Charles L'Enfant, French-born engineer. The president then entered into negotiations with the proprietors of the land which was to be used for the new Federal City and frequently had to reprimand them for fighting among themselves and for asking too much for their lands. Washington was able to overcome the difficulties and succeeded in getting the proprietors to agree to the following conditions, explained in a letter to Thomas Jefferson,

The terms are that all the land . . . including a breadth of about a mile and a half, the whole containing from three to five thousand acres, is ceded to the public, on conditions that, when the whole shall be surveyed and laid off as a City, (which Major L'Enfant is now directed to do), the present Proprietors shall retain every other lot, and for such part of the land as may be taken for public use . . . they shall be allowed at the rate of Twenty five pounds per acre. . . . No compensation is to be made for the ground that may be occupied as streets or alleys.[6]

By August 1791 Andrew Ellicott was busy laying out streets, squares, and lots, and it was expected that the public buildings would be begun in the spring of 1792. L'Enfant was busy choosing sites for the various public buildings and having disputes with the commissioners over who had supreme authority in handling the affairs of the new city. On 29 June 1791 Washington informed the proprietors of the sites selected for the legislative and executive buildings and showed them a plan of the city. The proprietors, many of whom would be involved with Nicholson, were Robert Peter, David Burnes, James Lingan, Uriah Forest, Notley Young, Daniel Carroll, Overton Carr, Thomas Beale, Charles Beatty, Anthony Holmead, William Young, Abraham Young, William Prout, Elipus Douglass, W. Warren, James Warren, William King, Edward Pierce, and James Pierce.

One part of L'Enfant's plan for the city which ultimately affected Nicholson was his desire to cut a canal to connect the Potomac with the Anacostia. Tyber Creek was to form the route of the canal and L'Enfant hoped that the initial buildings would be constructed along its banks. He hoped that building would begin at various points "not merely because settlements of this sort are likely to diffuse an equality of advantages over the whole territory allotted . . . but because each of these settlements by a natural jealousy will most tend to stimulate establishment on each of the opposed extremes. . . ."[7] As the reader will discover, this is exactly what took place, but instead of fostering the development of the city, the rivalries retarded its growth.

In September 1791 the commissioners advertised the sale by public auction of the 15,000 city lots obtained from the original proprietors. L'Enfant was upset because he thought that the sale was premature, that local speculators would acquire the lots for a pittance, that those around the president's house would go first, and that his plan for encouraging the simultaneous growth of the city at various points would be thwarted. As a result, he procrastinated in drafting a plan of the city which would show the lots to be sold at the auction held on 17 October 1791. Consequently, only thirty-five lots were sold, for a total of about $2,000. Washington and the commissioners then decided to hold another public sale but not before a clear plan of the city was drafted and copies of the plan printed and circulated to attract prospective buyers. L'Enfant still was tardy in doing the work, so Washington dismissed him for his procrastination and his disputes with the commissioners and assigned Andrew Ellicott the task in 1792. Even with the publication and circulation of the Ellicott map, the second public auction sale in October 1792 proved to be just as disappointing as the first; fifty-two lots were sold. An observer, William Winterbotham, related that the land obtained from the original proprietors, which produced the 15,000 lots, was supposed to provide enough money to "not only erect the public buildings, but to dig the canal, conduct water through the city, and to pave and light the streets, which will save a heavy tax that arises in other cities, and consequently render the lots considerably more valuable."[8] The paltry sums obtained, even when augmented by grants of $120,000 from Virginia and $72,000 from Maryland, proved insufficient for the construction of the public buildings and the development of the city. So President Washington and the commissioners decided to try other means. A lottery was advertised to be held in September of 1793 to raise $350,000. And to promote the sale of lots, in 1793 Washington authorized the commissioners to conduct private sales. It was at this point that our speculators moved into the story.

When Robert Morris was approached by Greenleaf, he left Nicholson in Philadelphia to handle their joint affairs and went on a ten-week trip to appraise the feasibility of investing in the city. Morris was favorably impressed with the speculative prospects and so informed Nicholson.[9] Nicholson was also being informed of the progress in the city by other agents who advised him in May 1793 that the foundation of the president's house had been laid; that the outline of the Capitol had been established, but that it would take a lot of money to finish these and other buildings. He was also informed about the proposed private sales of lots to be made in September 1793. Nicholson asked his agent to find out the boundaries of lots of the original proprietors as well.[10]

Nicholson did not take part in the sale of 23 September 1793, but James Greenleaf did and purchased 3,000 lots at 25 pounds per lot to be paid for in seven annual installments, without interest, commencing 1 May 1794. Greenleaf was required to build ten two-story houses yearly and not to sell any lots before 1 January 1796, without the stipulation that the purchaser build a house on every third lot within four years from the date of sale. Greenleaf then contacted Morris, who, acting for himself and Nicholson, formed a partnership with Greenleaf. Morris contracted with the commissioners on 24 December 1793 to buy an additional 3,000 lots—each containing 5,265 square feet—on the same credit as the first contract but at the cost of 35 pounds ($80) per lot. Of the 6,000 lots purchased, 1,500 were to be chosen in the northeast quarter of the city on land originally owned by Notley Young. This land was situated in one of the more remote areas of the city, but the commissioners desired for it to be developed as well. To compensate the trio, another parcel of Notley's land, consisting of 428½ lots, desirably situated along the Potomac River, was conveyed to them and the balance of the 4,500 lots could be chosen anywhere the partners desired. Over a period of seven years Greenleaf, Morris, and Nicholson were to pay about $68,000 yearly to the commissioners for the lots, or a total of approximately $480,000. These purchases represented about forty-two percent of the total number of lots available for sale in the Federal City, but the commissioners justified the quasi-monopoly by saying that the promotions of the combine would draw buyers and people to the city and hasten its development.[11]

Nicholson and Morris's participation in the speculation was predicated on James Greenleaf's promise to secure loans in Holland to help finance the venture. Indeed, the commissioners, as part of the agreement with the speculators, agreed to take one-third of the payment in Dutch bonds to be repaid at the end of six years. Washington lots were to be used as security for repayment. The loans would total two million guilders (about $1,200,000) at five percent interest annually. On 2 November 1793, Greenleaf contracted with Sylvanius Bourne, Vice Consul at Amsterdam, to try to execute the loan using Washington lots as security. He contacted Daniel Crommelin and Sons to negotiate a public subscription for the loan in Holland. Greenleaf later joined Bourne to try and secure the funds. As of 1795, Greenleaf was still in Holland trying to raise the money, and Morris feared that the French invasion of Holland would thwart his efforts. Morris's fears proved to be correct, as Dutch gold, instead of flowing into Washington to aid its development, flowed into the wars of the French Revolution. The wars also diverted prospective individual buyers of Washington lots to various battlefields where they would serve as cannon fodder. After Greenleaf left the combine in 1795, Nicholson and Morris found out that $190,000 had been subscribed to the loan in Holland but that Greenleaf used the money to cover his drafts and notes, leaving the other two partners without any of it.[12]

Since Nicholson and Morris desperately needed this money to pay for their lots and also for lands incorporated into the North American Land Company (another scheme formed with Greenleaf), they dispatched James Marshall, Morris's son-in-law and brother of future chief justice of the Supreme Court John Marshall, to Europe with certificates for 2,000 lots to be used as security in raising another loan. They also wanted him to inquire about Greenleaf's activities in regard to the first attempts. Greenleaf had even charged Nicholson and Morris $23,000 in six-percent stock of the United States to secure the loans which he had used for his own purposes. Later, when Marshall informed them that he was having difficulty raising a loan using the lots as collateral, Nicholson and Morris advised him to try to sell the 2,000 lots.[13]

While these efforts were being made to secure loans abroad, the partners were also buying lots from the original proprietors. Isaac Weld remarked that the original proprietors had willingly ceded their alternate lots to the government knowing that those they retained would increase in value as the city developed[14] This was true as several of these proprietors then sold lots to the partners at a higher price than they received from the government. The purchases from private proprietors included all of the following: 220 lots from Daniel Carroll of Duddington contracted for in September and December of 1793; 428½ lots from Notley Young, 26 December 1793; 239¼ lots from Uriah Forrest and Benjamin Stoddert, 15 July 1794; 108 from William King, 14 July 1794; 79½ from William Bailey, 15 July 1794; 40 from Peter Casanove and George French, September 1793; 6 from William Prout in 1794–1795; 60 acres purchased from William Deakins and 316 acres from Benjamin Oden, 10 July 1794.[15] When these purchases are added to the 6,000 lots obtained from the government, a total of 7,234 lots were procured, representing approximately sixty percent of the public lots and twenty-five percent of the lands of the original proprietors.

All of these purchases were under credit arrangements and contingent upon the building of houses on the lots. The president and commissioners set stringent building requirements in an attempt to achieve some uniformity in their construction. Houses were to be brick or stone with walls 35 to 40 feet high built parallel to the line of the street. Some wooden houses were permitted for workers quarters but these were to be razed when the work was completed. Each of the lots contained enough space for three or four houses with the deepest lots covering an area of 270 feet by 70 feet, fronting the streets. Henry Wansey, in observing all of these requirements and conditions, remarked, "the question still with me is, whether the scheme is not too magnificent for the present state of things."[16] How true these words were, for Nicholson, Morris, and Greenleaf encountered all types of difficulties in trying to fulfill these contracts and regulations while at the same time attempting to pay for the lots they had acquired.

One of the difficulties lay in trying to get some of the original proprietors to survey their land and mark off the lots designated for the partners. As late as 1796, most had not done this, and the surveys had not been completed. This was due to the fact that Morris and Nicholson were in dire financial straits; some of the proprietors anticipated their collapse and realized they would not be paid for their conveyances. Also by 1796, Nicholson and Morris had not made all of their payments to the proprietors and many were bringing legal suits against them. Adding to their problems was the fact that the commissioners had not made the divisions between the public and the original proprietary lots on some of the lands paid for by the partners, and no sales could be made of this property until this was done.

To fulfill the building requirements, the partners had to erect 370 houses on the 6,000 lots purchased from the government. To meet this stipulation, the partners sold lots with the condition that buyers build houses. With this stipulation, the partners sold about 1,000 lots within eighteen months of the governmental purchase, mostly to Thomas Law and William Duncanson, who paid about $293 per lot. Thomas Law, the major purchaser of lots, had amassed a fortune of 500,000 pounds in India as an official of the East India Company, and he came to America in August 1794 looking for lucrative investment possibilities. When he heard of the Washington project, he became eager to participate. He arrived in the Federal City in February 1795 and later married Eliza Park Custis, the granddaughter of President Washington's wife. Many travelers dined or stayed with the Laws, who had a reputation for providing what refined living there was in the new city.[17] One traveler, Thomas Twining, related

The clearing of ground and building of small houses amongst the woods of the Potomac, seemed an uncongenial occupation for a man of so accomplished a mind, and whose former habits and employment had been so different. As chief of a large district in Bengal, he had been accustomed to the discharge of important official functions, and to the splendor and consequence of a prince. In England his family was opulent and distinguished. One brother was a bishop of Carlisle, another was a barrister of the first eminence. . . . His inexperience in commercial affairs, amidst rivals so experienced and intelligent, might expose him to litigation and disappointment, and involve a considerable diminution of his fortune.[18]

Unfortunately, Twining's prophecies were to come true.

On 24 December 1794, Law agreed to purchase 445 lots for $133,-333 but with the condition that he had the right to reject the purchase within the first eighteen months. Furthermore, he was not required to build until after he had made the bargain absolute. So instead of having to complete his buildings within four years as was customary, he had five and one-half years. Then Law was persuaded by Greenleaf to forgo his conditional eighteen-month grace period and begin building immediately. Law, however, was shrewd enough to obtain mortgages on North American Land Company property as security for the delivery of the titles to the lots. Later, Law complained to Morris and Nicholson that he still had not received his titles for the lots either from the commissioners or from them.[19] This was due to the fact that Nicholson and Morris were behind in their payments to the commissioners, and the officers were withholding titles until all payments had been received.

Complicating this situation was the fact that the partners had conveyed to Law lots that were originally purchased from Daniel Carroll. As of 1796, they owed Carroll $13,000 for these lots, and Carroll would not deliver the title to Law until he was paid. Since neither Nicholson nor Morris had $13,000, Carroll agreed to take 100 shares in the North American Land Company representing $3,700, $5,000 in cash, and a 60 day negotiable note for $2,300. Only then would Carroll convey the titles to Law. Nicholson then wrote to Morris asking him where they were going to get the $5,000 and $2,300 in notes! Nevertheless, Morris and Nicholson were able to make token payments to Carroll, and the commissioners' and Law's titles were to be delivered on the condition that Law finish his buildings immediately. According to Nicholson, "Law bounced around the room this morning like a mad man, when he found that the comm[rs.] would not grant the titles without the convenant to build."[20] Nicholson and Morris again pleaded with the commissioners to deliver the titles. Finally, attorney-general of the United States

Henry Lee entered the case and decided that Law should have his titles and be allowed until 1800 to complete his buildings. Title disputes were a major problem for the speculators, and they experienced the same difficulties in their attempts to complete the contract made with William Duncanson for 103 lots. Duncanson had an additional cause to lament because he made a loan of $25,000 to Nicholson which in the end turned out to be a permanent gift.[21]

In addition to title difficulties and encumbrances on the lots in deals with buyers, the partners were hard-pressed in their attempts to fulfill the building requirements on the majority of their lots that they had not sold and in making their payments to the commissioners. Nicholson and Morris blamed all of their problems on Greenleaf and his failures in Europe—his use of monies obtained there for his own purposes, his defaulting on notes endorsed by Nicholson and Morris, and his flagrant appropriation, for personal use, of funds given him by Nicholson and Morris to pay the District commissioners. In 1795, Morris wrote to Greenleaf that "having supplied you with Seven Thousand Dollars toward my Share of the Payment which was to be made to the Commissioners of the Federal City . . . I naturally expected that you would have completed my Share of that Payment . . . but as it seems you have applied the money to your own use, the Commissioners remain unpaid. . . ." Morris strongly requested that Greenleaf inform the commissioners that Morris was not responsible for the failure to make payments. Greenleaf even used money gained from the partners' joint sales to Duncanson for his own benefit and again did not make the payments to the commissioners.[22] President Washington criticized the partners for their failures to make their payments and Morris wrote explaining that he was in arrears $15,000 and Nicholson $25,000 due the Greenleaf's failure to negotiate the Dutch loans.[23]

Greenleaf was also in financial difficulties in this period and blamed Nicholson and Morris for some of his problems. Greenleaf wrote to Nicholson, "your own acceptances & engagements for which I have rendered myself responsible are flowing fast upon me under the disgrace of protest & for which I am obliged to provide even by submitting to the most humiliating & unjustifiable sacrifices." He later told Nicholson that he would endorse no more of his notes. Greenleaf also maintained that he had to provide $15,000 for the Washington project because Morris and Nicholson did not forward their shares. This was a case of all the partners being in the same chronic state of financial distress, and therefore unable to help each other out of their respective quagmires. Morris summarized the plight of each when he wrote "money grows Scarcier [sic] and the probability of obtaining it on almost any terms becomes daily more doubtful. . . ."[24]

To raise money for the Washington venture after Greenleaf's failure in Holland, Nicholson and Morris agreed to form the North American Land Company, with Greenleaf as a participant. The details of this operation are discussed in a later chapter, but at this point, it is well to note that Greenleaf failed to provide his share of the money needed to pay for some of the lands in the company. Morris and Nicholson paid for his share of the lands, but they could not make their payments to the commissioners of the Federal City. Greenleaf was causing problems for both concerns which were financially linked. Morris wrote to Greenleaf, "I do not see how it is possible to pay the Installments at the Federal City unless you will pay what you owe us on the Land Purchases, which you ought to have done before, but certainly it should now be done in this hour of pressure."[25] But Greenleaf either would not or could not comply and his derelictions continued to plague the other partners.

Finally, thoroughly disillusioned with Greenleaf, Nicholson and Morris decided to dissolve the three-way partnership and buy Greenleaf's holdings in 1795. Morris explained the change and the partners' conditions to the Dutch bankers in this manner:

> The unhappy engagements which I had been tempted to make with that man, [Greenleaf] have proved a source of vexation & misfortune to me, beyond anything I could have conceived possible. My whole time and attention is necessarily called so to extricate myself; as one means of doing it Mr. Nicholson & myself purchased him out of all the concerns in which he held an interest with us, in doing this . . . we were obliged to issue a large number & amount in negotiable notes. At the Same time such a general scarcity & want of money has arisen in this Country that we cannot sell the property or obtain loans. Our ready money run out and not being able to pay as the notes fall due they have depreciated down to nothingness, and we are held in continual scenes of distress.[26]

Morris also explained that they bought Greenleaf's Washington lots to ". . . balance his shares in our land purchases." This refers to the money Greenleaf owed the partners for land bought for incorporation into the North American Land Company. Nicholson and Morris agreed to give Greenleaf $1,150,000 with payment, as Morris stated above, in Morris's and Nicholson's drafts on each other. The pledge was to be secured by using Washington lots as collateral, and the mortgage was to be canceled when the notes were paid. Morris explained that now instead of he and Nicholson being Greenleaf's creditors, they had "turned the tables" on him and now were his debtors.[27] Greenleaf explained that one of his reasons for abandoning the Washington project was because the commissioners favored the eastern part of the city in which they themselves held a personal interest over the other sections where the partners had most of their lots. He said it had cost the partners $150,000 for their operations in 1794 alone (four times what it should have cost), partly due to the bias of the commissioners. Other owners of lots, such as George Walker, a Philadelphia merchant, also accused the commissioners of favoring one section of the city over another, but the western not the eastern part. There probably was some truth to these assertions, as Liancourt recorded that two of the commissioners possessed lots near Georgetown, which was located a mile above the city on the Potomac, and they encouraged building there first.

With Greenleaf removed from the partnership, Nicholson took over the active management of the Washington project. He appointed Lewis Deblois, a resident merchant, to assist him, and Morris retained Greenleaf's chief agent, brother-in-law, and lawyer for the North American Land Company, William Cranch, to act on his behalf. Cranch was a nephew of Abigail Adams, wife of vice-president and future president John Adams, and would later serve as a federal commissioner and as a judge of the federal court. Morris later planned to establish his son William in Washington to manage his affairs.[28] Morris summarized Nicholson's chief flaw as a manager of their joint concerns when he wrote, "I know that you are never idle, it is not in your nature or habits to be so, but I think you are too often employed in doing what ought to be done by others, correct this error and you will accomplish more real business in a short time than any other man living."[29] Nicholson went to Washington in 1795 and stayed through 1797, trying diligently to expedite the project and make it a success. When he arrived, "the only public buildings carrying on . . . [were] the President's House, the Capitol, and a large hotel"; the partners' buildings were in a similarly incomplete stage.[30] So one of Nicholson's greatest tasks was to have their building constructed. As was mentioned, the partners had to build 370 houses on the 6,000 lots purchased from the commissioners or face forfeiture. Nicholson wrote to his agent for a progress report on the buildings they were constructing. He predicted that "I will with a capital of 100,000 Dollars cause the buildings which we are to have made in the federal city by Contract with the Commissioners, Mr. Carroll & Mr. Young erected and finished within the time contracted for."[31] Nicholson made a supreme effort to fulfill this prophecy.

By 1795 the partners had spent $120,000 for construction purposes but had little to show for it. So Nicholson proposed giving contracts to various individuals to build twenty houses annually on the best terms that he could make. He accused Greenleaf of having too many salaried employees on the payroll with little or nothing to show for the expenditures.[32] The partners hired architect William Lovering, at a salary of $1,500, to finish the buildings already under way in an eighteen-month period. John Henderson was retained to finish his six houses on square 74, located about midway between the president's house and Georgetown, and Joseph Clark was retained to finish eight three-story houses on squares 503 and 504.[33]

Clark had finished twenty houses on squares 501, 502, and 503 in 1794 at a cost of $144,000. These were located near the Potomac River and had a good wharf adjacent to them. Nicholson, because of the need for cash, offered these for sale in Europe for seventy-five pounds each. He said they were really worth $400 each and predicted that in a few years ten times that sum would not buy them. He attributed the cost of $144,000 to mismanagement which he intended to rectify.[34] Lovering was instructed to "avoid contracting with men of ill fame or bad character altho they should offer cheaper than others for we wish only to employ honest industrious men. . . ." Unfortunately for Nicholson, not all of the workers that were hired were honest, for the partners received reports of building materials being stolen.[35]

Under Nicholson's reorganization scheme, he and Morris agreed to build their own houses, hire their own supervisors, supply their own contractors, and the like. Nicholson instructed Deblois and Morris instructed his chief agent Cranch to supervise all of their respective operations and to check on Lovering's activities. Nicholson hired William Prentiss and his associate, Adonijah Stanburrough, to do most of his building at the rate of $3,400 for a double house and later contracted with William Tunnicliff to finish the construction of and manage a hotel-tavern in Washington to attract buyers. Deblois was not too pleased with the hiring of Prentiss and wrote, "I am sorry you did not find funds to finish the houses that are began, people here laugh at the idea of Prentice [sic] & building new houses for you, when you & Mr. Morris cannot supply funds to finish those that ought to have been finished some months since

& many have it in their mouth that your property here is to be sold to pay the commissioners."[36] But Nicholson insisted on trying to fulfill the complete building requirements and this necessitated the construction of new buildings.

Nicholson and Morris had lots all over the Federal City and thus had to supply building materials to various points.[37] Prentiss and Stanburrough were building on Greenleaf's Point, located on the Potomac River, just above the entrance of the Anacostia. When Nicholson took over the management, the name was changed to Nicholson's Point. Weld, in his *Travels*, recorded that the greatest number of houses in any one place by 1795 were at the point.[38] Here Nicholson operated two wharves and a store in which the workers could obtain supplies. By 1796, Prentiss had finished the work at the point and was proceeding to build houses along South Capitol Street, moving north toward the Capitol building. Houses were also being built on Carroll's Hill near the confluence of the Potomac and the Anacostia and on Capitol Hill near the eastern boundary of the city beyond the Marine Hospital grounds and his hotel was under construction near the Anacostia.

This lack of concentrated development was observed by Weld when he wrote that houses were scattered all over. "To be under the necessity of going through a deep wood for one or two miles, perhaps, in order to see a next door neighbor, and in the same city, is a curious, and I believe, a novel circumstance." In addition, most of the houses that were built were not occupied by cash-paying tenants. Weld observed, "the number of inhabitants in the city, in the spring of 1796, amounted to about five thousand, including artificers, who formed by far the largest part of that number." Winterbotham remarked that he observed the same situation when he visited the city.[39] Liancourt helped to explain the spotty development when he wrote that the city did not grow as fast as the speculators wanted. "The Proprietors then became rivals." Each built in his own quarter, tried to establish the reputation of his section and damned the other sections. One group had bought lots near Georgetown and wanted this developed first; a second at Greenleaf's Point (Nicholson and Morris) who stressed its advantageous position in regard to trade and commerce and its central location between the Capitol and president's house; a third near the Anacostia (Nicholson and Morris again, but not exclusively) and they stressed the proximity to the Capitol; and a fourth group around the Capitol itself (Nicholson and Morris had some lots here). The Frenchman also observed that the commissioners were accused of favoring the Georgetown interests at the expense of the other three, thus hurting Nicholson and Morris.[40]

Not only were these difficulties besetting Nicholson, but he was hard-pressed to supply his contractors with the necessary building supplies. In fact, invariably all of his principal employees faced bankruptcy in the end, along with Nicholson himself. Prentiss's case was typical. Jail was his reward for using his credit to obtain the supplies he needed to finish the houses for Nicholson and Morris. When the partners could not pay Prentiss, he was ruined. He lamented in 1797, "What am I to do—My credit was sacrificed—my property gone and wasting to pay engagments [sic] for you—my Family even in want of necessaries." In October 1797 he informed Nicholson that he had been in jail for five weeks with no one paying his bail.[41] By this time, Nicholson himself was just one step ahead of the sheriff and could offer no relief. The reply he gave to Lewis Deblois, who wrote him that, "Death would be preferable to the harried State I am in,"[42] was typical of his replies to all such pleas: "My distress for your Situation is extreme—depend upon it I will not leave you in it long. Another post or two and I will remit for your relief. I cannot describe my feelings for your case—but let it not sink you and we both shall soon see happier days." However, neither Deblois, Prentiss, Tunnicliff, nor Lovering saw those happier days.[43] In fact, not even the workers were paid. As early as 1795, the laborers held a mass meeting and decided to petition the "General Assembly of the State [Maryland] for powers to sell [the] property . . . to pay us our just demands for Services rendered."[44]

It was not the lack of persistence that brought Nicholson to the brink of financial collapse. He worked tirelessly to try and supply his contractors and pay his workers. He refused to leave Washington even though creditors were bringing suits against him in Philadelphia. He once wrote to Morris (who was in Philadelphia trying to escape debtor's prison), "I've got now into the habit of drinking Porter & Water & Sugar at night—it has a pleasing effect—after I went to bed last night I did not wake till Six this morning—and I have been enabled to do more business than when I have a Sleepless Night—God bless you."[45] But Nicholson was not always so kind to Morris. Once when Morris criticized him, he retorted, "I bear misfortune as well as most men, but this I find it very hard, very hard to bring my mind to say I will bear it with resignation. It is now 4 oclock in the morning, you are enjoying sweet repose, your mind

127

needs it. . . . I have been up now . . . on your business as well as mine. I should do it with more Satisfaction if I had not heard your mind. . . ."[46]

Part of the efforts to which he was referring were his attempts to furnish supplies and aid the development of the city. Nicholson established some of the first stores in the Federal City which supplied its residents with flour, wines, soap, candles, molasses, and other necessities. These supplies were shipped from Nicholson's manufacturing complex at the Falls of the Schuylkill. Some of the stores were established along the waterfront near Nicholson's Wharves, and since the waterfront was supposed to be reserved for future public use, he had to obtain President Washington's permission to locate them there.[47] Nicholson also established a branch of T.B. Freeman and Company of Philadelphia (a firm in which he held a partnership) in the Federal City to supply chimney pieces, paintings, and luxury items for the expected elite of the new city. When these items failed to find sufficient buyers, Freeman wrote, "I lament to say what I sincerely believe that America possesses few such Men as yourself who at the risk of private fortune endeavor to establish useful arts."[48] Nicholson also financed the construction of the largest hotel in the Federal City in the 1790s, the Eastern Branch Hotel, located on the southwest corner of Pennsylvania Avenue and Ninth Street. Many congressmen took lodgings here when the government moved to the new capital in 1800. In addition, Nicholson established some of the first bakeries, wine stores, and ice houses in Washington, and in 1797 agreed to pay one-half of the cost of constructing a sugar house. Law, Carroll, and Duncanson all subscribed to this project.[49] In another instance of Nicholson's attempts to link his enterprises, he supplied iron for his buildings in Washington from his furnaces and forge near Chambersburg in Franklin County, Pennsylvania—a complex he ran in partnership with General James Chambers. He supplied glass for windows from his complex at the Falls of the Schuylkill and established a glass house in the new city. Flour was supplied to the bakers and stores in the Federal City from his numerous mills throughout Pennsylvania, and he formed a partnership in a mill in the Washington area.

Nicholson also maintained lumber yards in the capital and secured additional supplies by running freight boats, which plied the waters from his wharves to Georgetown, one mile above the city, and Alexandria, seven miles below. Jesse Dewees managed his affairs in Georgetown where Nicholson had a tavern. Many items such as bricks and lime came from Alexandria and Georgetown, and many of the laborers who worked in the Federal City resided in those towns. Nicholson even extended credit to others who wanted to establish enterprises in the city. But when one wanted to form a partnership to establish a race track, Nicholson refused stating, "it is not by such means the Credit or Population of the place or the advantage of individuals will be promoted."[50]

Nicholson and Morris also became prominent members of a company formed to improve the navigation of the Potomac by building canals around the Little Falls, nine miles above Georgetown, and the Great Falls, fifteen miles above Georgetown. George Washington had proposed in the 1770s that the navigation of the river be improved, but it was not until 1784 that the Potomac Company was incorporated with Washington as its president. Henry Lee, governor of Virginia, served as one of its directors. James Rumsey, who Nicholson would later help finance in steamboat development, was recommended by Washington to superintend the construction of the canals, but as the projects were beset by labor, weather, and financial problems, Rumsey resigned in 1786, and the work stagnated. The construction of the Federal City renewed interest in the company and the canals, with Nicholson, Greenleaf, Morris, and other speculators becoming large shareholders.[51] They realized that the completion of these projects would enhance the value of their lots and buildings. Through the sale of new stock, the company by 1795 had $270,400 at its disposal; the states of Maryland and Virginia contributed to this total by purchasing shares. By 1796 both canals were finished, as well as a bridge, with a span of 120 feet, over the Potomac located above the smaller canal. The Georgetown Bridge Company was formed to construct the span and both Nicholson and Morris were shareholders.[52]

In addition to the canals and the bridge, the partners also bought land around the Great Falls from Governor Lee and planned to utilize the power of the falls for a saw mill and grist mill. This property was known as Matilda Ville and Nicholson took charge of its development. But Nicholson, acting for himself, Morris, and Greenleaf, postponed improvements at the falls until Lee informed them as to whether or not they could take water from the falls and the canal for their proposed mills. Nicholson wanted this right conveyed to the partners in the titles to the property. By 1796, the matter still was not settled to Nicholson's satisfaction, work had stopped and the partners ran out of funds.[53] In 1797, Morris and Nicholson tried to sell their shares in the property to Greenleaf and, failing that, to Henry Lee. They owed Lee $21,500, and he was threatening them with suits to collect. Eventually, to pay their creditors, this property was forfeited as were their shares in the Potomac Company. All of these efforts to promote the city and its development, as well as their own prospects, brought little relief for the partners, but they did bring the following words of praise from President Washington, when his secretary wrote to Nicholson,

> By the President's direction, I have the honor to acknowledge his receipt of your letter of the 23rd instant & its enclosure giving a detail of the progress which has been made in several elegant and useful arts and manufactures in this City [Washington, D.C.] chiefly thro your attention and support.
> The President directs me to inform you, Sir, that your laudable exertions to introduce & bring to maturity these manufactures in our own infant country demand & receive his Sincere wishes for their future progress & usefulness, and cannot, he conceives, fail to obtain general approbation. . . .[54]

Nicholson may have received some general approbation but not from the commissioners nor his creditors. According to their contracts of 1793, the partners were to pay $62,214 to the commissioners on 1 May of each year for seven consecutive years until they had paid for all of the lots. Since Greenleaf failed in his attempts to raise the loan in Holland, the only way they were able to pay the commissioners was through the sale of lots or, failing that, through loans. Nicholson and Morris, before and after they purchased Greenleaf's interest in the city, published broadsides, maps, and other promotional literature in order to induce sales and sent these with their agents to Europe. Speculators in the Federal City deliberately exaggerated the progress and advantages of the place to lure prospective buyers. Nicholson and Morris in 1796 painted glowing pictures of its prospects for their agents. Morris concluded one with, "I am delighted at the place, Nature has done it for all that could be desired and I see that man will do the rest."[55] As a result, when the Englishman Thomas Twining visited the city in 1796, he expected to see it well developed. Instead he found that,

> Having crossed an extensive tract of level country somewhat resembling an English heath, I entered a large wood through which a very imperfect road had been made. . . . Although no habitation of any kind was visible, I had no doubt, but I was now riding along one of the streets of the metropolitan city, I continued in this spacious avenue for half a mile, and then came out upon a large

spot cleared of wood, in the centre of which I saw two buildings on an extensive scale and some men at work on one of them. . . . Advancing and speaking to these workmen, they informed me that I was now in the centre of the city, and that the building before me was the Capitol, and the other designed to be a tavern. . . . Looking from where I now stood I saw on every side a thick wood pierced with avenues in a more or less perfect state. . . .[56]

Twining's countryman, Francis Bailey, observed the same primitive state when he toured the place and wrote, "The truth is, that not much more than one-half the city is *cleared*; the rest is *in woods*. . . ."[57] Helping to convey these false impressions to foreigners were the partners' European agents including—in addition to their major salesmen James Marshall and Enoch Edwards—Joseph Barnes, James Tate, William Temple Franklin, and Morris's son, William. Although they were able to draw capitalists like Thomas Law and William Duncanson to the city, most rejected their offers. Twining remarked that Law was fooling himself if he hoped to entice others from India to come and "smoke their hookahs on the banks of the Potomac."[58] Again, the European wars hurt their efforts and people with money to invest wanted safer avenues. They had no success in trying to raise loans in Holland and England using Washington lots as security, and adding to their woes was the fact that Dutch financiers refused to return the titles to lots used as security for monies advanced to Greenleaf and appropriated for his own use.

Failing in Europe, the speculators secured loans from various individuals at home giving lots as security for payment. They also were heavily indebted to a bank they had helped to establish—the Bank of Columbia, begun in 1793 and located at Georgetown. They once had to give 980 lots to secure a loan from the bank needed to pay the commissioners and consequently could not sell these lots, even if there were buyers. The same was true of other loans they had obtained using lots as security. In the end both individual creditors and the bank placed attachments against their Washington property in an attempt to collect debts.

Further complicating the situation was the fact that the commissioners refused to convey many of the titles for the lots because the partners were behind in their payments. By 1797, Nicholson and Morris claimed to have 7,235 lots remaining in their hands and the commissioners were pressing them for payments. One prospective buyer wrote, "Under these circumstances and in the present hazardous and precarious times, it is highly necessary that we should be well assured of our safety before we venture into advances. . . . Unless we receive such Property from you [that] is in every respect to our wishes, both as to clearness in Title of incumberances, & also as to its Value, we shall prefer remaining as we are."[59] President Washington was quite perturbed with them for their failures to pay the commissioners. They owed about $40,000 and the president feared that a cloud would be thrown "over the public and private concerns of the city. . . ." Robert Morris wrote sincere letters of regret to the president informing him that he and Nicholson could not get money either by selling lots or negotiating loans. He blamed Greenleaf for most of their difficulties and assured Washington that they would continue their efforts to fulfill their contractual obligations.[60]

Their failure to pay compelled the commissioners to go to Congress in 1796 to seek a loan to carry on operations. The alternative was to sell the lots for whatever price they could get and this the commissioners refused to do. They also threatened to confiscate all of the partners' lots and auction them off to the highest bidder. The sale was to take place thirty days after the 1 May 1796 payment became due. A commissioner wrote that this would be "a measure which will give much pain to the President, to my Colleagues and to myself, but it is indispensable; and at the President's desire I give you this notice." But as Morris stated in his letters to President Washington, this would not help the city but injure it, because Nicholson and Morris would contest the right of the commissioners to sell their lots in the courts, and the partners would make greater attempts to secure the funds to fulfill their contracts if their lots were not attached.[61] Morris and Nicholson helped to apply pressure to Congress to have the loan passed. Their efforts were successful and $300,000 was approved.[62] This postponed the sale of their lots by the commissioners.

The partners blamed the commissioners for some of their other difficulties, and they were not the only ones who complained. Dr. Nathaniel Appleton, who did some of the construction in the Federal City for the partners, said that the public was being defrauded by the commissioners. Appleton was referring to their favoring the Georgetown interests over the others and speculating in lots themselves. Nicholson said in 1797 that one of them, Dr. William Thornton, "was an Ass" and that another, Alexander White, was "the honest dupe." He said they were injuring the partners' sections of the city.[63] Nicholson also complained that the commissioners were tardy in dividing the lots with the original proprietors, thus delaying development of the city. Nevertheless, Nicholson sold lots to some of the commissioners to encourage their speculations and borrowed money from some of them using lots as security for repayment.[64] In fact, because the commissioners did not have enough funds to proceed with the construction of the public buildings, they had to borrow $100,000 from the state of Maryland in December 1796 and Nicholson and Morris brashly asked the commissioners if they could borrow it. Their request was denied.

Also, Morris and Nicholson were still complaining about the building requirements in their contracts. Without funds, how could they possibly finish 370 houses in the time allotted and still make their payments to the commissioners? Titles to the lots, even if obtained by payments, were and would be conditional—they had to meet the president's building regulations, which required a building on every third lot within four years after the purchase, or face forfeiture. The partners wanted the president to abolish the regulations so that the developers could proceed at their own pace. Morris said all would benefit from this in the end. He said the King of Prussia tried to build a city with these types of regulations "but with absolute authority & money at Command he could not do it & only impeded its Progress by the attempt." The building requirement also applied to individuals who bought lots from the partners, such as Thomas Law. Law was complaining about these stipulations and Morris replied that if the commissioners would suspend the regulations on their contracts, Morris and Nicholson would eliminate Law's need to build houses so quickly. The partners could not aid Law because they had to have Law build to help them fulfill their own contractual obligations.[65] The building stipulations also held for lots they had purchased from the original proprietors and this was to provide the partners with additional traumas, especially for those they had purchased from Daniel Carroll of Duddington.[66]

By 1796–97 Nicholson and Morris were pressed from all sides. Workers were staging demonstrations because they were not being paid; builders like Prentiss and Lovering were seizing some of the partners' building materials to recoup some of their losses; creditors were hounding them; title disputes were frequent occurrences; the commissioners were threatening to attach their property; and Greenleaf's notes were still haunting them. Not only were Nicholson's employees selling his building materials but he too was selling them in an attempt to salvage what he could from the fiasco. In fact, by 1797, Nicholson was finding it difficult to avoid Sheriff Joseph Boone of Prince Georges County, Maryland, who wanted to bring him to

Maryland to face his creditors there. He was urged by Morris to return to Philadelphia but refused, stating that he was staying in the Federal City to try to extricate the business entanglements despite his fear of being arrested. He concluded with, "I am safe yet and hope to continue so altho all Hell should turn loose. . . ."[67] Nicholson's hopes were not realized for he was arrested by Boone when he crossed the bridge into Georgetown from the Federal City. His friends raised bail for him and Boone, probably a kind man at heart, let Nicholson return to Philadelphia to try and raise some money to appease his creditors. Nicholson told Morris that he was taking the backroads to Philadelphia, ". . . I should not make a triumphant Entry into your Babylon, lest it might turn out a Babylonish Captivity. . . ." Since he also had creditors in Philadelphia who were anxious to see him, the reference to Babylonish Captivity was not inappropriate. Nicholson made frequent journeys between Philadelphia and the Federal City for a year. One of his creditors was going to bring suit against Boone if Nicholson did not return to Washington and Maryland in his custody, but Nicholson avoided Boone rather than return.[68] This brought all kinds of recriminations against the Sheriff and Boone wrote, "I hope my dear friend Mr. Nicholson you will consider Mrs. Boone and her Poor Little Children. Break away that Heavy Cloud which has been hanging over me for nearly 12 months."[69]

One creditor that was pressing the sheriff to take action against Nicholson was the State of Maryland. Nicholson and Morris had bought some land in the Federal City from Maryland, part of which contained a hopyard. They gave their usual notes in payment which they later were unable to pay. William Marbury, of *Marbury v. Madison* fame, brought suits against the partners on behalf of the state, and Maryland then attached some of their lots in the city. Nicholson and Morris wrote to Marbury and asked him not to sell their lots but to give them more time to raise the money to pay. Maryland eventually did sell the lots as did other states. Pennsylvania placed a lien against some of Nicholson's Washington lots, and the Washington commissioners attached the lots in 1797.

With states, creditors, bankers, the Washington commissioners, employees, and contractors all undertaking attachment proceedings, there were not enough lots to satisfy all. Nicholson and Morris had used so many lots as security to appease various creditors that no one, including Nicholson and Morris, knew just how many lots, if any, remained unattached by 1797. Their agents had not kept accurate records and neither had they. Their debts pyramided, built partly on the flimsy structure of their cross-endorsement of notes, using the lots and land company shares as additional collateral.[70] Beleaguered on all sides, Nicholson even contacted the owner of a brothel in Philadelphia and asked him if he would like to lease a hotel of his in the Federal City for the same purpose. With the failure of these attempts, Morris advised Nicholson to flee the city. Nicholson replied, "What can my Crossing the Potomack do for me my dear Sir, if I were to take the wings of the morning and fly to the uttermost parts of the Earth, even there should my Debts follow and my Bills and Notes oppress me, both Sides of the Potomack are alike insecure."[71]

As a last resort, Nicholson and Morris decided to bring some order out of this chaos and to salvage what they could by placing their Washington property in the hands of the trustees of the Aggregate Fund in June 1797. This body was organized by Nicholson, Morris, Greenleaf, and all of the creditors who had claims against them in regard to the Federal City project. The creditors banded together in the Aggregate Fund with the hope that a united effort would enable all to secure money owed. The trustees of the Fund included Henry Pratt, John Ashley, Thomas Francis, John Miller, and Jacob Baker, and they were empowered to arrange for effective security for the debts owed by the partners by selling or mortgaging town lots and by selling other lands and land company shares held by Greenleaf, Morris, and Nicholson. The partners hoped that once debts were paid, a surplus would remain for them.[72]

The partners could not sell any more lots after July 1797 as the trustees of the Aggregate Fund now had this responsibility; this was the case with the business with the commissioners as well. The trustees insisted on Morris and Nicholson supplying them with property, other than the lots, to satisfy their debts accumulated in connection with the Federal City. This, of course, further drained the already depleted financial resources of concerns such as the Population Company, the North American Land Company, and the Asylum Company. The partners also had to convey Kentucky property to the trustees to keep Maryland, Carroll, to whom they owed $13,000, and the Washington commissioners, to whom they owed $60,000, from selling their lots at public auction.[73]

By November 1797 the resources were no longer sufficient as the trustees refused to accept land company shares or Kentucky lands as security in their attempts to raise loans to save the Washington property. The partners replied that this was all they had left. Morris dejectedly wrote Nicholson, "You may as well piss against the wind as offer the trustees Georgia and South Carolina lands after their refusal of Kentucky. I see [our] poor Washington property will be disgraced and sacrificed."[74] Morris and Nicholson could not even pay their lawyer fees by 1797; Greenleaf was in jail and Morris and Nicholson would soon join him. The trustees of the Aggregate Fund tried to stop the commissioners from selling the partners' lots at public auction, but when no money was received, the commissioners had no other alternative. As public officers, they had the responsibility of seeing that the public buildings were constructed and that funds were available for this purpose. If they had not sold the partners' lots, they would have been dismissed in disgrace. The sale was advertised for 31 May 1797 to raise the $60,000 the partners owed in back payments through 1 May 1797.[75]

To the end, even from the confines of their prison, the partners blamed James Greenleaf for all of their woes. Nicholson was so angry with Greenleaf that he started a newspaper onslaught which had the overtones of a personal vendetta. Morris was angry with Nicholson for bringing their affairs into public print and wrote his son-on-law, James Marshall, that "you will see or hear that Mr. Nicholson & Mr. Greenleaf have entered into a news paper War, which has injured not only them but me, altho I have as yet kept myself clear of it. . . ." Morris did try to get them to stop their quarrels in the papers but to no avail, as Greenleaf insisted on continuing until one or the other was exonerated in the public's eyes.[76] Greenleaf was using notes endorsed by Nicholson which Nicholson claimed he had never authorized. Consequently, he published the following:

"Caution" to the public on January 23, 1797:

Whereas a large number of notes and acceptances wherein I am payer and acceptor, generally drawn in favor of or payable to James Greenleaf, or endorsed by him have fraudulently or improperly obtained from me by the said James Greenleaf and many of them have been detained from me by him which ought to have been delivered up, having from a misplaced confidence he unsuspectingly led to give such notes of *acceptances* twice and in some cases even thrice for the same debt and many of them given for property here in which he had no title & can give none. The Public are hereby cautioned not to receive or purchase any of the said notes or acceptances, as they will not be paid by me.[77]

Morris as well as Nicholson had endorsed notes for Greenleaf with the expectation that he would repay them upon completion of the Dutch loan. Of couse, when he failed to consummate this loan, the partners were left with his defaulted notes to pay. Broker Mordicai Lewis of Philadelphia alone held over $194,000 of Greenleaf's defaulted notes which he expected Morris and Nicholson to pay.

Coupled with this was the fact that Greenleaf used what monies he did obtain from the Dutchmen for his own benefit and used in a similar manner funds given to him by the other partners to pay the Washington commissioners. Greenleaf even tried to persuade Alexander Hamilton to let him use his name in a feeble attempt to solve his financial problems, but Hamilton wisely replied, "I think myself bound to decline the overture."[78] Greenleaf also made agreements and sales and gave lots and land company shares as security for debts without the knowledge of other partners. The shrewd Greenleaf also deceived the partners when he sold his personal property interests in the city to them. Nicholson complained to Greenleaf, "in your offer of the 8th July you state your 800 lots to be near to the President's house and near to the Capitol, neither of which is the case. The two parcels are generally at the extreme parts of the City, or near it."[79] Nicholson said $200 was the value of the lots Greenleaf conveyed whereas the ones they should have obtained, around the president's house, were worth $1,000. Nicholson informed Greenleaf that he owed the partners the $800 per lot difference and then asked his lawyer, James Gibson, to bring suits against Greenleaf for his illegal practices.[80] Greenleaf already had instituted suits against both Morris and Nicholson. He maintained that he had to sell $600,000 worth of his property in New York to take up the protested notes and bills of Nicholson and Morris and that he was taking them to court to collect.[81]

Once Greenleaf instituted the suits, Morris entered the battle arena and blasted him with the same charges Nicholson had made. Morris informed Commissioner Scott that Greenleaf had opened a Pandora's box that would bring his own ruin. He also wrote that he would never forgive himself for having been duped into schemes with Greenleaf. Greenleaf said he was the one who had been duped, and Morris quipped that Greenleaf also said "his wife seduced him to her Bed before Marriage in Holland." He concluded with, " 'poor innocent' as if it was not known what great pains he took to obtain his wife, and to lead M & N into his Schemes, but that he should have Succeeded is the Wonder."[82]

Pennsylvania Speculator and Patriot: John Nicholson

The dispute between the partners did not end until the deaths of Nicholson and Morris. It continued even after Greenleaf took up residence in the debtor's apartment of Prune Street Prison in Philadelphia in 1797. He was released in 1798, a declared bankrupt, but Morris in the meantime had joined him in the debtor's apartment, and Nicholson took up residence soon after Greenleaf's release. While Nicholson and Morris languished in jail, Greenleaf wrote this final self-righteous note, "My veracity is, at least, untainted by any abuse of public trust, my conscience will never be disquieted by the embezzlement of a widow's or orphan's portion; and I shall never be so callous as to smile . . . on the penury and ruin which I inflicted on others."[83]

While the Washington venture proved disastrous to John Nicholson and Robert Morris, competition and emulation were the parents of progress, and their interest in the Federal City motivated others to invest and thereby to launch the development of the capital of the United States. I reject the evaluation of Nicholson and Morris made by one historian who maintains that the legacy they left was a bad reputation for the capital as a place for investment—a reputation which handicapped the city for years to come.[84] The speculators moved into the city when the public auctions had failed to bring in funds sufficient for the construction of the public buildings and the development of the city. Although this was an example of premature enterprise, as was frequently the case with speculations, that the city existed at all in the 1790s was due very largely to the efforts of Nicholson and his partners. President Washington's praise of Nicholson for his efforts in regard to the city's development was not misplaced. The government moved to the new capital in 1800 as planned, and the public officials found almost 600 buildings finished and the President's House and Capitol building well under construction. This would not have been possible without the efforts of Nicholson and his partners.

9
NICHOLSON'S
ROLE AS AN
EARLY AMERICAN
ENTREPRENEUR

At the time when he was embroiled in land company and city development schemes, John Nicholson was also becoming involved in a variety of other business enterprises. Like others of his time, he attempted to bring to fruition many of the recommendations made by Secretary of the Treasury Alexander Hamilton in his "Report on Manufactures" submitted to Congress in December 1791. In the report, the secretary called for a balanced economy in an attempt to make the United States more nearly self-sufficient. Since agriculture was the dominant economic activity, he stressed the need for manufacturing, the use of labor-saving machinery, and the utilization of immigrants in manufacturing so as to avoid a drain on agricultural labor. Hamilton believed that a protected and adequate home market was essential to the growth of the nation and this necessitated the combination of manufacturing and agriculture.[1]

Aiding Hamilton in the development of these ideas was Tench Coxe, friend and business associate of Nicholson. Coxe had been pressing for a balanced economy since the 1780s and Hamilton appointed him assistant secretary of the Treasury shortly before Hamilton submitted his report to the Congress. Like Coxe and Hamilton, Nicholson stressed the need for non-agricultural pursuits and acquired an interest in manufacturing. He had become a member of the Pennsylvania Society for the Encouragement of Manufactures and Useful Arts when it had been established in 1787 under the presidency of Nicholson's friend, Thomas Mifflin. A manufacturing committee of the society had been formed with Nicholson and Tench Coxe as members.[2] The society had been formed to promote American industries and new labor-saving inventions with financial aid offered to inventors by the individual members and by the society in the form of awards for the best machinery for use in textile manufacturing. The funds were to be raised partly through the sale of subscriptions of not less than 10 pounds each.

Part of the efforts of the society were directed toward bringing to the United States Englishmen skilled in the textile industry and toward acquiring models of textile machinery. The exportation of machinery from England had been forbidden since 1774, consequently these activities were illegal. Nevertheless, models were brought to America, and the Pennsylvania Society acquired many of them. The society then proposed to establish a cotton manufactory of its own in Philadelphia, but on 24 March 1790 a fire destroyed the building which housed the machinery and, along with it, the society. In offering rewards to textile innovators, the society did entice such individuals as Samuel Slater to come to America in 1789, and it was he who built the first successful Arkwright mill in the United States at Pawtucket, Rhode Island, in 1790.[3]

In addition to supporting the Pennsylvania society, Tench Coxe stressed the need for the formation of a national society to encourage manufacturing and the balanced economy and Hamilton agreed with him. Consequently, on 22 November 1791, two weeks before the secretary submitted his report to Congress, the New Jersey Society for Establishing Useful Manufactures (S.U.M.) was incorporated by the Legislature of that state. Hamilton and his associates sought, through this society, to put their idea of a balanced economy into practice by establishing a manufacturing center to serve as a model for the nation. In August and September 1791 the notification of the project was made in the newspapers. The initial capital was to consist of a minimum of $500,000 in $100 shares, and subscriptions could be made either in specie or in the public debt of the United States. By December 1791 $625,000 had been subscribed (Nicholson participated by taking at least ten shares), but many of the total shares subscribed were never paid.[4]

Hamilton had been contacted on 9 August 1791 by several of the directors of S.U.M., including Nicholas Low, William Duer, William Constable, and Abijah Hammond, to help obtain workers and artisans skilled in cotton textile manufacturing. Thomas Marshall and William Pearce were recommended to the society as two Englishmen who knew the principles of the Arkwright inventions and could establish a cotton manufactory.[5] Machinery was acquired and these two and others began to construct a manufacturing complex at the Falls of the Passaic to utilize the available water power. The State of New Jersey, in incorporating S.U.M., had granted it a city charter over a six square mile district at the falls which later became the site of what is now Paterson, New Jersey. Work proceeded slowly and the project was almost ruined when many of its backers went bankrupt in the Duer Panic of 1792.[6] The society was also blasted in the newspapers as many associated the project with Hamilton's banking and assumption programs, or another attempt to create a government-sponsored monopoly.[7]

Hamilton had not intended to take direct command of the operations of S.U.M., but the panic forced him to assume this role to save the experiment from failure. The project suffered from the inexperience of American supervisors and workers in operating power-driven machinery for cotton production. Therefore, on 9 November 1792, Hamilton made an agreement with John Campbell, a Scottish stocking weaver who had supervised cotton manufactures in England and Scotland, to bring back from the British Isles stocking frames, tools, and other machinery, as well as twelve skilled workers to operate the machines. On behalf of himself, Nicholas Low, and Abijah Hammond, Hamilton further agreed that $3,000 would be advanced by S.U.M. to establish "a Manufactory of Stockings under the management of the said John Campbell at such place within the United States as they shall think proper. . . ." Campbell, on his part, agreed to supervise the manufactory for seven years in exchange for one-third of the profits. The terms were settled, and Campbell brought his machinery and men to Paterson in 1793.[8]

But the project was doomed to failure, even with these new additions, for a number of reasons. Traveler Henry Wansey, himself a cotton manufacturer in his native England, gave some of the causes when he quoted Dr. Joseph Priestley's reasons for not establishing a cotton manufactory of his own after viewing Paterson. Priestley wrote that Paterson "had been brought forward at a very heavy expense, is badly conducted, and will become a heavy loss to the first undertakers; . . . such undertakings will continue to decline till the country is so full of inhabitants, as not to employ themselves on the land, which at present commands a great preference." Wansey added that textiles could be produced much more cheaply in England because the wages paid to workers were lower due to the larger supply.[9] Another visitor to the project, St. Mery, recorded that "the shares have already lost much in value, which demonstrates the impossibility of profiting from a business venture when wages and labor are too high."[10] Other reasons for the failure were: 1. the project had to operate without the government bounties which Hamilton had said were necessary for infant enterprises to be successful; 2. women and children constituted the bulk of the labor force and they were unskilled; 3. there was a greater demand in the 1790s than ever for America's agricultural products due to the European Wars, thus resources and capital stayed in agriculture and in shipping; 4. the invention of the cotton gin in 1793 also made agriculture more profitable, again thwarting heavy concentrations in manufacturing; and 5. too much of the capital of S.U.M. was sunk in machinery, land, and buildings and too little remained for operating expenses. So by 1795, Paterson had become an agricultural village and Hamilton went into land speculation to recoup his losses. When Liancourt visited the site in 1797, all that remained was "a variety of machinery, but all in a state of decay."[11]

Most of the machinery had not decayed, however, because it had been sold to an individual who still had faith in the dream of a balanced economy and the profits that could be obtained by a manufacturing entrepreneur. This individual was, of course, John Nicholson. He attempted to duplicate and excel Hamilton's proposed manufacturing complex at Paterson with one of his own at the Falls of the Schuylkill near Philadelphia. Late in 1793, John Campbell, the man whom Hamilton had hired to save the Paterson project, was introduced to Nicholson by their mutual friend William Pollard. The latter was an Englishman who, in 1791, had obtained an American patent for a water frame to spin cotton, was perfecting it, and was being financed by Nicholson. Campbell, probably sensing the failure at Paterson, offered to form a contract with Nicholson and to move the machinery and men from the Paterson project to Nicholson's proposed complex at the falls. Nicholson wanted Campbell to keep their negotiations a secret, probably because Nicholson was also a member of S.U.M. Campbell informed Nicholson through Pollard,

> Mr. [Nicholas] Low questioned me concerning the plan upon which I intended to carry on the business. I told him that I had formed a Connection at Philadelphia & intended moving off Directly but agreeable to your request mentioned no names; he wishes very much to know the persons concerned—at the same time it appears to me that he was Sorry that the Machinery & C [ompany] should leave Paterson, that he expected that I would carry on the business there. . . .[12]

The agreement between Nicholson and Campbell required Nicholson to pay to Nicholas Low and the society $1,440 for the "whole stock of the Paterson manufactory" on 5 February 1794, and on 6 February, after the money was sent, Campbell informed Pollard that he was beginning to ship the machines from Paterson to Philadelphia. Campbell also informed Nicholson (who they now knew was the purchaser) that Low and his associates wanted him to sign an agreement freeing them of any future claims Campbell might make against them. The agreement also was to cover Campbell's workers whom he was bringing with him to Nicholson's employ. Campbell concluded with "I think that Mr. Nicholson can support a Manufactory equal to Mr. Low or his party & in Justice to him I deem it necessary to retain the men."[13] On 8 February 1794 Nicholson signed an agreement with Low, Alexander Hamilton, and Abijah Hammond certifying that Campbell had dissolved his contract with S.U.M. and was now working for Nicholson, who would assume all future claims of Campbell and his men.[14]

When the Paterson project was under attack in the newspapers of Philadelphia, S.U.M. published a rebuttal entitled "observations on the Letters of a 'Farmer,' addressed to Yeomanry of the United States." The supporters of the Paterson project defended their enterprise and suggested that the "Farmer" promote a similar manufacturing complex in Pennsylvania on the Susquehanna. They said this would draw capital to develop American industries like they were doing in New Jersey and help to eliminate foreign competition. The primary author of this piece could have been Tench Coxe, an avid supporter of S.U.M., who in 1787 and again in 1793 had suggested that a manufacturing complex be established along the Susquehanna near the forks of the east and west branches.[15] Evidently, Nicholson was the man who was attempting this feat in Pennsylvania, for by 1793 he was making queries about the English cotton industry of such people as Dr. Thomas Cooper and Dr. Joseph Priestley, while he was negotiating land sales. Interestingly enough, the land Nicholson owned was at the forks of the Susquehanna. Coxe, for his part, must have given up on the idea because he offered his 90,000 acres in the Wyoming Valley to Nicholson.

Further evidence of Nicholson's plans and promotions of manufacturing was presented by the promoter's membership in the American Philosophical Society of which his friend, Dr. David Rittenhouse, served as president. In 1793 Nicholson was asked by the society for advice on manufacturing. He wrote that the various manufacturing societies and individuals could help by contacting foreign experts about coming to this country to aid in the development of American enterprises and that more efforts should be made to secure American patents for foreign inventors who came to the United States with their inventions. Nicholson took his own advice by financially supporting William Pollard and his water frame and by contracting with Pollard to build cotton machines for him. Nicholson also instructed his European agent and friend, Dr. Enoch Edwards, to procure "artists and manufactories" for use in his proposed factory. He said in the letter, "my present ideas are to employ my factory principally on the articles of Hosiery and low price cottons—without going generally into the trade until some little experience of the success of the enterprise is obtained. . . ."[16] Pollard was enthusiastic about the prospects of the projected plant and wrote these words of praise to Nicholson: "I cannot doubt but it will gain you the merited esteem of your Country at large for being the first promoter (to an extent) of this kind of manufactures." Nicholson then commissioned Pollard to build machines using 1,000 spindles and to look for possible sites for the manufactory. By 31 May 1793 the factory was under construction at the Falls of the Schuylkill. Pollard was also hiring workers brought from England and Holland and keeping them from going to the Paterson complex.

It was at this stage that the contacts with John Campbell were made, the agreement with him consummated, and the shift of the Paterson machinery and workers made to Philadelphia. It was ironic that even Governor William Paterson of New Jersey was helping to move the looms. While the falls factory was being completed, Campbell established his men and machines in Nicholson's building at 451 North Front Street in Philadelphia and converted it into the Fleecy Hosiery Manufactory. Campbell also helped with the construction of the Falls Mill as well as two others, the Kensington Mill in Philadelphia and the Globe Mill near Reading. By October 1794 Pollard informed Nicholson that "we shall be ready to Card & prepare our Cotton for Spinning at the Globe Mill by next week. . . ."[17]

While these mills were being constructed, Nicholson also made contracts with others who had experience in textiles in England. Charles Taylor, who had built the Albion Mills in England, and John Bowler, "who invented a new machine which Cards, rolls & Spins the finest thread at the same time & . . . with which . . . one person . . . can do the work of 15 men in a day," were hired by Nicholson to work for him. Taylor was to build steam engines while Bowler was to make cotton machinery. Taylor knew how to build the Watt-engine, and it was predicted that with the additions of himself and Bowler "a clear profit of 10,000 pds. a year would accrue after deducting 3,000 pds. for workers, wages & ordinary expenses." Taylor was to supervise a steam engine factory at the falls and the iron foundry that was also being constructed there.[18]

Another Englishman who went to work for Nicholson was John Lithgow who had operated stocking manufactories in England and Scotland. Nicholson asked his advice as to the best possible location for a cotton manufactory, and Lithgow advised against any seaport town because, although materials and machines could be obtained easily in them, it was almost impossible to get competent workers at reasonable rates in Philadelphia or any other port. They wanted one dollar a day and England would undersell American hosiery at these rates. He advised Nicholson to move his hosiery works from Philadelphia to an inland site near villages where boys might be used. Lithgow agreed to come to his complex under construction at the Falls of the Schuylkill for one year on a trial basis to try and help make it a success, but he preferred a more inland location. Lithgow also insisted that his friend William England, another expert in hosiery manufacturing, come with him to the falls and supervise the workers; Nicholson agreed.[19]

One of the reasons for the failure of the Paterson project was S.U.M.'s concentration on cotton instead of diversifying and manufacturing other products. Nicholson tried not to duplicate their mistake but instead promoted a variety of manufacturing enterprises, all of which were eventually located at the falls. These included a glass works, button works, iron foundry, stone quarry, dye house, and a supply store in addition to the cloth and steam engine manufactories already mentioned. The glass works and button manufactory had been started in Philadelphia but in 1795–96 these were moved to the falls.

Henry Wansey described the Falls of the Schuylkill as "nothing but an obstruction of the rapid stream from several large rocks having fallen into it from the neighboring heights. Skilful [sic] pilots know how to pass them in loaded boats, without danger."[20] Liancourt visited Nicholson's manufacturing center in 1795 and described it as follows:

Above the falls, a Mr. Nicholson possesses large iron works, a button manufactory and a glass house. But none of these works are completed. The buildings, however, which appear to be well constructed, are nearly all finished. A particular building is assigned to every different branch of labour; and the largest is designed for the habitation of the workmen, of whom Mr. Nicholson will be obliged to keep at least a hundred. . . . The situation of this settlement is extremely well chosen; for, on the very spot where the navigation of the river is intercepted, all the materials necessary can be procured. . . . The sand required for the glass-house is brought from the banks of the Delaware; the cast-iron from the higher parts of the Schuylkill, and the pit-coal . . . from Virginia. . . . Everything promises success to his undertaking.[21]

In short, the promoter was constructing what must have been one of the first company towns in America. In addition to the manufactories, he built workers' quarters and a store to supply their needs. Nicholson in 1796 instructed the manager of his store, Thomas Joubert, to have the workers take their wages out in produce at the store.[22] He had different supervisors for each enterprise: William Eichbaum, the glass works; Nathaniel Mix, the button works; William Pollard, John Campbell, James Lithgow, William England, and Charles Taylor, the stocking manufactory, dyehouse, and steam engine works, at different times; Thomas Bourne and Thomas Flood, the iron foundry; Henry Elouis, the stone quarry; and Thomas Joubert, the store. Nicholson even brought a German family to America to run a farm of his at the falls for the purpose of supplying the workers and supervisors with food. Nicholson had ambitions of expanding this complex and bought all of the surrounding estates from such notables as Governor Mifflin, Alexander J. Dallas, William Rawle, Dr. William Smith, and John Dickinson. In fact, Nicholson explained his ultimate goal later when he was forced to abandon most of these projects. He intended to establish a great manufacturing center connected to Philadelphia by a canal cut between the Schuylkill and Delaware rivers.[23]

The Philadelphia venture remained a dream as financial problems plagued all of his enterprises at the falls. Nicholson went into the glass business because there was the demand for window glass and bottles in the 1780s and the 1790s. He had the necessary raw materials: potash and pearl ashe, from places like Asylum, which were used as flux for common and white glass respectively; manganese, which again helped produce transparent glass, obtained from suppliers in Philadelphia like William Davy and Company; charcoal obtained from the surrounding forests with the help of John Jacobs; sand and clay from the river bottoms; glass furnace grates supplied by Nicholson's foundry; and competent glass blowers from Westphalia like the Eichbaum family who supervised the work. Nicholson began the business in 1793 upon receiving advice from Thomas Bedwell and Thomas Town, who had operated a glass business in England. They advised that since the workers only spent nine months of the year at the glass furnace, the other three should be spent in preparing the furnace for the next blast. Not only did Nicholson insist on this, but he told Eichbaum, when the workers complained that they had not been paid, that he had paid them for twelve months when the factory was being built and that they owed him money instead of the reverse.[24]

The factory produced all sorts of glass ware. In addition to window glass, some of which was shipped to Federal City for use in Nicholson's buildings, the factory produced snuff bottles, claret bottles, quart and pint bottles, mustard bottles, and glass tubes and apothecarial glasses for doctors. One of the more unusual demands came from Charles Willson Peale who ordered glass eyes for some of his statues.

But the glass works suffered like the others from Nicholson's lack of financial resources. The profits for 1796-97 were only $77.[25] Eichbaum constantly complained about the need for money to buy the necessary supplies and the situation became chronic by 1797 when there was no coal available to keep the furnaces going. The workers, some of whom were drunkards, went unpaid and many left to find employment elsewhere. In the end, the glass works was attached by the sheriff and sold at public auctions.

The button works was also begun in 1793. Nicholson was influenced in the business by the Mix family of New Haven, Connecticut, whose button manufactory was producing nearly 2,000 gross of metal and metal-rimmed buttons a year by 1789. The Mix's designed their own machines and made their own plate metal. Nicholson contacted them about the details of their operations and John and Jonathan Mix sent him a sketch of a button manufactory.[26] Nathaniel F. Mix later agreed to come to Philadelphia and run an operation similar to theirs for Nicholson. By 1795, Nicholson's Philadelphia works was producing 100 gross per day. His vest buttons sold for $.50 per gross, coat buttons for $1.50.[27] Then, in 1795, he shifted this operation to the falls complex with Nathaniel Mix and Thomas Bourne running the operation there. At the same time, he started a button manufactory in New Haven, Connecticut, under the direction of Jonathan Mix because the Mixes said buttons were cheaper to make there. Nicholson supplied his Federal City stores with buttons produced at his factories and even had customers in Kentucky. Nicholson also made military buttons and sold these to the United States government and the government of the French Republic. By 1797, this enterprise, like the others, was in serious financial trouble. Nicholson could not furnish enough raw materials like lead and copper to keep the production going, and workers were not being paid and started to leave the falls. In Connecticut, Jonathan Mix wrote that Nicholson had not financed the manufactory as he promised; Mix pleaded for money, and in 1798 told Nicholson that he had paid $3,000 out of his own pocket to keep the manufactory going and had deprived his ten children in the process. He asked Nicholson for relief, Nicholson could offer none, and the button manufactories were also eventually sold at sheriff's sales.[28]

The same kinds of difficulties beset the hosiery manufactory and dye house. John Campbell failed to solve Nicholson's problems, just as he had failed at Paterson. Nicholson accused Campbell of misusing funds he had given him and Campbell pleaded his innocence and wrote,

> Had I been a person who had bad intentions, I could when I went to Scotland staid and kept from the late Secretary of the Treasury [Hamilton] . . . three Hundred guineas, the government of that Country would a made me a presant [sic] for doing so in Ninty four, you intrusted me with a considerable sum of money, which might have been an object for a bad man to go of [sic] with. . . . I hope you will look upon me as an honest man, altho poor.[29]

However, Nicholson did not accept this defense and, in fact, even had to bail Campbell out of jail when the latter was apprehended for smuggling out of Scotland three textile workers who had broken a contract in their homeland. Then Campbell did not pay his workers with funds Nicholson had appropriated for that purpose and the workers came to Nicholson with their complaints. In the end, Nicholson instituted a lawsuit against Campbell to force him to account for the monies he had appropriated.

Nicholson had no better luck with William Pollard, John Bowler, Charles Taylor, or the others in their attempts to make the hosiery manufactory a success. Pollard wrote, "it is painful to me to be troubling you so often but I have not a Dollar to go to Market with for my own Family, or to give to some poor Widows who board some of my people. I have given several of my People who had no Shoes, order on my Shoemaker, who has had faith & God knows my own Bill for Shoes is of long standing. . . ." Nicholson could not pay the workers in this manufactory either, and as a result, they began to leave. He tried to use his note endorsed by Morris for this purpose but Pollard wrote, "I can not do anything with it."[30]

As for John Bowler, he caused Nicholson more trouble than Campbell. Bowler was brought from England at Nicholson's expense and advanced $10,000. In September 1795 he absconded with the money and sailed for Cork, Ireland. Not only did he flee, but he had also been building machines for others while supposedly working for Nicholson. This breach of contract carried a penalty of 1,000 pounds in this era. Nicholson wrote to his friend and agent, Samuel Bayard, who was also the American Claim's officer in London, to apprehend Bowler and charge him with damages of $13,000.[31] There was no evidence that Nicholson ever gained satisfaction.

Charles Taylor was hired by Nicholson to build steam engines for his hosiery manufactory and also for steamboats in which Nicholson had an interest. Taylor complained about the same lack of funds as the others and Nicholson typically answered that Taylor was misusing the monies that had been appropriated. Nicholson also had visions of using Taylor's talents to devise an engine that could be used to pump water for the cities of Philadelphia and Washington but this also would take capital. In 1796 Nicholson promised Taylor that he would devote his full attention to this project as soon as his affairs in the Federal City were unsnarled, but this was never accomplished. By 1797, the sheriff was at the falls complex attaching Taylor's engines, and Taylor was informing Nicholson that he had no money even to feed his own family.[32]

Unfortunately for Nicholson, the same fate befell his store, iron works, and quarry at the falls. He used the iron works, managed for him by Thomas Flood, to supply material for his glass house and hosiery manufactory as well as his buildings in the Federal City. He even had a working agreement with one of the famous ironmaster families of Pennsylvania, the Potts family. The Potts's works, located north of Nicholson's complex along the Schuylkill River at Potts-grove in Montgomery County, supplied his foundry at the falls with gray pigs.[33]

Nicholson's stone quarry supplied stone for the Lancaster-Philadelphia Turnpike and for the canals that were under construction in the Philadelphia area. Eventually, the quarry, supervised by Henry Elouis, would become part of Nicholson's Pennsylvania Land Company and would ultimately be sold at a sheriff's sale. Nicholson expected his store at the falls to be a major center of supplies for the Washington, D.C., project and for his numerous other stores in Pennsylvania, such as those at Philadelphia, Asylum, Wilkes-Barre, George Town, Fayette County, and Shippensburg. Everything from glassware to hosiery filtered through the falls store operated by Thomas Joubert. The goods were disseminated by Nicholson, in part through the use of his own fleet of boats which plied the Schuylkill from the falls to Philadelphia. His plans for the store, like his other plans, went awry.

In addition to the enterprises at the falls, Nicholson was the major partner in T.B. Freeman and Company of Philadelphia. As indicated earlier, this company was a supplier of pictures, chimney pieces, and luxury items for the Federal City project. His other partners in this company included Tristram and Benjamin Freeman, Richard Claiborne, and James Trenchard of Philadelphia, Burgess Allison of Baltimore, and William Annesley of Bordentown, New Jersey. The partnership was formed for "the business and art of Engraving Copperplate printing in plain and in colours, publishing prints, Carving and Gilding Composition ornaments, Colours, Earthen ware and stone composition. . . ."[34]

The company was located at 102 North Second Street in Philadelphia, and the articles of agreement called for it to last for seven years. Nicholson and the others imported artisans skilled in the above crafts from England, and they produced, in addition to chimney pieces, prints of Anthony Wayne, George Washington, and others, gold picture frames, fine china ware, and eye glasses. Dignitaries like General Anthony Wayne posed for engravings, and Judge Thomas McKean, a future governor of Pennsylvania, came to be fitted for glasses. Charles Parrish ran a branch store of the company in Charleston, South Carolina, and another was opened in the Federal City. But the company was not a financial success because it produced and supplied luxury items to a market that basically demanded necessities. Nicholson complained that he carried most of the financial load for the company and that his partners were not paying for their shares. By 1797 he could not afford this additional burden and withdrew from the firm and sold the stock he claimed.[35]

Nicholson also had an interest in mining operations which would add to the value of his lands as well as supply raw materials for his manufacturing activities. He participated in founding the first iron works west of the Allegheny Mountains. He formed a partnership with John Hayden in 1792, and they built a blast furnace at Fairfield, seven miles from Uniontown, Pennsylvania.[36] Unfortunately, Nicholson did not investigate Hayden's character until later. One informant wrote Nicholson that Hayden had "miraculously brought about things no one thought possible. His good intentions have brought aid even when parties weren't that much interested. Yet I do not think he is fully calculated for extensive trust."[37] This characterization was proven correct because after Nicholson had established a store at George Town under Jessee Evans's management, Evans informed Nicholson that Hayden was in debt for 1,000 pounds and was obtaining goods from Nicholson's store on credit. Later Evans had to draw on Nicholson to pay some of Hayden's debt. Shortly thereafter, Hayden started to steal part of the receipts that belonged to Nicholson and to convey part of their joint lands to his son; by 1797 Hayden was cutting the timber and defacing the land.[38] Ultimately, Hayden came to Philadelphia to dissolve the partnership at Nicholson's insistence. Since Hayden owed him 6,570 pounds, Nicholson took over most of the property. The property was incorporated into the Pennsylvania Land Company and eventually sold by the sheriff to satisfy Pennsylvania's lien on Nicholson's property.[39]

Nicholson was also in partnership with General James Chambers in the Loudon Forge and Furnace at Chambersburg in Franklin County and this venture proved to be as unsuccessful as his partnership with Hayden. By 1796 Chambers was writing, ". . . my Expectation has fallen short but hope soon to be able to realize our most Sanguine Expectations,"[40] and by 1797, Nicholson was pleading with the General to send him his share of the profits with ". . . surely the profits by this [time] must have amounted at least to something or it is a wretched Concern indeed."[41] This was a "wretched concern" and so were his other furnaces at Asylum and in northern Virginia along the Potomac River. He also had an interest in the famous Hopewell Furnace, forty miles up the Schuylkill from Philadelphia, operated by James Old, but he had to sell his share to pay creditors.

Just as Nicholson could enhance the value of his lands and supply his building needs with iron production, the mining of coal could bring similar rewards. Therefore, he had become an organizer and part owner of the Lehigh Coal Company which was located about thirty miles from Bethlehem, Pennsylvania, on the Lehigh River. He formed a partnership in this concern in 1792 with Colonel Jacob Weiss and Robert Morris. Nicholson became president of the company in 1794 and took an interest in improving the navigation of the Lehigh River to improve the company's prospects, but this venture met the fate of all the others. Nicholson could not pay the assessments on his shares that had to be made to keep the company in operation and on 6 March 1798 had to forfeit them. His efforts to make this company a success helped lay the groundwork for the Lehigh Navigation Company founded in 1818.[42]

Nicholson also had an interest in lead, silver, and copper mines. Lead was used to make buttons, and silver and copper were used in his engraving business. Nicholson hired John Nancarrow, who had been in the mining business in England, and Thomas Bedwell to tour the country in 1793 and empowered them to purchase and lease mines they thought were worthwhile.[43] These two inspected mines in Pennsylvania, New Jersey, Virginia, the Southwest Territory (now Tennessee), and Connecticut. Eventually Nicholson purchased lead, silver, and copper mines in all of the above states and territories. His lead mine in the Southwest Territory was a partnership venture with William Blount, governor of the territory, George James, and David Allison. Judge James Wilson of Pennsylvania was a partner of his in a Frederick County, Virginia, lead mine, and Thomas Bedwell and John Mason joined him in a partnership in a lead mine near Hartford, Connecticut. Nicholson also had three lead mines in Pennsylvania near Reading and Philadelphia. His copper and silver mines were located near Frederick Town, Virginia, and in Northampton and York counties in Pennsylvania. Most of these mines were either sold to pay Nicholson's creditors or attached to satisfy liens.[44]

Added to all of the above enterprises were tanyards, saltpeter and powder works, a carpet works, a hat manufactory, and, probably feeling that an alliance with something Divine might help, a "Hot Pressed Bible" concern. All of these were consuming much of Nicholson's time and money, neither of which he could afford. None of them were providing enough profits to help him, and most were injuring him. In 1796 he started to become disillusioned with all of his manufacturing enterprises and wrote to two men who asked him to join in another, "if you could ensure me half the profits you State I would go into it but estimates are not always realized especially in manufactures with me they have seldom been so. . . ."[45] Mrs. Nicholson wanted her husband to abandon most of these and so did Robert Morris. Morris told him, "they consume your time, pick your Pocket, Suck your blood, make Complaints & never will retribute one shilling for a Pound. Therefore cast them off & save thyself."[46] And when Morris was offering this advice he was writing from personal experience. He had a manufacturing complex in New Jersey that was costing him large sums of money and providing him little in return. He spent $300,000 on the complex and had to mortgage it for $100,000 because he needed money.

Nicholson did not abandon these projects but had to sacrifice all of them to pay his creditors. Liancourt, describing Nicholson's falls complex, aptly summarized the major causes for failure when he wrote,

> All these natural advantages must vanish if ever there should arise a want of money, large and prompt supplies of which are required to give activity to the whole; as well as judgment, industry, and economy. There is in America a scarcity of persons capable of conducting a business of this kind. There are also but few good workmen, who are with difficulty obtained, and whose wages are exorbitant. . . . Mr. Nicholson's situation does not afford the most flattering prospects of success, if his returns be not rapid, as well as large.[47]

To enhance the prospects of having returns "rapid as well as large," Nicholson engaged in all kinds of internal improvement projects. As early as 1788, he promoted a road to pass from Northampton and Luzerne counties of Pennsylvania to the New York border by way of the Lehigh and northern branch of the Susquehanna. This Northern Road was an artery financed by private subscriptions, but Nicholson and other promoters wanted the assembly to help support it. Tench Coxe asked Nicholson to apply pressure on those with whom he had influence in the Pennsylvania legislature in order to pass the bill. He wrote, "the house appointed a commission. . . . Our object is now to get them to gather as soon as possible in order that we may be absolutely certain of getting the Bill thro this Session. Will you give it your helping hand?"[48]

Nicholson did use his influence, and when he found that James McLane of Cumberland County was delaying the bill pending in the assembly, he wrote and urged McLane to vote for the bill because it would increase the value of the state lands in northeastern Pennsylvania, bring population to that part of the state, and benefit the state more than land speculators like himself. He concluded with "I know ten or twelve families that have agreed to go up this year upon the strength of getting those roads."[49] The assembly passed the bill, and Nicholson became one of the managers who supervised the construction of the Northern Road. Nicholson owned some choice land along the road's right-of-way which later became part of his Asylum and North American Land companies.

Until 1791, the Commonwealth of Pennsylvania was, of all the states, almost the sole promoter of transportation facilities at public expense. Then it became apparent that public construction alone was not enough. In March 1789 the elite of the Pennsylvania business world gathered in Philadelphia and formed the Society for Promoting the Improvement of Roads and Inland Navigations. It should occasion no surprise that the directors and sponsors of the society were among the major land speculators of the era: Robert Morris, William Bingham, John Adlum, James Wilson, Henry Drinker, Thomas Mifflin, and, of course, John Nicholson. Their private speculations in Pennsylvania would benefit from improved transportation facilities. The society was instituted with the avowed purpose of "the Improvement of the natural advantages of Pennsylvania and the encouraging [of] useful designs and undertakings for promoting its trade, agriculture, manufacturing and population by means of good roads and internal navigation."[50] Omitted from the specific goals was one dealing with the increased value of lands and the aid to manufacturing and mining operations which would accrue from such projects. The society made concerted efforts to apply pressure to the Pennsylvania Assembly so that the state would allocate more money for internal improvements and to obtain corporate charters so that private parties could build and profit from these improvements.

Early in 1791, the society presented the assembly with a memorial proposing a series of internal improvement projects. In April 1791 the General Assembly approved twenty-four road projects and appropriated 30,000 pounds. They also granted 23,000 pounds for stream improvement. (This made a total of about $143,000.) In connection with this, Nicholson proposed to Governor Mifflin a road project which would connect Philadelphia with his Population Company lands in Erie and helped to persuade the governor to lend his support to the Lancaster-Philadelphia Turnpike, incorporated in 1792. The need for improved roads was vividly illustrated by Henry Wansey when he wrote, "it is a disgrace to so fine and large a city as Philadelphia to have such bad roads near it, we could go scarce four miles an hour, although it is the month of June. It was a deep miry clay, drenched with water. . . ."[51] Nicholson's friend, Dr. David Rittenhouse, was one of the commissioners who "market out" a road from Philadelphia to Lancaster, and on 9 April 1792 the legislature passed an act enabling the governor to incorporate the Lancaster Turnpike Company to construct the artery. In Philadelphia, 2,276 people sought at least one of the 600 shares allotted to the city with the $300,000 worth of subscriptions quickly raised. Nicholson initially subscribed to $4,000 worth of the stock or about fourteen shares and was elected to serve on the Board of Managers.[52]

Nicholson played an important part in the construction of the Lancaster turnpike, the first of its kind in the United States. It started a movement that helped to unite the young nation. This road increased the value of Nicholson's falls complex, and, in fact, his stone quarry at the Falls of the Schuylkill supplied stone for a part of the road. Liancourt observed that the quarries near the road were doing a good business. Not only did Nicholson supply materials, but he used his influence as a member of the Board of Managers to have John Townes appointed as one of the supervisors of the road's construction and John Thompson appointed as an assistant supervisor. He also gave Tobias Barrett, a former clerk in his comptroller's office, a similar post with the Turnpike Company. Evidently, Nicholson was a favorite with the construction supervisors. William Pollard, who was in charge of the care of the road, and who also was connected with Nicholson at the falls complex, wrote on the eve of an election for the Board of Managers, "I sincerely hope that [William] Bingham, [Tench] Francis & [William] Smith may be out, the first has treated me with greater hauteur than I ever was treated by my Master during my youthful apprenticeship, the second I ever dispised, the third I have no reason to admire. . . ." He asked Nicholson to use his influence to have these three removed.[53] Nicholson increased his interest in the company by making several subsequent stock purchases and then borrowing money on the strength of these shares. The road opened in 1794 and cost $465,000 or about $7,500 for each of the sixty-two miles. In 1793 Thomas Cooper, another foreign traveler, revealed some of the benefits that accrued from the project when he wrote that a waggoner told him that he could only haul twelve barrels of flour in his wagon before the road was built but on the parts that were finished, he now could haul twenty-four barrels. Henry Wansey said that the German farmers originally complained about the road because of the tolls, but after its completion, they rejoiced because of the benefits it brought them. And Francis Baily summarized most people's opinions when he said the road was "a masterpiece of its kind . . . paved with stone the whole way & overlaid with gravel so that it is never obstructed during the most severe seasons."[54]

Nicholson was proud of this road and used his influence with the governor to have other roads constructed and streams improved so that settlers could come out to his lands in the interior and so that his manufacturing and mining operations would be facilitated. He acquired the contract for the construction of the Wilkes-Barre to Lehigh Portage Road which would increase the value of his lands in that area, helped to improve the navigation of the Lehigh and Delaware rivers which would facilitate his Lehigh Coal Company operations, and was one of the several promoters who contracted to improve the navigation of the Susquehanna. He also contacted the governor, who also owned property near the falls, about improving the navigation of the Schuylkill River above and below his manufactories. The legislature appropriated 1,000 pounds for the improvement of the river—600 pounds for the portion above Reading and 400 pounds for that below. Nicholson was awarded the contract but later returned 600 pounds to the governor because he only improved the area below Reading and near his manufactories.[55]

Not only was Nicholson interested in constructing roads and improving streams to better his prospects, but he also played an important part in canal construction. The Society for the Improvement of Roads and Inland Navigation proposed a series of canal projects to the governor, and Mifflin pleaded the society's case before the legislature. On one occasion he said, "If their opinion is sanctioned by your approbation . . . a certain foundation will be laid for connecting the western waters of the Ohio and Great Lakes with the eastern streams, flowing into the Atlantic particularly with the tide waters of the Delaware, in the neighborhood of Philadelphia."[56] These canal projects would benefit not only the state but also Nicholson's land schemes and projected factories, and so he gave them wholehearted support. He wrote an article in the newspaper advocating the opening of a canal between the Susquehanna and Delaware rivers and urged the public to support a company that was being formed for this purpose.[57] On 29 September 1791 the legislature authorized the governor to incorporate a company to build a lock canal between the Susquehanna and Schuylkill rivers, and on 10 April 1792 authorized a company to build a canal from the Delaware to the Schuylkill above the falls. The latter canal would combine with the Susquehanna-Schuylkill Canal to provide an eastern link of a water carriage route to the west. Liancourt helped to explain Nicholson's activities in these projects when he commented upon observing the construction at Nicholson's falls manufactories, "the completion of the canal, which is to unite the Schuylkill with the Delaware, will greatly facilitate the sale of manufactures."[58] William Pollard predicted that once the canal was finished, a major town would develop around Nicholson's complex.[59] John Fenno, in the *Gazette of the United States*, painted a glowing picture of the benefits that would accrue from the canal projects, predicting that their construction would open a six-million-acre hinterland in the state, and when that was accomplished, connections could be made to Lake Erie and the Ohio. Pennsylvania would then be able to reap the benefits of the Mississippi and Missouri trade as well as that of the Great Lakes.[60]

Nicholson was enthusiastic about the prospects. He became a major shareholder and manager of both the Susquehanna and Schuylkill Navigation and the Delaware and Schuylkill Navigation companies, and Robert Morris became president of both. It was also decided to build a canal around the dangerous Conewago Falls in the Susquehanna, and on 3 July 1792 the state executed an agreement with seventeen men, one of whom was Nicholson, to construct the canal.[61] Nicholson also contracted to do some of the work on the other canals. Not only were he and the other speculators increasing the value of their holdings by engaging in these projects but they were also collecting two dollars a day from the state for their services as construction supervisors.

William Weston, a British engineer, was hired to direct the construction of the two major canals while James Brindley was to undertake the Conewago construction. Nicholson was solicited by both of these engineers for assistance. Weston complained to him about the German farmers who would not provide him with enough teams to carry bricks, lime, and sand to the locks. He asked Nicholson to come to the Lebanon valley and use his influence with them. Nicholson also served on the Committee of Purchases to procure supplies for Weston's use and contracted with Daniel Olcott of Hartford, Connecticut, for this purpose. As late as 1798, the two companies had not paid Nicholson for the supplies that he had purchased for their use; this was because he still owed money for his stock in the corporations.[62] Nicholson also was able to have his brother-in-law, William Duncan, appointed as a canal supervisor for both major canals, and he supplied both canal projects with stone from his quarry at the falls. And while he was busy having relatives appointed and supplying the construction crews, he was also using his shares in the canal companies as collateral to obtain credit to carry on his land speculations.

By 1794 Nicholson had taken complete control of the management of the Conewago Canal and gave out contracts for the excavation of the various sections. The Conewago Canal Company had begun to flounder because of financial difficulties, partly caused by the lack of promised appropriations from the state. Another problem with the Conewago Canal was that various members of the Board of Managers were constantly bickering with construction engineer John Brindley and Nicholson had to serve as a referee in these disputes. He was anxious to settle these disputes because the canal cut through his lands, as well as land owned by Governor Mifflin. Thus the governor was also eagerly awaiting the canal's completion. The consequences of this desire for the canals to cut through the lands of the promoters was aptly summarized by Liancourt when he said that the engineers wanted the canal beds to be laid on solid foundations but that the promoters insisted on them passing through their lands, which were oftentimes sandy. In commenting on the Delaware and Schuylkill Canal he said the engineer "recommended that it might be dug on the opposite bank of the Schuylkill as it would be much more solid there; but as it was much to the interest of the directors of the company, that the canal should pass through their estates, they were deaf to every other proposal and the canal is now executed on the most difficult and most circuitous plan, with little prospect of success."[63]

As a result of these pressures and other factors, all of the canal projects encountered financial difficulties. Adding to the problems was the fact that many of the stockholders, like Nicholson, did not pay for their shares in cash but in notes. When the notes fell due, Nicholson could not pay. Also, Nicholson did not pay for the assessments that had to be charged on the shares because of the financial problems of the companies. Because of these financial difficulties, the legislature had to grant the Susquehanna and Schuylkill and the Delaware and Schuylkill canal companies permission to conduct a lottery to raise $400,000 to finish the construction. Five thousand tickets were to be sold at $10 each with $100,000 in prizes. The lottery was to be held on 1 September 1795. However, the subscriptions were not filled by that date and the promoters were still trying to sell the tickets throughout 1796. Eventually, the value of the companies' stocks fell to zero.[64]

Constructing and promoting internal improvement projects, financing manufactories and mines, and promoting land schemes all were costly enterprises but this fact did not discourage Nicholson from also helping to finance the operations of prominent inventors of the period like Oliver Evans, John Fitch, and James Rumsey. Oliver Evans was one of the greatest of the early American engineers and innovators. Evans received patents for his flour milling machinery and advertised for financial help to build them, and Nicholson answered his ad.[65] Nicholson advanced him money to build his machines and also furnished funds for Evans to publish his book, *The Young Mill-Wright and Miller's Guide*. Evans had applied unsuccessfully to the Pennsylvania Legislature for funds to publish his Guide. Nicholson must have thought that this instructional guide would be an asset to farmers and millers who settled on his lands. The book went through fifteen editions between 1795 and 1860 and became an indispensable tool for millers. Oliver Evans wrote, "I could not find the means of publishing it, and it would probably have been lost had not John Nicholson, Esq. . . . assumed the expense to the amount of 1,000 dollars. . . ." However, even Nicholson's support of Evans backfired because Evans never did repay him for the advances.[66]

Part of Nicholson's motivation for financing Evans stemmed from the fact that he had flour mills throughout Pennsylvania and was a major flour merchant of Philadelphia in the 1790s. Nicholson's countinghouse at the corner of Seventh and Race streets was reported to be "as busy as the Bank of the U.S.," while his store at the falls was the receiving center for his Pennsylvania mills. He shipped flour to France under contracts with the French minister Joseph Fauchet, and he also made shipments, many in partnership with Robert Morris, to places such as Havana and the West Indies, England and the British Isles, Calcutta, India, and Lisbon, Portugal. Nicholson was a pioneer in the India venture. Talleyrand observed about Philadelphia shippers that "in 1794 I witnessed the return of the first American expedition which had gone to Bengal. The shippers made immense profits, and the very next year fourteen American vessels set sail for India . . . to dispute with the English the rich profits of that trade."[67]

But all kinds of difficulties beset Nicholson in his attempts to make trade profitable. He, like other American shippers, was caught in the middle of the wars of the French Revolution and many of his cargoes were confiscated by the British. His shipments to France under the Fauchet contract caused him grief because the French government delayed making the payments for the flour shipments. In addition, his ships were being harassed by the Barbary pirates as they plied the Mediterranean. When his shipments were confiscated and cargoes delayed and not paid for on time, Nicholson was left little or no money with which to pay the creditors who helped to finance these shipments. Difficulties of this nature prompted him to write that they had "dampened my ardour for further concerns in trade. . . . I have now had a concern in Commerce with the East Indies, West Indies, France and other parts of Europe. Some of these in prospect flattered so highly and most of them have turned out so badly, that I have resolved to withdraw myself from foreign trade, and commerce in general. It is after all, to land I am indebted that this . . . business hath not ruined me wholly."[68] In the end, his cargoes and ships were attached and sold to pay his creditors.

Nicholson's efforts in regard to the steamboat activities of John Fitch and James Rumsey also proved to be fruitless ventures. The Fitch-Rumsey rivalry presented an important chapter in the history of steamboat development, and Nicholson played a role in the dispute. James Rumsey and John Fitch both worked on boats propelled by steam in the 1780s and each claimed priority over the other as the inventor of the steamboat. After the Revolution, Rumsey experimented with self-propelled boats at Bath (now Berkeley Springs), West Virginia. In 1784 he showed his boat to George Washington and Washington certified that he had seen Rumsey's boat run against the stream by the force of water acting on a wheel to which setting poles had been attached. Washington confessed that steam was not used but that Rumsey had discussed its use with him prior to 1785.[69] Rumsey then built a boat propelled by steam and demonstrated its use on the Potomac in 1787.

Rumsey wanted to patent his invention but since there were no national patent laws in the 1780s, petitions had to be submitted to the individual states. Consequently, in 1787, Maryland and Virginia granted Rumsey the exclusive privilege of making and selling his boat for a period of ten years.[70] However, in 1785, Fitch also petitioned the Maryland legislature for a monopoly for his boat which he claimed was run by steam. Confronted by two conflicting claims the legislature of Maryland referred the matter to a committee and the decision was made to accept Rumsey's claim and to reject Fitch's because Rumsey had the idea of using steam to move boats before 1785, the year Fitch first conceived of it.[71] A heated debate took place in 1788 between the two. George Washington championed Rumsey's cause in the dispute, Thomas Jefferson called Rumsey "the most original and the greatest mechanical genius I have ever seen," and even a biographer of the man who most often is given credit for the first successful steamboat, Robert Fulton, stated that Rumsey was the "first to bring to a practical issue" hydraulic jet propulsion.[72] Another who supported Rumsey's claim and efforts was John Nicholson.

Both Fitch and Rumsey, in their attempts to monopolize the field, sought financial help to construct their boats. In March 1788 Rumsey informed Washington that he was going to go to Philadelphia to try to obtain financial support and that his brother-in-law, Joseph Barnes, who helped him build his first boat, would follow with the machinery. Barnes later served as one of Nicholson's chief land agents in Europe, operating from London. When he arrived in Philadelphia, Rumsey was confronted with the opposition of a company Fitch had formed with Henry Voight, later chief coiner of the Mint of the United States, as its major supporter. To end the conflict, Rumsey offered to form a partnership with Fitch, but when Fitch only offered him one-eighth of the proceeds, Rumsey refused.[73] Rumsey then formed a company of his own called the Rumsean Society to enable him to finish his work on steamboats and to finish an engine for use in various kinds of mills. According to the Articles of Agreement, Rumsey was to retain one-half interest in his inventions and the other half was divided into fifty shares with subscribers ultimately to pay sixty Spanish milled dollars per share. Rumsey gave land as security for the completion of his work. Among those subscribing were William Bingham, Benjamin Franklin, James Tenchard and Burgess Allison, two future partners of Nicholson's, and the man who took out shares for Nicholson, Benjamin Wynkoop. Meanwhile, Fitch had secured patents from New York, New Jersey, Pennsylvania, and Virginia and was on his way to Europe to seek patents there. Rumsey then applied to the society for an additional $1,000 so that he could also go to Europe to seek patents and the request was granted.[74]

Joseph Barnes remained in America to supervise the construction of Rumsey's engines and machines and to seek a patent from the United States Congress, as the first patent law was pending in 1789. The Rumsean Society, during Rumsey's absence, made efforts to have Fitch's patents in New York, Pennsylvania, New Jersey, and Virginia repealed, and in 1789 they succeeded in persuading Pennsylvania to issue Rumsey a patent for his steam engines.

While in Europe, Rumsey was able to obtain an English patent for his steam engine and proposed in February 1789 to build a ship, which according to Brissot de Warville, "should go to America by the help only of the steam engine and without sails. It was to make the passage in fifteen days. I perceive with pain that he has not yet executed his project. . . ."[75] Rumsey's greatest difficulty was the lack of funds, so he sought to form a partnership in England with steam engine inventors James Watt and Matthew Boulton. However, they insisted that he terminate his connection with the Rumsean Society, but Rumsey refused, and so these efforts failed. Rumsey went into debt in trying to build his models and blamed the society for not sending him enough money. In 1790 he succeeded in forming a partnership with Samuel Rogers and Daniel Parker in England but these two also failed to supply the necessary funds. Rumsey did succeed in building a boat, the *Columbian Maid*, and was preparing for a trial run on the Thames when he suddenly died.[76] Joseph Barnes was sent to England by the society to settle Rumsey's debts, to try and retrieve the 1,000 pounds the society had given Rumsey's English partners (the society had been excluded from Rumsey's English patent), and to take possession of his property.

While all of the above was taking place, Nicholson was busy trying to secure a monopoly of the Rumsean Society shares. He was motivated in his support of Rumsey by the desire to utilize the latter's engines in his flour mills, saw mills, and manufactories. He also wanted to use Rumsey's steamboat designs for his own fleet of ships. By 1797, Nicholson and the treasurer of the Rumsean Society, Benjamin Wynkoop, had secured four-fifths of the shares of the society. By August 1794 Wynkoop was experimenting with nautical machinery of his own and offered to sell his shares at $300 each to Nicholson so that he could carry on his work. Nicholson did not buy the rest because he was awaiting developments in England with the Barnes mission. In addition to securing most of the shares, Nicholson also secured part interest in Rumsey's British patent, so he was very anxious for Barnes to succeed in England in collecting the monies due him and in bringing back Rumsey's machines. Samuel Rogers and Daniel Parker carried on Rumsey's work after his death and so Barnes had to deal with them. Rogers and Parker both owed the society and, indirectly, Nicholson money and Barnes advised Nicholson that he thought it would be best to terminate the work on Rumsey's experiments in England and to return to America. But Barnes had difficulty unsnarling Rumsey's affairs and collecting money owed his promoter. By 1795, he was still involved with this; he was also trying to peddle Nicholson's land company shares and lands. Nicholson became impatient with Barnes's efforts in 1795 and told him to concentrate more on his land sales and less on trying to settle the Rumsey business. In 1798, Nicholson was still trying to collect monies owed him from the estate of James Rumsey.[77]

While Nicholson was engaged in these activities with Rumsey, he was also taking care of the possibility that John Fitch's work might prove to be more beneficial than Rumsey's by negotiating deals with Fitch. Fitch, like Rumsey, always seemed to be in dire financial straits, and he sought support from anyone with capital to invest. By 1791, Fitch's company had withdrawn its support and he was living on charity. In 1793, he decided to go to Europe to try and obtain financial aid and to build a boat for Aaron Vail in Paris. But Vail withdrew his support and Fitch's European efforts failed; it was at this stage that Nicholson became involved with him. Nicholson contracted with Fitch to build him a boat large enough to haul two tons of machinery, two tons of horses, and six tons of passengers and baggage. Nicholson planned to utilize a fleet of boats like this in the carrying trade along the Delaware River. He and Fitch also planned to try to obtain a twenty-five-year congressional patent on the boat. Fitch told Nicholson that $20 a day in profits per boat could be expected. Nicholson also agreed to support financially a cattle boat that Fitch had been constructing. But the connections with Fitch, like those with Rumsey, proved to be disappointing. Almost immediately Henry Voight, formerly Fitch's principal supporter, contested Fitch's right to construct the boat for Nicholson, claiming that he had the patent rights for it. Coupled with this was the fact that Fitch, in typical fashion, misapplied funds Nicholson had given him to be used for the boat. Fitch also took long absences from his work and went to Boston and New York. He kept asking Nicholson for more money, and Nicholson disgustedly wrote that he never would advance him more "now nor ever will be world without end amen." He concluded with "I wish you & your project had never been seen or known by me."[78] So Nicholson withdrew his support, Fitch never did gain financial solvency and died in a drunken stupor in 1798.

Historians of the steamboat era have concluded that much would have been gained had Fitch agreed to form the partnership with Rumsey on terms Rumsey could have accepted. They maintain that an operational steamboat would have been developed a generation ahead of Fulton's *Clermont*. One historian has made the point that steamboat inventors were all handicapped by the idea that they should have exclusive privileges on streams and the sole use of their inventions. He claimed that all of them failed to appreciate the frontier's potential productive capacity or how much freight would be available for all of them to share.[79] Had Fitch and Rumsey cooperated it probably would have aided Nicholson's operations and certainly would not have been as costly for him. Nevertheless, the tendency of inventors and entrepreneurs throughout the history of the United States has not been to encourage cooperation and competition but to eliminate competitors. Competition usually has been regarded as "wasteful," to paraphrase John D. Rockefeller, so if one is to condemn John Fitch and James Rumsey, then the indictment applies to most American inventors and entrepreneurs.

Nicholson's chief mistake as an entrepreneur was not his efforts to eliminate competitors but his failure, along with others like him, to realize the lack of the "industrial mind" in the United States in the 1790s. Alexander Hamilton failed in his manufacturing efforts because they were attempts "to tilt against the fundamental economic conditions of a new and an agricultural nation." Nevertheless, Nicholson's and the others' short-lived manufacturing and enterpreneurial activities helped to prepare the American mind for the transformation to the Industrial Age, and they showed, by example, what could and could not be done in these fields in the new nation.

10
THE NORTH AMERICAN LAND COMPANY AND ITS AFTERMATH

John Nicholson engaged in so many divergent pursuits that to keep accurate records of all of them seems an impossible task. Nicholson did, however, make one major attempt in his life to consolidate several individual land enterprises into one giant corporation, which some historians have called "the largest trust ever known in America."[1] But in the end, this enterprise became a tangled nightmare like all of the others. The corporation, called the North American Land Company, began 20 February 1795 as a result of the Federal City project and was also another venture in partnership with Robert Morris and James Greenleaf. Greenleaf's failure to negotiate the Holland loan as he had promised left his other two partners drastically in need of funds so Morris and Nicholson developed this scheme to try to raise money and included Greenleaf despite his past derelictions.

This company was a giant consolidation of the scattered land holdings of the partners, which totaled six million acres. They proposed to sell shares to the public or to convey them to their creditors as payment for debts. The land holdings were assigned to the company at fifty cents an acre. The speculators were to issue 30,000 shares of stock at a par value of $100 each, guaranteeing at least six percent dividends annually on the $100 shares. To secure this guarantee, they each gave the trustees 3,000 shares of their personal stock. These shares were in addition to those on the market, and they were to be sold if the owner defaulted.[2] Since 9,000 shares were kept by the trustees as security, only 21,000 shares of the stock were available for sale; of this total the partners retained 6,000 shares—Morris 3,000, Nicholson 2,000, and Greenleaf 1,000. So only 15,000 shares were put on the market for sale by the company. Furthermore, the partners could not fill the six-million-acre schedule, primarily due to Greenleaf's failure to pay for his share of the lands. Greenleaf was permitted to participate in the company by the other two because he promised to supply Nicholson and Morris "with money to sustain & relieve their advances" which had been given to Greenleaf so that he could negotiate the Holland loan. But Greenleaf was no more reliable in this company than he had been in the Federal City project. In addition to the above, the plan called for a two and one-half percent commission for all land sales to be given to the Board of Managers and for the company to exist for fifteen years or until all the lands had been sold. Nicholson and Morris also agreed to furnish the advance capital for the company, and Greenleaf was to supply his portion one year after the project was in operation.

After formulating the general plans, the partners' next task was to secure trustees and this proved to be a major assignment. Nicholson and Morris wanted the presidents of the three major banks in Philadelphia to serve: John Nixon of the Bank of North America, John Barclay of the Bank of Pennsylvania, and Thomas Willing of the Bank of the United States. All three initially agreed, but then Willing withdrew his services because, upon consultation, his board of directors advised him that a conflict of interest might develop. Jared Ingersoll, attorney-general of the Commonwealth of Pennsylvania, was selected to succeed him. Then Barclay and Nixon began to hedge, fearing that they would be liable if the company failed. Nicholson tried to reassure them that they would not, and Nicholson and Morris even agreed to pay their salaries for the first year until the stockholders could select a Board of Managers who would then assume the responsibility of paying the trustees. But the partners could not convince these two to remain as trustees and in March 1795 both resigned, giving as their reasons

> The Nature of the Business generally, the Extensiveness of the Plan, the length of Time to compleat it . . . & the Responsibility annexed to us as Trustees in the Execution renders this undertaking notoriously tedious & extremely troublesome . . . [and] hazardous to us individually and of course may involve ourselves & Friends in difficulties which no pecuniary offers could compensate. . . . For these reasons & others which could be given, we must now decline the acceptance of the Trusteeship of your Land Company.[3]

Nicholson then secured the services of Frederick Muhlenberg, formerly speaker of the United States House of Representatives, and Matthew Clarkson, mayor of Philadelphia, to replace these two and to join Jared Ingersoll as trustees. Care had to be taken in the selection of trustees as holders and conveyors of titles because, as Nicholson explained to his European brokers, all trustees had to be citizens and men of prominence. Nicholson said this helped to attract European buyers because only Pennsylvania permitted aliens to hold lands in the United States. If Europeans bought lands of the company lying in other states and "should it be said that the specific shares are held by aliens, the answer given will be that the title is rendered unquestionable by a transfer of the shares to Citizens . . . so the property probably never will be questioned on the basis of alienage."[4]

The difficulty in securing trustees was a harbinger of the persistent problems that beset the company during its existence, despite the optimistic expectations of the promoters. One of the reasons for the optimism was because of the variety of lands that the company offered to prospective buyers. The company incorporated all of the following acreages: Kentucky, 431,043; Pennsylvania, 647,146; North Carolina, 717,299; Virginia, 932,621; South Carolina, 957,238; and Georgia, 2,314,796. The Pennsylvania lands included the following counties and acreages: Northampton, 72,000; Northumberland, 217,046; Luzerne, 4,500; Mifflin, 34,328; Huntingdon, 29,172; Westmoreland, 40,000. Also included were 250,000 acres north and west of the Allegheny and Ohio rivers.[5]

Part of the Pennsylvania lands conveyed were those originally intended for the Cooper-Priestley settlement near Northumberland, but when this project aborted, the lands reverted back to Nicholson and Morris and became part of the North American Land Company. The Pennsylvania lands, although the most desirable because of their fertility and the alien ownership feature, also caused problems because of the residence requirements of the land law of 1792. The requirement that a family be placed on every 400-acre tract within two years of purchase or face forfeiture held for this land company just as it had for Nicholson's other Pennsylvania companies.

Coupled with this was the fact that many of the Pennsylvania lands in this company were secured by Nicholson and Morris from the state without obtaining Indian titles. Squatters had come onto these lands, bought the Indian titles—regardless of Nicholson and Morris's state claims—and hoped that the speculators would be unable to fulfill the residency requirements and make their payments to the state. Then they would have the best claim to secure the state titles at reduced rates. Nicholson and Morris tried to make allowances for this contingency by sending gifts and money to Cornplanter to protect their northern Pennsylvania lands.

Pennsylvania Speculator and Patriot: John Nicholson

Further difficulties stemmed from the fact that the Holland Land Company, another well-established land company in Pennsylvania, was operating north and west of the Ohio and Allegheny rivers. Land disputes between the two concerns, involving 90,000 of the 250,000 acres claimed by the partners in this area, developed almost immediately. The disputes were taken before the Board of Property where the partners' claims were argued by Moses Levy and Jared Ingersoll. The company also hired Hugh Henry Brackenridge of Pittsburgh to help with the litigations which lingered on even after both Nicholson and Morris had died.[6]

It was imperative, because of these disputes, to hire agents, to have the surveys made speedily, and to promote sales. Consequently, John Hogue of Pittsburgh and, later, Thomas Rees of Erie were hired for the Pennsylvania lands at a rate of $3,000 each for provisions and expenses and $3,500 per agent for surveying fees. Similar fees were paid to Thomas Davis for Georgia, C.W. Burd for Kentucky, Robert James for Virginia, Joseph Karrick for North Carolina, and S. Swansey for South Carolina. To induce sales a prospectus was published which outlined very liberal terms for prospective buyers of the company's lands.

The terms and modes of settlement were patterned after Captain Charles Williamson's policies in the Genesee area of New York. Williamson came from London late in 1792, set up an office in Bath, and managed a tract of one million acres which Morris had sold in 1791 to Willamson's employers, the Pulteney Associates, for 75,000 pounds. On 12 January 1795 Williamson sent Morris an account of the lands sold from the purchase as of 31 December 1794. He had sold 463,017 acres for 263,186 pounds or 657,965 dollars in New York currency. Williamson further estimated that the returns for the entire tract would not be less than 3,157,965 dollars for the land which Morris sold for 75,000 pounds. Morris wrote that he was happy for Williamson and that he expected to do the same with the North American Land Company using Williamson's "hothouse" method of luring buyers. This method would involve sending out an agent to a tract of the company's land and having him build a saw and a grist mill for the use of the expected settlers. He was also to build a farmhouse, where he was to reside, a barn, and clear 500 to 600 acres. Then he was to lay out a town in the vicinity of his farm and mills in order to entice artisans, such as blacksmiths, shoemakers, and carpenters, that would be needed for the settlement. Next he was to sell the town lots at moderate prices and survey and lay out the rest of the tract into farms of 100 to 500 acres, numbering each on a general plot. The Board of Managers, following the agent-surveyor's advice, then determined which farms were to be sold first and which retained for future sale. Initially the company was to sell the land at two dollars per acre, payable in annual installments with interest, and when thirty to fifty families were settled on the tract, the price was to be raised to three to four dollars per acre, "and as the settlement progresses, the price keeps advancing untill [sic] it mounts beyond what I dare at this time to name lest you might suppose me extravagant in my Ideas."[7] This pattern was to be followed in all states where the company held lands. Nicholson was also enthusiastic about the Williamson method and sent a surveyor to see the captain and observe his work. He counted on the company's shares to rise 100 percent in value before a year was over and exclaimed, "I could not hold a more rising property."[8] Morris had such faith in the scheme that he told a prospective buyer that if the plan did not succeed he would buy back the shares at cost plus interest, and he relinquished his seat in the United States Senate to devote more time to the company.

However, not everyone was as enthusiastic about Williamson's methods. Weld recorded in his *Travels* that a Wilkes-Barre farmer lamented that his son

> had been to Bath, the celebrated Bath, and has returned both a speculator and a gentleman, having spent his money, swapped away my horse, caught the fever and ague, and what is infinitely worse, that horrid disorder which some call terraphobia. We hear nothing from the poor creature now (in his ravings) but . . . of ranges, of townships, numbers, thousands, hundreds, acres, Bath, fairs, races, heats . . . etc. etc. My son . . . is not worth a sou and never will be, at this rate.[9]

The partners' agents were then sent throughout the United States and to Europe to sell the shares and lands. Sylvanius Bourne was hired at a salary of $2,000 a year to sell in England, Ireland, Switzerland, what is now Germany, and France and so were Joseph Barnes, Griffith Evans, Omer Talon, James Marshall, William Morris, Benjamin Parsons, Adonijah Stanburrough, William Temple Franklin, and Dr. James Tate. All except Bourne were given $1,000 salaries, five percent commissions on their sales, passage money and expenses, plus one-half of the proceeds above the minimum price of the lands which ranged at different times from twenty-five cents to two dollars per acre. If the agents could not make sales, they were instructed to try to obtain loans using the company shares as security. The agents were given a two and one-half percent commission on any loans that they were able to negotiate. In addition to the agents, Nicholson and Morris also sent shares and plans of the company to their European brokers and contacts including Colborn Barrell and Henry Servanti, Bird, Savage and Bird, George Barclay and Company, Samuel Bayard, the American Claims Officer, all of London, and Christian Frege of Leipzig and John Parrish, the United States Consul at Hamburg.

But even with all of these agents and contacts, the company's shares and lands still did not sell, despite Nicholson's expectations that Jay's Treaty would help the land market in Europe and that the disruptions in France would induce French capitalists to invest in American lands and companies. However, many factors contributed to the depressed land market in Europe. The war situation kept draining European capital; there were those who wanted to come to America but they were mostly poor; French capitalists, if not supplying money for the war effort, were buying confiscated estates; and then there were the rumors spread by the French minister Fauchet that American land companies were poor investments. Fauchet attacked Morris and Nicholson personally, and the partners circulated rebuttals in Europe through such papers as the one financed by Nicholson, *The Level of Europe and America.* Nicholson's friend, Edmund Randolph, secretary of state at this time, and Robert Goodloe Harper, congressman from South Carolina and shareholder, defended the company in the United States.

The failure to consummate sales was a major blow to promoters like Nicholson and Morris who had invariably bought on credit using their notes as security and who counted on land sales to enable them to discharge their notes. This paucity of ready cash was especially felt in an enterprise as extensive as the North American Land Company. Morris assured prospective buyers that

> The proprietor of back lands gives himself no other trouble about them than to pay the taxes, which are inconsiderable. As Nature left them, so will they be till circumstances give them value. The proprietor is then sought out by the settler who has chanced to pitch upon them, or who has made any improvement thereon, and receives from him a price which fully repays his original advance, with great interest.[10]

This was indeed a fallacy because the reverse was true. The total taxes on a scheme as vast as this were crushing and the settler often did not seek anyone nor pay anything; he merely squatted. The tax burden remained for the speculators to pay and this was especially acute on lands in states like Georgia.

S.G. McLendon stated that the 2,314,796 acres of Georgia lands included in this venture constituted the "unsolved riddle of Georgia's land history." This referred to part of one of the biggest land swindles in United States history, the Yazoo land frauds. He also stated that four Georgia governors granted lands to single persons in very large quantities "without the slightest authority under the law . . . ," but was at a loss to explain how Nicholson, Morris, and Greenleaf acquired the Georgia lands which constituted the largest amount of any state's lands that were incorporated into the North American Land Company.[11] Several memoranda in the Nicholson manuscripts throw light on the Yazoo affair and his connection with it.

There were actually two Yazoo sales. In 1789 three companies—the South Carolina, Virginia, and Tennessee Yazoo companies—tried to purchase from Georgia part of its western territory. On 21 December 1789 the legislature of the state did provide for the sale of twenty-five million acres to these companies for about $207,000. However, in 1790 the state had second thoughts and refused to accept payment in public certificates of debt as specified in the granting act and demanded specie at the state treasury. Until the second and more notorious Yazoo sales of 1795, these companies tried to compel the state to honor the first commitment and to convey the lands. It was during this interval that Nicholson entered the Yazoo operation. Nicholson was not involved in the earlier history of the first three Yazoo companies, but later he did become a partner in the South Carolina Yazoo Company. The major participants in this company were Alexander Moultrie, John Stockdale, and Wade Hampton, all from South Carolina. Moultrie led the fight to have his company's claims honored by Georgia. The company claimed fifteen million acres between the Yazoo and Mississippi rivers.[12]

Nicholson joined the others in the company in 1792 and tried, along with them, to have the 1789 sale validated. He made political alliances in the State of Georgia and helped to draft the petitions that were presented to the legislature on behalf of the company. His chief political ally was state senator Francis Wade of Hermitage, Montgomery County, Georgia. The senator's son John had worked for Nicholson as a clerk in 1790–91 and Nicholson had used his influence with Governor Mifflin and President Washington to obtain a commission in the United States army for him. Young Wade then served as an officer with General James Wilkinson's expeditions against the Indians. Nicholson also loaned him money to further earn the gratitude of the senator. In December 1792 Senator Wade warned that there were a "nest of secret enemies" out to do Nicholson harm and that he had been snubbed for not joining in the move to block Nicholson's efforts. But Nicholson assured the senator that he was sufficiently fortified against his enemies, who Wade said were accusing Nicholson of disseminating bribes totaling 15,000 pounds to have the 1789 sales consummated.[13]

However, Nicholson and the South Carolina Yazoo Company's efforts proved futile. By 1794 the legislature of Georgia was contemplating a second sale of Georgia's western lands to four new companies whose agents were liberally passing out bribes in order to consummate the new sales. Nicholson and Moultrie sent John Stockdale to Augusta to find out what was taking place. He arrived on 16 December 1794 and reported to Nicholson that the Georgia legislature had declared the South Carolina Company contract void and was offering the lands that the partners claimed to the highest bidder. He said that he had arrived too late to prevent it and further informed Nicholson that four companies, the Georgia, Tennessee, Upper-Mississippi, and Georgia-Mississippi companies, had been formed for the purpose of buying the lands; they bought an estimated twenty-eight million acres. The legislators, he said, had been persuaded by "the purchase of votes" to authorize the sale, and the bill had been sent to Governor George Matthews for his signature, which was expected on or before 29 December 1794. He further stated in his report that "I have done all I possibly could do to postpone the sale of the Lands until next session of Assembly but the Companies outbribed me. . . ." He concluded with a warning that the land jobbers in these four companies knew that Nicholson and Morris were buying lands for their North American Land Company and all hoped

> to make their fortunes out of you & your Company & Every Land Jobber in the South Expect the Same—they think you will purchase anything called land. I can only observe to you if you want to purchase Lands & to have Choice and at a low price it will be wise in you to lock up all your Money & Take Every Step to put a Stop to all purchases untill [sic] the rage is over. . . . General [James] Gunn [major promoter of the Georgia Company] is your Great Enemy beware of him.[14]

Evidently, the large purchases made by Nicholson and Morris of lands for incorporation into the North American Land Company were major factors in precipitating the second Yazoo sales.

After the January 1795 sale to the four companies, Alexander Moultrie, on behalf of the South Carolina Company, brought suit against the State of Georgia in the Supreme Court of the United States, claiming that the state had violated the clause in the United States Constitution which prohibits a state from violating obligations of contract. This referred to Georgia's refusal to honor the 1789 sale. The suit was pending until the case was heard in 1798, and during the interim, Moultrie prepared his case. He asked Nicholson to supply him with a copy "of the Petition presented by the old South Carolina Yazoo Company to the Legislature of Georgia in 1789 for their purchase."[15] In addition, Nicholson, Moultrie, and Stockdale thought that Zachariah Cox could provide valuable information on the sale, since he was a participant in it with his Tennessee Company, and so they made him a member of the South Carolina Company by giving him two shares. In 1796 the partners held several meetings to chart their course of action, and Moultrie was a guest in one of Nicholson's mansions in Philadelphia while the case was pending.

On 19 February 1796 the newly elected Georgia Legislature rescinded the sale made to the four companies in 1795 because of the wholesale bribery that had taken place. So the partners of the old South Carolina Company decided to seek an alliance with some of the participants in the 1795 sale so that through a united effort something might be gained for all parties concerned. Consequently, on 24 September 1796 Moultrie and Stockdale set out for New York to attend a meeting with Senator James Gunn, Wade Hampton, and others involved in the 1795 sale. Then they went to Boston, New Haven, and Hartford and met with others who were involved. Moultrie was informed on this tour that Alexander Hamilton, then practicing law in New York and speculating in lands himself, wanted to see him, and Moultrie wrote Nicholson that "I almost think Hamilton will join us in the Georgia business, You see now Georgians are completely routed every way."[16] All of the speculators in the Yazoo affair were anxious for Hamilton, who knew the meaning and intent of the United States Constitution as well as anyone, to issue a statement on Georgia's rescinding act, and they were not disappointed. In 1797 Hamilton said that the Georgia Legislature had no right to rescind sales because the Constitution specifically stated that "no state shall pass a law impairing the obligations of contract. This must be equivalent to saying no state shall pass a law revoking, invalidating, or altering a contract."[17] This would apply to the South Carolina Company's case, as well as to the new companies, so Moultrie, Nicholson, and the others must have been pleased.

Complicating the activities of the Georgia speculators was the fact that by 1790 Georgia was the only state which had not ceded her western land claims to the central government. These extended north into what is now the southern Tennessee border, south to Spanish Florida, and west to the Mississippi River. So the state was in constant conflict with the national government over Indian policies, treaties, and Spanish machinations. Consequently, speculators had to concern themselves with Indians, the State of Georgia, and the activities of the federal government. In 1797 Georgia finally ceded her western territory to the central government in return for $1,250,000. Thereafter, the Yazoo claimants had to deal with the central government which established a commission to investigate the claims.

In their attempts to validate the South Carolina Company claims, Nicholson and Moultrie now had to try to secure aid from federal officials. However, Moultrie did not have too much confidence in these appeals. He explained to Nicholson, ". . . they might as well appeal to Brutus or even Anthony [sic] as to the President & Congress. What has the Executive or Legislative to do with a Cause legally before the Judiciary?" He concluded by advising Nicholson that in April 1797 he would bring "such a *form* & *force* of Evidence with me (before the Court) that we *must* prevail. . . ."[18] Moultrie was expressing the same confidence in August, and Nicholson was reinforcing his optimism by supplying him with petitions and contacting lawyers like Jared Ingersoll for their opinions which favored the company's claim. He thought that a favorable decision would be rendered and was satisfied that they had done all they could to assure this.

Despite this optimism, when the case was finally brought before the docket of the Supreme Court in 1798, the court refused to hear the case because, since the adoption of the Eleventh Amendment to the United States Constitution in 1798, the court had no jurisdiction in a suit brought by a citizen against a state. However, Moultrie continued his efforts, even after Nicholson's death in 1800, and when the rest of South Carolina Company's western lands were ceded to the central government in 1802, he made an appeal to the United States Congress. Congress created a commission comprised of James Madison, Albert Gallatin, and Levi Lincoln to decide the question, and in 1803 they ruled against the company on the grounds that the legislature of Georgia had the right to demand specie instead of public debt certificates in payment for the lands and that this option was left open to the state in the 1789 sale.[19]

While all of this was taking place with the South Carolina Company, Nicholson and Morris were busy buying other lands for the North American Land Company. Greenleaf was a partner, but not an active one, and the burden of buying and paying for the lands fell to the other partners. Several large purchases of Georgia lands were made in 1793 from different individuals and this was a major factor, according to John Stockdale, in the famous Yazoo sales of 1795. Before the sale in January 1795, the partners negotiated many deals with individuals who had secured the tracts from Georgia. Dr. John Hall conveyed 113,000 acres in 1793 and another 400,000 in 1794 in exchange for lots in the Federal City and 11,000 pounds. Hall, along with his partners George Dennison and Samuel Jack, also negotiated a deal in 1793 to convey one million acres of pine-barren lands to the partners—this was the famous "pine-barren speculation."

The pine-barren area of Georgia was located in Montgomery, Washington, and Franklin counties and it was a vast wasteland. When the lands were incorporated into the North American Land Company, Nicholson and Morris painted false pictures of the land in order to promote sales in Europe. Little could be sold in America because most buyers were well aware of the infertility of these "barrens." The sandy lands were described as being "traversed by streams & clothed with oak, walnut & hickory trees."[20] However, the company itself was duped by Hall, Jack, and Dennison, who gave false impressions of the lands to Nicholson and Morris. When the partners' agents were sent south they discovered the true quality of the lands. Nicholson asked Morris what they should do, and evidently Morris told him that they would keep them and sell the lands in the same way as they had bought them. One historian remarked that "a hundred years later people were still . . . looking for streams which did not exist and for walnut, oak and hickory tree markers in a land where only wire-grass and pine trees have ever grown."[21]

In addition, Nicholson and Morris arranged with Daniel Carthy in August and September 1794 to purchase tracts in small quantities using fictitious names so that Nicholson's and Morris's identity would be concealed, as all of the land jobbers knew they were buying lands and would probably try and cheat them. Carthy said the lands around Fayettville, Georgia, were selling at about three cents per acre and that he would acquire them there and in the back-country to avoid the jobbers.[22] And while Carthy was scouting these lands, land jobbers William Ewing, William Hanna, John Lee Gibson, Robert Ross, and Charles Newbold all offered Nicholson a total of 1,920,000 acres at about one-eighth of a dollar per acre in the same counties as the Hall-Jack deal. Since these counties only had a total of 1,323,600 acres, it seemed that Stockdale's warning that "all the partners of these Companies Expect to make there [sic] fortune out of you & your Company & Every Land Jober [sic], in the South Expect the Same—they think you will purchase anything called land" was valid.[23] Nevertheless, Nicholson and Morris also formed a partnership with James Seagrove, superintendent of Creek Indian Affairs and United States commissioner to the Spanish governor of East Florida. They jointly held 50,000 acres along the St. Mary's River, and Seagrove was their agent charged with showing the land to prospective buyers.

Then Zachariah Cox, who was acquainted with Nicholson through their mutual friend Senator Francis Wade, and Dr. John Hall contacted the speculators and offered them four million acres in Tellapie County for 60,000 pounds, undoubtedly part of Cox's old Tennessee Company. However, Nicholson found out that Georgia had set the price at 20,000 pounds for these lands, and when he confronted Hall with this, Hall said that he and Cox would sell them to him for the 20,000 pounds.[24]

Before this transaction could be concluded, however, the second Yazoo sale was about to be made and Cox approached the partners with another offer. On 15 and 28 June 1794 Cox asked Nicholson, Morris, and Greenleaf, whom he knew were buying large tracts for the North American Land Company, to join him in a new Tennessee Company as other speculators in Georgia were forming other companies and would seek grants from the Georgia legislature in its November 1794 session. He assured the three that

> I . . . can scarcely doubt but the assembly at their next session will agree to issue a grant for the Tennessee purchase provided the purchase money is paid into the State Treasury. The *real* confidence that I have of success in this business induces me to *advise* that you have the purchase money in Augusta as soon as possible. . . . This will enable me to take advantage of the most favorable moment.[25]

However, Morris took the advice that John Stockdale had given Nicholson when he wrote, "I can only observe to you if you want to purchase Lands & to have Choice and at a low price it will be wise to you to lock up all your Money & Take Every Step to put a Stop to all purchases whatsoever for the present here & Elsewhere Untill [sic] the rage is over. . . ."[26] Morris, for once in his life, was prudent and did not take part in the famous Yazoo purchases of 1795. He wrote to Wade Hampton, from whom he would later buy lands, "I feel quite satisfied in being Unconcerned in those great purchases, having little doubt, but there will be oppys [opportunities] of buying in hereafter when it may be more convenient than at present, Should I then incline to take an interest."[27] This was exactly what he later did do, but he also assured William Constable of New York that "I have avoided the Georgia Western Land Business after mature consideration. . . ."[28]

Nicholson was not as prudent as Morris in this instance, and he did become a participant in the Yazoo sale after knowing this his South Carolina Yazoo Company claims of 1789 would not be upheld. His entry into both the Georgia Company and the Tennessee Company was by way of Zachariah Cox. On 7 January 1795 Governor George Matthews of Georgia signed into law the bill authorizing the sale of thirty-five million acres of land, two-thirds of the state's land west of the Chattahooche River, for $500,000 or about one and one-half cents an acre. The land was sold to four companies: the Georgia Company, which received the most, the Georgia-Mississippi Company, the Upper-Mississippi Company, and the Tennessee Company. In the two companies that concerned Nicholson, Senator James Gunn of Georgia was the major promoter of the Georgia Company and Zachariah Cox of the Tennessee Company. It is a well-known fact that these and other participants distributed bribes in the form of shares in the companies and cash to have the sale consummated, just as Nicholson earlier had used bribes to try and get his South Carolina Company claims validated. There was a total of ten shares in the Georgia Company, each representing about a million acres, although, as Wade Hampton informed Morris, the associates did not hold "*nominally* more than about 500,000 acres each but in *reality* more than double the quantity."[29]

Even though Stockdale said that Gunn was Nicholson's major enemy, Nicholson became a member of his company through Cox who was also a member of the Georgia Company. Cox informed Nicholson that "I have reserved you an interest which I expect will amount to about three hundred thousand acres."[30] This, Cox later informed him, amounted to one-fifth of Cox's share in the Georgia Company. Cox also told Nicholson that the latter was too late getting in on this company, so he could not do as much good for him as he had done in Cox's Tennessee Company. Nicholson also obtained 100,000 acres of Georgia's marsh lands through Cox who offered to buy all of the marsh lands along the coast for him. Nicholson paid thirty dollars per 1,000 acres for these lands. The Tennessee Company was divided into 420 shares, and Nicholson acquired thirty, representing about 214,290 acres which were later transferred to the North American Land Company. According to the agreement made with Cox, Nicholson was to have powers equal to Cox's in negotiating the business of both the Georgia and Tennessee companies.[31]

However, Nicholson's association with Cox proved to be another fiasco. Cox was constantly asking Nicholson for money, and Nicholson endorsed his notes which he never honored. On one occasion Nicholson complained, "I continue to accept them [notes] but remember you place me in a very disagreeable Situation indeed if you do not as you promise deposit with me the funds sufficient to meet these drafts. . . . I am surprised that in none of your letters you do not specify from what quarter and means the funds are to come."[32] Cox never did pay Nicholson, who was sued in the Federal Court by John Ralston because he had endorsed notes for Cox which the latter did not discharge. Nevertheless, the partners retained the thirty shares in Cox's Tennessee Company until 1797 when they were placed, along with the Washington property, in the hands of the trustees of the Aggregate Fund.

While the second Yazoo sales were being completed, Wade Hampton informed Nicholson and Morris of what was taking place and concluded with, "should you think well of the business, there is no bounds to what may be done with proper exertion."[33] As said earlier, Morris declined and Nicholson participated, but after the sales were made, Morris forgot his earlier reservations and became involved. Hampton served as an agent for the partners and purchased lands and shares in Georgia from the companies. The lands and shares they purchased were probably in the Georgia Company for by 1797 Nicholson and Morris had acquired 2,500,000 acres of the Georgia Company's Land and conveyed these to the trustees of the Aggregate Fund.

In addition to Cox and Hampton, the partners also bought a million acres of Georgia lands from David Allison, who was an agent and partner of the Blount brothers of North Carolina—William, Thomas, and John Gray. The Blounts and Allison were members of Cox's Tennessee Company. David Allison was also a partner of Nicholson's in a lead mine venture, and William Blount, governor of the South West Territory, later joined Nicholson in the Territorial Land Company. The deal with Allison called for the partners to pay 100,000 dollars in twenty-four monthly installments. The balance of 50,000 dollars was to be paid when Nicholson ascertained the quality of the land. Nicholson also secured 500,000 acres in Franklin County and 400,000 in Montgomery County from E.B. Hopkins for ten cents per acre and 40,000 acres from Jonas Ingham at four cents per acre.

All of these purchases in Georgia were clouded by the frauds that were discovered by the newly-elected legislature of Georgia in 1796. Senator James Jackson, Gunn's counterpart from Georgia, resigned his seat in the United States Senate and returned to Georgia to lead a campaign to have the 1795 sale nullified. The bribes of Gunn and his associates were discovered, as well as those of the other companies, and the situation became so heated that Gunn challenged one of his accusers, Congressman Abraham Baldwin of Georgia, to a duel. The anti-Yazoo forces were successful in Georgia and the Rescinding Act was passed on 13 February 1796. This act left individuals like Nicholson and Morris, who had purchased most of their Georgia lands from participants in these companies, without recourse because a state could not be sued by citizens. Of course, it also left Nicholson's shares in the Georgia and Tennessee companies without value. Pamphlets were written and pleas made in behalf of the companies and the purchasers but the state maintained its position.

Then in 1797 Georgia conveyed its western lands to the central government, to which the speculators then had to make their appeals. Debates took place in Congress throughout the rest of the 1790s as to whether or not to compensate the Yazoo claimants. The opponents answered Hamilton and the others who claimed that the State of Georgia, with its rescinding act, had violated the United States Constitution's clause against impairing the obligations of contract, by declaring that fraud cannot be a valid basis for a contract and thus no legal contract had been made in the first place. Abraham Bishop of New Haven, Connecticut, wrote a pamphlet in 1797 entitled *Georgia Speculations Unveiled* in which he denounced the Yazoo frauds and stated that the Rescinding Act of 1796 allowed for the purchase money to be returned to the companies but that few had come to reclaim their money because they were still hoping to reap a fortune out of this fraud.[34]

Two of those who still had hopes of reaping this fortune were Nicholson and Morris. They did not reclaim money from the state, and as was stated above, Nicholson was helping Moultrie prepare his case concerning the first Yazoo sale of 1789 which was still pending in 1796–97 before the United States Supreme Court. Now he and Moultrie obtained the opinions of Jared Ingersoll and William Tilghman that favored the Yazoo claimants and added these to their defense.[35] In addition, although Georgia lands were not as valuable as their other lands, Nicholson and Morris were going ahead with their attempts to peddle them and so instructed their agents in America and Europe. They also tried to use these lands as collateral for loans and as payments for their notes held by creditors, but most of these attempts failed. The partners even sent agents like Levin and Edward Wailes and Robert Hoops to Georgia to start settlements based on Williamson's "Hothouse Methods." They were to be paid a two and one-half percent commission plus expenses for their work. Thomas Davis was also sent to conduct surveys of their lands.

These lands, like the others, proved to be a burden that helped to bring ruin. Sales, especially of Georgia lands, were never enough to pay for the cost of acquiring them and for the accumulated tax burden. Morris once wrote Nicholson that "it is indispensable that we send money to pay the Georgia Taxes. I cannot find money for your part, If I can for my own it will be a happy Circumstance, but go it must, & that immediately."[36] But they never did raise enough money to pay for the taxes on all their Georgia lands and some were sold at the sheriff's sales in consequence. The Georgia lands in the North American Land Company that remained were placed in the hands of the trustees of the Aggregate Fund in 1797. Nicholson never did receive any compensation as a purchaser of Yazoo Company lands. He died in 1800, and it was not until 1814 that Congress appropriated five million dollars to reimburse the purchasers of the Yazoo lands, this after the 1810 decision of John Marshall and the Supreme Court in *Fletcher* v. *Peck* which declared unconstitutional the Georgia Rescinding Act of 1796 on the grounds that it violated the contract clause in the Constitution. Perhaps Abraham Bishop, when he wrote his condemnation of the Yazoo participants, provided Nicholson's epitaph in the Georgia business when he related, "if he knew of the deceit practiced on him previous to his selling, and yet made use of the deceit to induce a bargain, the least he can expect is the total loss. . . ."[37]

None of the other lands that were incorporated into the North American Land Company were as extensive or caused as many problems as those in Georgia. Most of the lands obtained in North Carolina and South Carolina for incorporation into the company were bought from Wade Hampton and David Allison, who represented the Blount Brothers. Hampton sold them 900,000 acres in South Carolina at sixteen and one-third cents per acre, of which 300,000 were incorporated into the North American Land Company and the remainder divided between Nicholson and Morris for private sale. Nicholson and Morris later tried to sell these for fifty cents an acre. Allison sold them 150,000 acres of swampland which John Gray Blount assured Nicholson was of "good quality" and when drained "will become the garden spot of North Carolina."[38] In another transaction, Allison conveyed 500,000 more acres in North Carolina at twenty-five cents per acre which the partners included in their company. John Hall, another land broker, obtained some lands from the Blounts, and he, in turn, transferred these to Nicholson and Morris. However, many of the titles for these lands had not been conveyed as late as 1797 and the partners wrote to the Blounts asking for them. The reason for this was that Allison and the others had made the mistake of accepting Nicholson's and Morris's notes in payment and the partners never supplied the cash. In 1798 Allison was imprisoned for debt partly due to Nicholson and Morris's failure to pay and died of yellow fever.

The Virginia lands of the company were obtained from many different individuals and at various prices. Andrew Moore and John Beckley sold Greenleaf, Morris, and Nicholson 200,000 acres, and Wilson Nichols sold Morris about 800,000 acres which Morris then transferred to the company. These lands were located in Bourbon, Randolph, Bath, Wythe, and Montgomery counties. Interestingly, Thomas Jefferson's *Notes on Virginia* were used to describe the lands to the speculators. Nicholson also had other lands in Virginia that were not part of the North American Land Company, including 47,-057 acres in Bourbon County and another 100,000 mostly in Monongahalia, Harrison, and Randolph counties. All of these lands were also paid for with notes which the partners could not take up when they became due.

Finally, as for the Kentucky lands of the North American Land Company, Nicholson and Morris secured 247,000 acres from Richard Graham and bought Humphrey Marshall's contract with George Rogers Clark for 74,000 acres. The balance of the 400,000 acres incorporated into their company probably came from Benjamin Wynkoop and Samuel Young, who sold Nicholson 50,000 acres, partly surveyed by Daniel Boone, in Lincoln County, Kentucky.

While Nicholson was engaging in these transactions in Kentucky on behalf of the North American Land Company, he was also participating in other land deals there without Morris, and in so doing, tried to establish another English settlement in America. His purchases for the North American Land Company led him into this venture in partnership with James Trenchard, Dr. Burgess Allison, and Major Richard Claiborne. David Barber was brought from England to become the partners' agent in 1795. He was to secure settlers and lay out towns on the partners' 100,000 acres of lands south of the Ohio River, thirty miles below Louisville, Kentucky. This tract was called the Piomingo after an Indian chief. Nicholson's agents in London, Barrell and Servanti, were to secure settlers for the proposed settlement. According to William Winterbotham, who must have been involved with the scheme, three towns were planned for the Piomingo Track—Franklinville, Lystra, and Ohiopiomingo.[39] The plans for these towns were remarkably similar to those of the Federal City, probably revealing Nicholson's influence, as the houses were to be uniform and set back from the streets, which were to be named after the states. The Ohiopiomingo settlement was described as follows: "The town is to contain upwards of a thousand houses, forty-three streets, a circus and several capital squares . . . each settler in the township will be entitled, in fee simple, to one town lot of an hundred feet in width, and three hundred feet in length: a field of five acres, and another of twenty acres, will also be allotted to each of them. . . ."[40] This scheme was similar to that of another of Nicholson's projects, the Asylum settlement in Pennsylvania.

John Reps wrote that "like its companion cities of Lystra and Franklinville, Ohiopiomingo never existed except on paper." However, Winterbotham claimed that the town was being set up under the superintendency of a competent surveyor and that a college was also to be erected there. David Barber was that surveyor-supervisor; he was establishing a settlement there in 1795, and Nicholson contributed money to build a college. By 1796, settlers were arriving from Europe to settle on the company's land, but Barber was beset by rivals claiming that they had titles to the lands. He wrote, "there are now many families coming down the river and I have had many applications for land but do not know what to do." Nicholson told him to buy out the rival claimants, but this would take money, and Nicholson's lesser partners were not carrying their share of the load. Meanwhile, contracts were being made with settlers in England, Ireland, and Wales, and Barber was worried about their plight when they arrived and found their titles disputed.[41] Nicholson supplied what money he could and succeeded in buying off some of the rivals, but by 1797 his remaining funds were exhausted. Barber drew on Nicholson to purchase other claims, and Nicholson angrily called on Trenchard, Allison, and Claiborne to reimburse him or else he would keep all of the titles. Barber confessed that Nicholson was the only partner who advanced money for the settlement and for the taxes, and that the others all had defaulted. In August 1797 Barber severed all relations with Nicholson's partners, blaming them for the failure of the settlement and for his own ruin.

Then Nicholson severed his relations with the others and hired Barber to be his agent for his Kentucky Land Company. The Piomingo tract was incorporated into this 300,000-acre plan with Thomas Bedwell serving as the company's treasurer. However, this proved to be a short-lived venture because by 1797 Nicholson was very nearly bankrupt. He could not make the tax payments on these lands and they were sold at sheriff's sales in 1798 and 1799. Barber could offer Nicholson little solace: "the account of your present situation grieves me much, and I am sorry to say your affairs here are not like to mend it much."[42]

The fate suffered by the North American Land Company was as tragic as that of Nicholson's other enterprises and in it James Greenleaf again played his role of albatross. He failed to provide for his share of the payments for the lands in this project, just as he failed the partners in the Washington fiasco, and constantly maneuvered Nicholson and Morris into debt to his creditors. Greenleaf's creditors descended on the other partners for payment because they were the endorsers of his notes. Greenleaf even had the audacity to complain about the time he had to devote to the company and Nicholson retorted ". . . my Cause of Complaint as it invades my time and arrangements is much more."[43] After these repeated problems with Greenleaf, the other partners, as they had done in the Washington venture, decided to buy his shares and dissolve all connections with him. On 26 May 1796 the first payment was made of the $1,150,000 purchase price by transferring Washington lots to Greenleaf. They were to pay Greenleaf 100 dollars per share in four annual installments, the shares to remain pledged to secure the payments. When the partners failed to meet these payments, Greenleaf brought suits against them and attached their property and some of their shares in the company.

In addition to Greenleaf, collectors of unpaid taxes and their creditors plagued Nicholson and Morris. Agents from all the states where the North American Land Company had tracts sent the same pleas for payments of overdue taxes. When the payments were not paid, the lands were attached and sold at sheriff's sales. Then there was the fact that notes were used in payments for these lands with Morris endorsing Nicholson's and vice versa. When the notes were not paid, their creditors came to collect and brought suits. Morris and Nicholson kept trying to put them off by saying that sales were going to be made very soon and then they would pay what they owed. Morris in typical fashion wrote, "We have immense Property daily rising in Value & shall pay our Engagements punctually after the present Hurry is over." When they offered their lands as security for payment, the typical reply from their creditors was "with respect to Southern lands, like most other people, I have no good opinion of them at almost any price...."[44]

By 1797, Morris and Nicholson could not even pay the dividends to the stockholders. Morris told Nicholson that the latter would have to pay the dividends because he was out of money, but Nicholson was in the same state of pecuniary embarrassment. The agents and surveyors of the company also went unpaid in 1797, and many of them left the company's employ. The situation became so critical by 1798 that no one knew the location of the company's offices, who the secretary and managers were, or often even the whereabouts of Nicholson and Morris, as they were in seclusion trying to escape creditors and sheriffs.

Both partners became bankrupt and their shares in the North American Land Company were sold at seven cents each to honor their guarantee, but the new managers, proving that there was no honor among thieves, bought all 7,445 shares by using fictitious names. The company continued to exist for seventy-five years mainly due to court litigations, and the heirs of the creditors and of the partners participated in many legal disputes. The partners, optimists to the end, still persisted in their attempts to see rays of hope in the potential market of the teeming masses of Europe. Nicholson certainly would have agreed with Morris who wrote, "Here is unoccupied lands in this Country to an immense Extent capable of producing Food and Raiment for Millions and millions of men allowing to every family such comfortable space that they will not be willing to engage in Broils as they do in crowded Europe where Air & Subsistence can hardly be obtained by the great Mass."[45] The inscription on the Statue of Liberty, written nearly a century later, expressed almost the same sentiments but for different reasons.

11
THE END
OF A
SPECULATIVE
PATH

By early 1797 John Nicholson had almost reached the end of his speculative journey. He had taken many side paths, and his last two detours proved to be alternate routes to disaster. He tried two independent land ventures in an effort to recoup his losses, but instead of relieving his chaotic situation, they further entangled him. On 21 April 1795 he formed the Territorial Land Company to sell 310,904 acres of land in Hawkins, Knox, and Washington counties, Southwestern Territory, Tennessee. The 1,554 shares of 200 acres each were offered for sale at 350 dollars per share with the stipulation that the purchaser who held the shares for three years could get back 300 dollars per share from Nicholson or his heirs by transferring them to Nicholson. He also guaranteed dividends of 18 dollars per year per share, and if the sales did not cover it, he would make up the difference. Needless to say, Nicholson could not honor these pledges. His friend Edmund Randolph agreed to serve as trustee for this company along with Matthew Clarkson, mayor of Philadelphia, and James Biddle, president of the Courts of Common Pleas of the first district of Pennsylvania. His brother-in-law, James Duncan, served as secretary-treasurer of the company and General Walter Stewart, Viscount de Noailles, Governor William Blount, and David Allison served on the board of managers. Nicholson tried to sell this land at $2.25 per acre and sent copies of the Plan of Association to his agents in Europe. Since his agents were already trying to sell his other land company shares and lands without success, this was just another mill stone around their necks. Prospective buyers, thoroughly disillusioned with Nicholson and Morris, were asking such sharp questions as these: As buyers of shares, will we be responsible for debts incurred by the company? Could dividends be paid? What guarantees on our investment do we have? Since the desired answers were not forthcoming, efforts to sell Territorial shares in Europe failed like the others, and so did the company. By 1797, Nicholson was trying to use Territorial Land Company shares as security for debts, but his creditors would not accept them, basically because the titles were not clear of encumbrances. The lands of this company, like those of so many others, were taken by creditors or were attached for failure to pay the taxes and sold at sheriff's sales.

A drowning man gasping for breath, Nicholson made one last effort to recoup his losses and save himself. Like Robert Morris who made his final attempt in 1797 by forming The Pennsylvania Property Company, Nicholson organized his Pennsylvania Land Company. The capital for this company consisted of land and estates to which Nicholson claimed ownership in eighteen Pennsylvania counties and the City of Philadelphia. Morris shared an interest in some of these holdings and the total value of this property was set at $4,000,672.33. When someone doubted the value Nicholson placed on his Pennsylvania property, he wrote, "I know the whole of scheduled property to be richly worth at present what it is set at, and in ten years will quadruple the value."[1] The capital stock of these enterprises was represented by 40,000 shares, and a board of managers was established to handle the sales. This board consisted of Joseph Higbee, Michael Hillegas, William Nichols, and James Gibson. Nicholson again promised a guarantee of six dollars per share and used notes to provide $6,000 as a partial security for honoring this stipulation.

Robert Morris, also still deluded with hope, commented in 1797 that "it is the settlers that give value to the land, the continual rise of prices is inevitable until it arrives to a certain pitch. . . . Then one sells."[2] This assertion may have been true, but the land which was offered for sale had to have clear titles. The two partners had to use their lands and company shares as security for their debts so often by 1797 that none of their holdings was clear of encumbrances, and most burdened of all were their Pennsylvania lands. Included in the property consigned to the trustees of the Pennsylvania Land Company, and under various encumbrances, were Angelica Farm, the remainder of the lands he claimed in the Pennsylvania Population Company along French Creek, the store at the falls, the Iron Forge at Fairfield, formerly held in partnership with John Hayden, and an eighty-eight-acre estate next to Thomas Mifflin's in Philadelphia County. He also had innumerable lots and houses in Philadelphia that were conveyed including those on Arch, Market, Chestnut, Seventh and Race, Center Square, Kensington, Philbert, High,

186

Eighth, Spruce, and Third streets and his stables on Locust Street. Unhappily for Nicholson, even the Commonwealth of Pennsylvania had placed two liens on his property in the state—one in March and one in December of 1796—in an effort to collect what he owed for the shortages discovered while he was comptroller-general. So these claims destroyed whatever hopes Nicholson had for salvaging his fortunes through the Pennsylvania Land Company. He tried to secure debts using these company shares but his creditors would not accept them. One wrote, "no one knows of any such property—or any such Company & to be satisfied with such Security is Impossible, I can scarcely believe you can think it yourself." And another: "I have taken pains to obtain information concerning the Pennsylvania Land Company, I find that a prevailing opinion that the property of the Company would not sell in Cash for the amount of the Incumbrances. I wish you would point out some other method to secure my demand."[3] Those properties that were not subject to the liens of the state or the attachments of creditors were sold at sheriffs' sales to pay the taxes that had accumulated. One wrote, "I am sorry to be obliged to proceed to the sale of this property, but I will use my endeavors to make it bring the most for your interest."[4] By 1798, even the trustees were resigning. Since Nicholson had neither funds nor time to clear all of the conflicting claims on his property and no credit with which to secure them or to honor his promised guarantees, the Pennsylvania Land Company and his other projects failed, and with them, John Nicholson.

It may be difficult to comprehend how a man that was once recognized as being extremely competent in public finances, even by enemies like Albert Gallatin, could fail so miserably in his own private transactions. This question may also be raised in connection with Nicholson's partner, Robert Morris. Each was deluded with the hope that the cure for their ills was just around the corner, but like flies caught in a web, the more they struggled, the more entangled they became. By 1798 Nicholson owed individuals, bankers, insurance companies, commissioners of the Federal City, trading houses in the United States and abroad, architects, workmen, former agents of his land companies, manufactories, stores and mines, other speculators, land offices, county treasuries, widows' and ministers' funds, whose assets had been entrusted to him for "safekeeping," and the Commonwealth of Pennsylvania for funds which mysteriously vanished while he was comptroller-general. So completely was his credit destroyed by 1797 that his note for 8,000 dollars was only able to command 135 dollars.[5]

Pennsylvania Speculator and Patriot: John Nicholson

His creditors hounded him and brought litigation to bear. Pennsylvania, in December 1795 and again in March 1796 and December 1796, obtained judgments against him for $11,222.50, $58,429.24, and $63,729.86 respectively. Since Nicholson was dissatisfied with these judgments, a trial was held between him and the state in the Supreme Court, where in March 1797 a judgment was rendered against him for $110,390.89.[6] According to J.B. Anthony, who was later appointed by the state to investigate Nicholson's affairs, "Nothing appears to have been done by Mr. Nicholson, after judgment was obtained, to procure any credits or allowances nor were any errors shown by him in the amount."[7]

Since Nicholson could not secure the funds, liens were placed upon his lands. The state acted by virtue of authority granted by an act that "goods, chattels, moneys, effects and credits, . . . lands, and in short every other subject of property, are liable in Pennsylvania to attachment." Ironically, Samuel, Nicholson's brother, was appointed after John Nicholson's death to aid in collecting these liens. Samuel found that after his brother died, other speculators had "possessed themselves, by illegal sales of the immense spoils of John Nicholson, for a cent or two an acre. . . ."[8] As a result, the state, during the administration of Thomas McKean, appointed a special commission, the Nicholson Commission, to try to clear up the business and to bring litigation to bear against individuals who had the misfortune of endorsing bonds which Nicholson had given to the state as security for the "faithful execution of his office." The four trusting souls had been Barnabus Binney, Matthew Irwin, Blair McClenachan, and Dr. David Jackson, and they were made to pay for the Nicholson bonds.

Other individuals also suffered from Nicholson's folly. An example of this developed from Nicholson's membership in the Presbyterian Church of Philadelphia. He had used the Widow's Fund, which had been established by the church and which he supervised, for his own purposes. He used Widow Fund Certificates, given to widows of soldiers, for land speculation purposes and in 1795 had borrowed $37,166 from the fund, securing payment by mortgaging some lands in Susquehanna County. Nicholson settled forty German and Irish families on these lands and promised to furnish them with needed supplies. He could not keep his promise, and furthermore, when payments were due to the fund in 1799, he could not meet them. Consequently, the lands were sold to John B. Wallace of Philadelphia, and the settlers were left in a desperate state. A township in

The End of a Speculative Path

Susquehanna County, probably one of Nicholson's last remaining monuments—the other being a village in Wyoming County—was later named for him, possibly due to the fact that he encouraged the establishment of the first settlement in the area.

In addition to widows and immigrant families, Nicholson's agents also suffered from their connection with him. William Prentiss, one of his agents in the Federal City, went bankrupt and wound up in debtor's prison blaming Nicholson for his plight.[9] David Allison, who had accepted Nicholson's and Morris's notes in payment for lands they had purchased and never redeemed, suffered a similar fate and died an insolvent debtor. William Duncan, another agent, was being pursued by the sheriff and wrote, "I care not what I endure myself, But if I'm not relieved god only knows what will become of my Innocent wife & Little children. For Heavens Sake have mercy on them. For I cannot nor will not live to see them suffer."[10] However, Nicholson could not even help his own family, and they, along with his agents and friends, suffered from his folly. Mrs. Nicholson did not even have money for a gravestone for John's mother and had to borrow to acquire it.

In addition there were those who had had the misfortune to endorse Nicholson's notes and who received as their reward, when Nicholson defaulted, law suits and imprisonment.[11] Coupled with these were other speculators who had been persuaded to participate in Morris's and Nicholson's ventures and went bankrupt when these two fell. Dr. Thomas Ruston was one of these and Dr. Benjamin Rush lamented that Ruston had "lost all the habits of innocence, friendship and benevolence of his early life and became a sordid speculator and an oppressor even of some branches of his own family." Ruston became the occupant of a debtor's apartment in Prune Street Prison along with Nicholson and Morris. Another that the speculators put into a similar situation was Thomas Fitzsimmons, once a delegate from Pennsylvania who had helped to draft the United States Constitution. Fitzsimmons had taken shares in the land companies of Morris and Nicholson and had also endorsed their notes. When they did not take up these notes, it helped to cause his ruin. Nicholson kept putting him off with one of his typical responses to creditors, "I regret that I have so long been disabled from meeting my obligations to you . . . and further that I am unable to fix a day on which I shall be able to pay it, but I am taking measures which I hope to mature before the close of the present month which will enable me to do it. No effort shall be wanting on my part." Fitzsimmons, in reply, gave the typical creditors' lamentation, "you have injured me beyond a possibility of retribution."[12]

Part of the cause of Nicholson's difficulties, and those he caused for others, can be traced to the handling of his land companies. Three main methods were used by speculators of the era in disposing of lands: 1. they offered to sell large tracts of land to wealthy men in Europe and America; 2. they set up land offices and sold lands to small groups or individuals; or 3. they held them as an investment to resell when lands were in demand. Nicholson encountered difficulty with all three options. If he wanted to sell land, the trustees of his land companies had difficulties because he did not have the funds to liquidate claims against the lands. Furthermore, most of his lands and land company shares had been mortgaged or given as security for loans from banks or creditors, and those that had not been conveyed, such as those of the Pennsylvania Land Company, were not being accepted by his creditors. Individuals and groups soon became apprehensive about buying lands from either Morris or Nicholson, because even the speculators did not know if the land they were attempting to peddle was actually theirs to sell.

In paying for lands, Nicholson and Morris had a favorite device of endorsing each other's notes— "Ballons" [sic] Nicholson called them. In reply to a note from Nicholson soliciting his signature, Morris wrote, "I will most cheerfully give you my Name upon the notes you mention and to any others . . . to relieve you from the present painful situation." Nicholson reciprocated innumerable times and endorsed Morris's notes. The notes sometimes involved very large sums. Morris seriously wrote, "I have made a purchase of which I want $500,000 in your notes of this date in my favor payable in two years."[13] Part of Nicholson's trouble was that these notes issued in the 1790 to 1795 period began to fall due in 1797, and he had no money to take them up because land sales had not proven to be sufficient, nor did the returns from his manufacturing, mining, and entrepreneurial operations. Nicholson described the consequences admirably when he wrote, "enclosed are four notes for your endorsement. I am obligated to issue paper at 50 per cent per annum. It puts me in mind of the old continental paper money, which was decreased in value as the quantity augmented." As the notes fell due, creditors began to press the speculators from all sides. Morris wrote to his partner, "I find a number of your notes dated in December 1795 are coming in for payment, and of course, go to the Fraternity of 'Notarius Publicus', and as the Supreme Court is now setting, honorable mention will be made of our Names. We must my Friend make great Exertions & release ourselves from the worst of all Situations.[14] Nicholson took the barrage in stride and quipped that he would probably end before his troubles did and commented to a friend that problems are great or small only in one's estimate of them.

In fact, there was so much of Nicholson and Morris's paper in circulation that speculators began to speculate in their notes. One broker wrote to Nicholson, "a gentleman is to call on me this afternoon for 100,000 dollars in your notes of 2 years endorsed by Robert Morris Esq. for which he will give 4,000 dollars in cash." Nicholson was much better off with the cash than his notes, so he speculated in his own paper and so did Morris. Of course, this had to be kept a secret "so as to Effectively secure your Credit & Reputation," as one broker put it.[15] However, as the decade of the 1790s wore on, the notes of the speculators sank in value. By 1797, one broker wrote, "I can dispose of 100,000 Dollars of N & M notes at 10 Cents on the dollar." When Nicholson heard a rumor that his notes were rising in value, his lawyer, William Moulder, hastened to reply, "you have been wrong informed respecting your notes. . . . The fact is that they have [been] falling instead of rising—Billy Duncan tells me that they were sold this day for Five pence in the pound & Mr. Higbee says there is plenty offered for Eight pence at most." By July 1797 they had dwindled in value to the infinitesimal sum of two cents on the dollar.[16]

Nevertheless, Nicholson and Morris should have known the consequences of issuing notes without proper security because Morris had handled finances during the Revolutionary War and Nicholson had administered state finances afterward. One possible explanation is that both, like others of their generation, had a mania for land and, like others, they overextended themselves in trying to satisfy this passion. Another possible reason for the use of notes was that brokers in Philadelphia and elsewhere, just as they did before the Great Crash of 1929, encouraged credit buying and its concomitant speculation and, unfortunately for Nicholson and Morris, with the same results, financial collapse and ruin. The use of notes impeded the sale of land at home as well as abroad, because land agents in Europe could not persuade people to buy land to which titles were not certain.

If Nicholson wished to use his other option of holding onto his lands until a better price could be obtained, he was thwarted as well. His plight was immediate, he could not wait for his "pipe dream" to materialize. Furthermore, there was the problem of the tax burden which neither he nor his partner seemed to realize. As mentioned above, Morris thought the tax burden on lands was "inconsiderable." Taxes on a few acres might have been inconsiderable, but on millions they were crushing. Most of the North American Land Company holdings reverted to the states in which they were located because tax payments were not made.

Another cause of the Nicholson plight was the trust he placed on those selling him lands. Since he bought on faith and contracted for land so frequently, he could not take the time to examine the lands for quality or to check on the validity of his titles. He had to depend on deputies for this, and they were not always careful or loyal. A good example of this was the Nicholson-Morris purchase of the pine barrens in Georgia. The partners were entangled in the Federal City project at the time and could not inspect these lands personally. When they found out about the quality of the lands, they tried to recoup their losses by falsifying the description of these lands to entice buyers, but few came forth. The same situation developed in regard to other land projects.

Added to his unwise faith in those who sold him lands should be his misplaced reliance in those who helped entangle him in so many schemes. At the top of the list must come James Greenleaf. Two of Nicholson's most fatal blunders were the Washington project and the North American Land Company. Nicholson and Morris were led into these by Greenleaf with the latter's assurance that his contacts with European bankers and investors would be adequate to back the enterprises. When Greenleaf failed to secure the funds, the partners were left with financial burdens which could not be met. Greenleaf added to their distress by personally appropriating funds which were designed to pay the creditors and by defaulting on notes which Nicholson and Morris had endorsed, thus leaving these added debts to be paid. When Morris and Nicholson realized the treachery of Greenleaf, it was too late to save the situation. However, one of Nicholson's creditors said that he deserved no pity for being used so badly by Greenleaf. He said, "the world knows that you have ability, power and action to Retaliate with a pair of Shearers that will reach from the Falls of Labrador to East Florida nay to the East Indies."[17]

In addition to these problems, Nicholson and other large speculators were constantly at odds with the actual settler. The settler viewed the speculator in the same light that he viewed the Indian—individuals holding more lands than they could use and consequently depriving those in need of land for settlement. Numerous petitions to the legislature of Pennsylvania protested against the speculators and demanded that the improvement features of the state's land laws be enforced. Since the Republican administration of Thomas McKean was favorable to settler interests, from 1799 on Nicholson could expect no state sympathy in these land conflicts. Furthermore, when Nicholson sent his agents to inspect lands, the settlers or squatters had a tendency to show them the wrong parcels.

Added to all of the land problems were problems related to Nicholson's entrepreneurial activities. Most of these were premature ventures which neither the promoter nor the nation was equipped to handle. They drained Nicholson of needed funds, consumed his time, and helped, along with his land schemes, to bring him down.

As a result of all these difficulties, Nicholson found himself short of money but amply supplied with lawsuits brought by his innumerable creditors. For example, as of 31 August 1796 there were sixty-one cases brought against him, and by 24 May 1797 sixty-four more were added to the list. Nicholson did not even know how many were pending and occasionally asked the clerks of the courts if there were judgments rendered against him in particular sessions. Because of the suits, Nicholson was constantly pressed to stay one step ahead of the law. He explained these evasive tactics to his lawyer in this manner: "it is not the horrors of a prison as it respects my person that would make me avoid meeting those writs for one day but the knowledge of my power in [the] future to do what otherwise I hope to be able to effect, that is to settle with my Creditors, secure them and provide the means of payment as soon as possible."[18] So he avoided sheriffs like Joseph Boone of Prince Georges County, Maryland, and George Baker of Philadelphia in an attempt to extricate himself.

Nicholson tried everything to raise money, "settle with my Creditors, secure them and provide means of payment as soon as possible." He used his land company shares and Washington lots to appease the few creditors that would accept them, although most by 1797 would not. This was because, as one creditor found out, Nicholson had already given most of his shares to other creditors to appease them and had none left that were unencumbered. Nicholson tried to use canal and turnpike company shares but with the same results. He also recalled all of his European agents and instructed them to bring along whatever they had left to sell.

When these devices failed, he sold his furniture, his stock in firms such as T.B. Freeman and Company, and his remaining farms, plantations, sloops, and cargoes. However, he needed millions of dollars and he was receiving pennies. The situation became so critical that he had to assign all of his rights, title, interest and property "in the Person and Service of a Negro Man named Jim" and had to ask the Black Church that he once helped to aid him. To Joseph Higbee, one of his creditors, he wrote, "in part to secure you the balance owed you . . . accept . . . two Shakespeares, and one General Wayne. . . ." To another he wrote, "please receive the key to the house. There are eleven barrels of old cider turned to vinegar. Could not you sell it, perhaps someone will buy it?" In the margin of the letter appeared, "No Purchasers."[19] Even Robert Morris sometimes pressed Nicholson and complained because the younger man was in the Federal City leaving him to face their creditors alone. Once he wrote, "five cases are out against me, four of them your account, and one my own, they must be provided for, the amount about $12,000—the pressure is beyond anything you can conceive."[20] However, Nicholson was under just as much pressure in the Federal City trying to expedite their affairs and to stay one step ahead of the sheriff in the process; he could offer Morris no relief.

Nicholson tried to gain some relief from individuals who owed him money. The typical reply was that they would help at some future date, "in the meanwhile, you have my most fervent wishes, that you may be extricated from every difficulty."[21] Nicholson's account book listed one hundred persons who owed him money but these individuals, such as Daniel Brodhead, Aaron Burr, Robert Morris, James Greenleaf, and Oliver Evans, were almost as much in debt as Nicholson. There could be no help from them. Oliver Evans, the engineer, wrote, "if you could direct any of your acquaintances to me for a pair of mill stones it might enable me to discharge the note. . . ."[22] But Nicholson's creditors wanted cash, not mill stones.

As a consequence of all of these difficulties and of their lack of business judgment, both John Nicholson and Robert Morris became residents of the debtors' apartments of the Prune Street Prison in Philadelphia—Morris in 1798 and Nicholson in 1799. The latter half of 1796 and all of 1797 were years of woe for them. They had lost track of the innumerable notes they had endorsed for one another. They tried to bring some order out the chaos, and several messages a day would pass between Nicholson's residences at Seventh and Sassafras (Race) streets and Chalkley Hall overlooking the Delaware River, and Robert Morris's domiciles at Trout Springs and "The Hills" overlooking the Schuylkill River. Chalkley Hall became "Castle Defense" and "The Hills" became "Castle Defiance" in their correspondence during this period of gloom. When Morris finally realized the futility of the situation, he commented, "I wish to God these notes would serve to take up those that bear promise of payment. They are numerous already but if they would answer the other purpose, you would want more copying presses and a half a dozen paper mills."[23] At this point, their Philadelphia associates estimated their debts at twelve million dollars. Morris facetiously requested that Nicholson take up residence with him so they could plan ways to escape creditors and especially debtor's prison.

Their letters during the period of adversity became so voluminous that they began to number them. Morris wrote to Nicholson, "your letter No. 8 of yesterday is written with more animation & Spirit than the others. Oh what a charming delightful thing is a gleam of hope, how it clears the Soul & drives away that friend of Hell, despair." Once when Nicholson failed to write as expected, Morris quipped, "Good Morning to you, my good friend, what is the matter is your Ink out, Quills exhausted, or paper quite done, excuse those questions they arise out of circumstance of my not having heard from you all day."[24] It is surprising to find a sense of humor in their letters of this period. When Morris asked Nicholson to start numbering his letters, Nicholson replied, "you ask me to number my letters, but like my *printed notes* they become numberless—that is, numerable."

Morris observed about the creditors who were watching his house, "If I see them it is out of a Window I being upstairs and they down, when I sniff the open air it is on the Top and there is Something else to sniff there unless you keep to Windward."[25]

During this period, they became prisoners in their own homes, afraid to venture out for fear of being arrested. They conveyed messages back and forth through their sons or other trusted messengers and sometimes had to physically arm themselves to protect their lives and property. Once a creditor by the name of Dunwoody sent six men to the "Hills" to get Morris. Morris informed Nicholson that they were armed with sledge hammers and pick axes. "They would have had me in five minutes if every Pistol & gun in the house had [not] been manned and fixed at them, for we could not have killed all."[26] Nicholson once reported that two representatives of the law had been pacing back and forth in front of his "Castle" all day and so he left them there while he remained safely inside. To gain entrance to their "fortresses" one had to swear an oath of allegiance. One who wanted access wrote, "I pledge to you my most sacred word of honor, that I have no precept against you of any kind or sort whatever against you nor no other business but what I have maintained." Once Morris was going to risk a visit to Nicholson's domicile but "recollecting that Brenton's *Guards* may possibly have taken their Station & admittance be difficult I turned back & shall write what I meant to communicate. . . ."[27]

Nicholson, in this period of despair, still deluded himself with the hope of eventual salvation. With eager anticipation he wrote, "I have waited today in expectation of the money I was to have sent you at half past three but it is now 5 and I have not got it. I hope I shall get it by evening but if I do not, I shall certainly have it early Monday morning." On another occasion he assured Morris, "Thro God strengthening us, we will yet work, what the public will account a Miracle."[28] However, Morris doubted divine aid and wrote, "I believe if you or I were the Owners of the Heavenly Paradise, no security we could offer in this world would be accepted, so long as Trustees and creditors thought that the best."[29]

Nicholson and Morris were not the only ones facing bankruptcy during this period. There was a rash of business failures in Philadelphia in 1796 and Dr. Benjamin Rush remarked that the city was in great consternation. This was the period when the Bank of Pennsylvania was in a "perfect uproar" due to the defalcations by its president, John Barclay, and its cashier, Jonathan Mifflin. Keeping in tune with the temper of the times, even the good Governor Mifflin had improperly withdrawn $13,000 from the bank. Judge James Wilson was in and out of the debtor's apartment in this period prompting Nicholson to write, "Poor Wilson I pity him from my Soul; he is a good man." Speculator Blair McClenachan "conveyed his estate to his children to cheat his creditors." Rush reported that during a six-week period in 1796, one hundred businesses failed and sixty-seven people had shortly thereafter gone to jail; Robert Morris was one of these unfortunate souls.[30]

Morris began to resign himself to this fate in December 1797 when he wrote to his friend,

> For my part I begin to think the best way to get clear of the whole Host of them [creditors] is to submit and take up quarters in Pruen [sic] Street at once, nothing *there* can be worse than this continual harrassment & torment which we . . . now suffer.

On 12 December 1797 he wrote, "I fear my good friend it will be long before we sit down under our own vines and Fig trees, altho' it may not be long before we get among the Pruens." A little later he exclaimed, "Oh Lord oh Lord what are we come to? Answer? The

Stool of repentance." And on the eve of his departure for the Prison he lamented to Nicholson, "My money is gone, my furniture is to be sold, I am to go to prison and my family to starve, good night."[31] Nicholson related that it was the suits of George Eddy and the Bank of North America that were the immediate causes of Morris's confinement and he assailed the bank especially for this because Morris was its founder. Shortly before Morris's internment on 16 February 1798, both "Castle Defiance" and "Castle Defense" were sold to pay creditors, and Morris wrote this caustic vituperation to all of their creditors who were responsible for their plight. "Good Heavens! What vultures men are in regard to each other! I never in the day of prosperity took advantage of man's distresses, and I suppose what I now experience is to serve as a lesson whereby to see the folly of humane and generous conduct."[32] On the day before Morris's departure for Prune Street, Nicholson, trusted friend and faithful to the end, somehow scraped together 40 dollars and sent this to this compatriot. Morris returned it with, "as I believe you want money as much, if not more than I do at this moment I return the forty dollars received in your note of this day, with thanks for the kind intention."[33]

When Morris entered the prison, he found some familiar faces. Three fellow speculators were there as well—David Allison, Charles Young, and Henry Banks—but they offered him little solace. At first he did not like his confinement and thought it "disagreeable and uncomfortable." But after he had become acclimated, he wrote Nicholson that "my situation may be supportable . . . but this place ought to be avoided by all that can possibly keep out of it."[34] Nicholson was able to avoid debtors' prison for almost two years after Morris was confined.

During this period they maintained a constant correspondence, in which Morris offered Nicholson constant advice on how to avoid the same fate. In a book that he had read Morris came upon the following verse:

> A raven once an acorn took
> From Bosom's tallest, Stoutest tree
> He hid it near a limped Brook
> and lived another oak to see.
> Thus Mellancholy buries hope
> which Fear still keeps alive
> and bids us with Misfortunes Cope
> and all Calamity survive.

He sent this verse to his friend with a note of comfort saying, "you are young enough to bury the Acorn and see the Tree grow up again. . . . I am too old and therefore quiet acquiescence and submission to my fate is perhaps all that remains for poor R. Morris."[35] But fate ruled otherwise, for Morris outlived Nicholson by six years.

Nicholson attempted to provide for his family during the interval between his failure in 1797 and his imprisonment in late 1799 and tried to borrow to meet his obligations, but no one would accept his notes. Nicholson, dejected and despondent, wrote, "my family have learned like good Christians to endure all things patiently hoping & expecting in the next world that times will go better with us there than in this." Morris also lamented for his family as he wrote, "I consider my fate as fixed . . . the punishment of my imprudence in the use of my name and loss of credit is perhaps what I deserve but it is nevertheless severe on my family and on my account, I feel it most tormentingly."[36] Morris and Nicholson's families were in dire straits. Abigail Adams, wife of the president, visited Mrs. Morris while her husband languished in Prune Street Prison and wrote,

> She received me with all that dignity of manners for which she more than any Lady I ever saw, is distinguished. . . . She endeavored to smile away the Melancholy which was evident upon her whole countanance [sic] . . . I requested her to come and take Tea with me! I took her by the Hand. She said she did not visit, but she would not refuse herself the pleasure of comeing [sic] someday when I was alone. She then turned from me, and the tears burst forth. I most sincerely felt for her.[37]

While Morris was busy writing letters to Nicholson, others were trying to secure his release. William Morris tried to persuade the eight creditors who were responsible for the internment of his father to withdraw their suits or at least to give the sheriff permission to let Morris go home during the yellow fever epidemic that again hit Philadelphia in 1798. Five agreed, but three would not, and so Morris remained in jail. Nicholson as well did all that he could do to secure his partner's release. He challenged one of those responsible for Morris's imprisonment, John Ely, to a newspaper war but Ely refused. He also consulted lawyers but they could offer little assistance because all of the suits were legal. The former president, George Washington, visited his old friend in his debtor's apartment in 1798 but offered no assistance in trying to secure his release.

During this period, Nicholson visited Morris in the prison and

The End of a Speculative Path

came dangerously close to being arrested himself. Morris then cautioned him against coming to see him and wrote these prophetic words, "but you must not go to Pruen street, Parry the present difficulties, and fortune will smile hereafter, but if the key is once turned on you by the hand under any authority but your own God only knows when that door shall be opened to you; perhaps never, until you shall be insensible to the affairs of the world."[38] The key was turned on Nicholson in August 1799, and it was never turned back, for he died in prison in December 1800.

The irony of the debtor's apartment at Prune Street was that the prisoner, who was there because he had no money to pay debts, was compelled to pay rent and furnish the room the law forced him to occupy. The prison was located at the northeast corner of Sixth and Prune streets in Philadelphia. William Wood, the actor and playwright, spent seventy days there during Morris's confinement and described this unusual place. He wrote, "one side of the Prune street debtors prison was neatly laid out as a garden, and well kept, affording an agreeable promenade for the luckless inhabitants of this Bastille. . . ." He further related that Morris and some prisoners walked from 6 A.M. until 8 A.M. on one side of the prison while others rode on the other side. Of Morris, he said, "his person was neat, and his dress, although a little old-fashioned, adjusted with much care."[39] Among those whom Wood saw riding was James Greenleaf. The partners must have taken great delight in seeing that this man, whom they considered to be the chief cause of their failure, had not escaped the clutches of the law. Nicholson and Morris were not the only ones to have contempt for Greenleaf. Morris related that when Greenleaf requested that his slave, Cudjo, be buried with him, the Black replied, "No massa, no. . . . Maybe massa when de debil come for you, he mistake and take Cudjo."[40]

Another visitor to the prison said that the prisoners there were not under much restraint and did not have to be locked into their cells or apartments until nine o'clock in the evening. The jailer was responsible for the amount of debts that escaped prisoners were liable for "but the prisoners make it a point of honor not to subject him to this."[41]

The bankrupts received visitors of all kinds, principally creditors. One creditor even had the audacity to request "if you have got a Shirt to Spear [sic], you could not bestow it more properly nor more seasonably. . . ." Another pleaded to Nicholson with, "I am loath to call on you but necessity has no law—for god sake help me if you can."[42] The partners did have associates working in their behalf, including Alexander Hamilton and James Gibson who were offering legal assistance and Samuel Nicholson and Gouverneur Morris who were trying to raise funds, but the partners' "balloons" thwarted their efforts. The New York Morris visited the speculators several times in the prison and on one occasion wrote, "Morris and his family are in high spirits, and I keep them so by a very lively strain of conversation. . . ." Another visitor who called was Elizabeth Drinker, wife of speculator Henry Drinker. She wrote, "My husband & I visited John Nicholson in prison today—engaged to take his newspaper. Poor man! What a reverse of fortune—from affluence to Jail."[43]

As indicated by Mrs. Drinker's comment, Nicholson, to his credit, did not sink immediately into remorse but tried diligently to expedite his affairs and gain some relief for his family. While he was in prison, Mrs. Nicholson and the children lived at Angelica Farm until that was taken by creditors; they then rented a house at Eighth and Walnut streets in Philadelphia. To meet the expenses of the prison and to pay the rent for his family, Nicholson decided to publish a newspaper with the appropriate title *The Supporter*, or *Daily Repast*. He and Morris had too much pride to beg or to give their creditors the satisfaction of coming to them for aid. Under Pennsylvania law, if a debtor could not supply himself with food, he was to be given an allowance of seven cents per day, which was to be paid by the plaintiff upon whose suit the debtor was confined. Nicholson tried the newspaper in an attempt to avoid this. In 1799 he contacted Grace Raketon of Philadelphia to publish his paper but later secured the services of his old friends and leading publishers, Francis and Robert Bailey. The subscription price was 8 dollars a year or 2 dollars per quarter with single copies selling for six cents. One of the first subscribers to the paper was Dr. Enoch Edwards, an old friend and agent, who suggested to Nicholson that he use the paper in defense of his actions. Nicholson refused to do this and instead devoted space to items common for the day—European news, prices of goods, fires, robberies, and the like. Nicholson's friends and advertisers supplied him with newsworthy items and helped him obtain subscribers. Among the prominent subscribers and advertisers were President John Adams, the Pennsylvania Abolitionist Society, the Bank of North America and the Bank of Pennsylvania, the Georgia Land Company, and, ironically, the Bankruptcy Committee. The paper did furnish a profit in 1800 as expenses totaled $252.94 and receipts $964.10, but this venture unfortunately turned out like all of his others, a failure. He had difficulty obtaining supplies of paper, competent delivery men, and new subscribers. In the end, even Robert Bailey left his service because of the unpaid bills that he had accumulated in Nicholson's behalf. So in the end, not even this final venture could provide John Nicholson with peace of mind.

12
JOHN NICHOLSON'S MIXED LEGACY: PRIVATE DISHONOR AND PUBLIC HONOR

John Nicholson, burdened with despair, died at age forty-three on 5 December 1800 leaving a wife and eight children. His spectacular legacies of private debt and dishonor must be weighed against his less celebrated public bequests of enduring achievements. Some of the legacies he left were debts totaling twelve million dollars, three to four million acres subject to the liens of the Commonwealth of Pennsylvania, numerous tracts of encumbered land in other states, dilapidated manufactories and buildings, an army of creditors, the development of Washington, D.C., developing inventors and internal improvement projects, and some land settlements. Yet little attention was paid to his death. Only one obituary notice, probably written by Robert Morris, appeared. It noted his service as comptroller-general and his business activities.[1] Another friend wrote, "John Nicholson died in the Debtor's apartment, a day or two ago. Poor man, he has paid the last debt."[2] Nicholson may have paid his last debt, but his creditors could not forget the debts owed them and brought litigations against his family. These cases continued to plague Nicholson's heirs for over forty years.

In addition, the Commonwealth of Pennsylvania pressed Nicholson's heirs for settlement. In 1806 a special Nicholson Court and Commission was established to collect $121,613.39 due the state based on the court decisions of 1795 and 1797 against Nicholson.[3] The commissioners were to trace Nicholson's land holdings, place liens, and sell the lands to collect the debts. This went on until 1839 when Commissioner J.B. Anthony issued a thorough report on Nicholson's affairs and submitted this accurate characterization: "It may be difficult for many to comprehend, how Mr. Nicholson, who was a gentleman of active habits, of untiring industry and high intellectual attainments, should become so deeply and irretrievably involved. . . . Great financial skill and eminent talents, shone, conspicuously throughout his public career. The principal cause of his failure may be attributed to his immense land speculations. . . ."[4] By 1842, the state had collected $147,718.35 but had no more lands on which to place uncontested liens. Rather than contest the right of the state to lands, formally part of the Pennsylvania Population Company and sold to over 40,000 settlers, the state withdrew its liens in 1843, closed its books, and abolished the Nicholson Court.

As for Nicholson's partner, Robert Morris, he was released in 1801 under a federal bankruptcy law after spending over three years in prison and went to live with his old friend Gouverneur Morris. He and his wife lived on 1500 dollars a year paid by the Holland Land Company as the price of Mrs. Morris's assignment of dower until the financier's death in 1806. Morris's estate was not settled until forty years after Nicholson's. One consolation that both he and Nicholson could take was that their imprisonment helped to focus attention on debtor's prisons and accelerated the movement for their abolishment.[5]

Both Nicholson and Morris were brought to ruin by their speculative private finances, but they were brilliant in public finance. One creditor who wanted pay but did not know how the partners could supply the funds wrote, "to point out ways and means to the greatest financiers of the age, would be presumption in me—it would be like the arrogance of one who should attempt dictating to Hannibal on the art of war."[6] However, the partners overextended themselves and could not find the means to salvage their fortunes. Abigail Adams, wife of President John Adams, aptly summarized the consequences of this when she wrote, "what distress what Ruin have these immense speculators involved themselves, their families, their connections, and thousands of others in? What is past cannot be remedied. We seldom learn experience until you get too old to use it, or we grow callous to the misfortunes of the world by Reiterated abuse . . . I have been led into these reflections in contemplating the unhappy situation of Mr. Morris, Nicolson [sic] and others,"[7] One of Nicholson's creditors added, "I remain essentially astonished at so much Sense being so much abused and so much a Speculation for every Vulgar fellow to charge you with epithets too indelicate to put on paper."[8] While they lived, both Nicholson and Morris took the abuse philosophically, and Nicholson would have agreed with Morris when the latter quipped,

> Here is your Health and mine too
> Here is those that love you and I too,
> and those that hate you and I too
> may kiss your a— and mine too.

If a psychologist wanted to embark on a case study of a man with delusions of grandeur, John Nicholson would be an ideal subject. Speculation after speculation and peripheral entrepreneurial activities followed the idea that his fortune would be made with one more effort. Energy and perseverance characterized the man even during his last years as he struggled against the current of adversity, cherishing the delusion that he could avoid prison, pay his debts, and salvage his life's work. He refused to sink into the morass of self-pity and wrote to a fellow in distress, "my case is widely different, where you have one demand against you, I have at least 900, yet I call in the aid of reason, and do not let my mind be unfitted for business at a time when it ought to be fitted. . . ."[9] However, Nicholson did not use the judgment with which he was endowed, for his failure to accept his limitations was the chief cause of his downfall. If his vast schemes and numerous land companies brought him at last to bankruptcy, the cause lay less with the conditions of the external business world than with his failure to use sound judgment in his private affairs. He recognized the importance of being a good creditor and paying his debts for he once wrote, "I will yet meet all by Creditors face to face and with 20 [shillings] in the pound pay them all—anything said by malice to the contrary notwithstanding God damn them."[10] However, to have fulfilled this pledge and to have been successful, he would have had to stop overextending himself and thereby becoming entangled in the webs of worthless notes. Given his temperament and his grandiose expectations, one doubts if Nicholson could have overcome this weakness enough to control it. Dr. John Ewing once sent to Nicholson the following verse from John Bunyan's, *Pilgrim's Progress*:

> I will tomorrow, that I will,
> I will be sure to do it,
> Tomorrow comes, tomorrow goes,
> And still thou art to do it.
> And thus Repentence is deferred
> From one day to another,
> Untill the Day of Death does come,
> And Judgment is the other.[11]

This could serve as Nicholson's epitaph.

Nicholson's Mixed Legacy

Nevertheless, John Nicholson cannot be abandoned to abuse without a few words of commendation to ease his burdened soul. He provided yeoman service as the financier of Pennsylvania and many would agree with William Lewis, a prominent Philadelphia attorney, who commented during the interval of Nicholson's impeachment that "the Committee of Investigation had, with unwearied industry, traced all the uncounted millions and tens of millions with which he had been entrusted, and it now appeared that the *Temptations However Great Could Not Corrupt Him*. . . . He has undergone this fiery ordeal of more than inquisitorial persecution, and . . . his character must, like pure metal doubly refined by an over severe heat, appear with unexampled lustre." [12] There were also many who felt that Robert Morris was treated unjustly by a nation he had served so well during the gloomy days of the Revolution. Samuel Breck expressed the opinions of many when he wrote, "I visited that great man in the Prune Street debtors apartment, and saw him in his ugly white washed vault. In Rome or Greece, a thousand statues would have honored his mighty services. . . . In America, republican America, not a single voice was raised in Congress or elsewhere in aid of him or his family. . . ." [13]

To John Nicholson and others like him can be given some credit for the growth of the new nation. His interests in promoting settlements, manufactories, mines, and the like may have been self-centered—in this he was acting no differently than John D. Rockefeller, Andrew Carnegie, and countless others—but the results were of national importance. His work in the fields of land and water transportation had a unifying effect, not only in his own state of Pennsylvania but throughout the United States. The Lancaster Turnpike which Nicholson helped to build was used as a model by the other states and his work with canals anticipated the great canal-building era of the 1820s and 1830s in the United States. His promotion of inventors like John Fitch, James Rumsey, and Oliver Evans helped to enable them to conduct their experiments and develop their machines and engines which advanced the cause of American technology. Furthermore, his promotion of manufactories, even if somewhat premature, helped those who followed to benefit from his mistakes and those of his counterparts. But even with these futile attempts, he was displaying the creed expressed so well by Alexander Hamilton in his Reports on Manufactories in 1791 when he wrote, "it is a truth, as important as it is agreeable, and one to which it is not easy to imagine exceptions, that everything tending to establish substantial and permanent order in the affairs of a country, to increase the total mass of industry and opulence, is ultimately beneficial to every part of it."[14] This is the philosophy that helped to motivate Nicholson and men like him, and it is a central theme of American history.

In addition to the above, his interests in promoting the cause of immigrant groups helped to stimulate Europeans to make the ocean journey and thereby to populate the nation and to man its farms and later its factories. He also supported the independence and freedom of Blacks. Dr. Benjamin Rush, a leading man of medicine in the United States, once wrote Nicholson that "I wish to suggest to you an idea of offering 10,000 or more acres for sale on moderate terms and on a credit for a few years, *to Africans only*. . . . I think the offer would succeed, and thereby a precedent be established for colonizing in time, all Africans in our country." After Nicholson expressed some interest in the project, Rush wrote, "may Heaven prosper you in all your great and extensive pursuits and may you long continue to enjoy the highest and only rational pleasure that wealth can offer."[15] Nicholson did offer aid to the Blacks in the form of a $1,000 loan to construct a church. He then attended a dinner with Rush to commemorate the raising of the roof. Rush related "never did I see people more happy, some of them shed tears of joy. An old black man took Mr. Nicholson by the hand and said to him, 'May you live long, and when you die may you not die eternally.' "[16] Nicholson's reputation as a benefactor of Blacks must have been widespread, for another, seeking employment, wrote to Nicholson that "I have been advised by some worthy men of my colour that if I would apply to you I should stand a very good chance of employmen [sic] . . . they tell me they are more indebted to you for several reasons than all the gentlemen in the City. . . ." Nicholson loaned Blacks money several times during the 1790s and they called him one of "the fathers of our Infant undertakings." He also refused to participate in the slave trade even though his agent pointed out the monetary rewards.[17]

Nicholson also had a reputation for benevolence in regard to other unfortunate individuals who needed a helping hand. One wrote, "it is not so much your character of being a *rich* man, as your character of being a *humane* and *benevolent* man which has induced me to address you. . . ." Another requested aid with "I venture to address myself to you as being a father of a family, and the friend of the unfortunate victims of a reverse of circumstance. . . ."[18] Nicholson gave money to those who wanted to start their own businesses, to families of men imprisoned for debt, to sufferers from natural and accidental calamities, to widows and orphans, and even found jobs for those out of work. He also gave money for the support of theaters, actors, musicians, and schools.

We must also credit Nicholson for his pioneering efforts in the construction of the national capital. With partners, he was directly responsible for constructing many of the early private buildings in Washington, and he entered this venture at a time when others were reluctant to do so. He also promoted manufactories in the new city as well as internal improvement projects which drew the praise of President Washington. Again, while his motivations were primarily personal, his building projects did much to attract others to invest in the Federal City, and thus helped to stimulate interest in the capital and in the young nation.

For these contributions and more, John Nicholson should not be buried beneath dusty manuscripts. He was a man who exploited his speculative path to the utmost as others have done after him. He tried to fulfill the "rags to riches" dream that America has provided for her people. His greatest calamity was that he overextended himself, but even this can be partly excused because this flaw stemmed from a too firm faith in the growth of the new nation. Had he lived, Nicholson might have taken comfort in a decision rendered in 1805 by Chief Justice of the United States John Marshall. In the case of *Huidekoper's Lessee* v. *Douglas*, Marshall ruled that prevention from settlement due to Indian hostilities was sufficient to give title to lands and that settlement was not necessary. With this decision, his unoccupied lands in Pennsylvania would have been safe from squatter encroachments, and since Nicholson was a man with much perseverance, he might have found a way out of his morass. Had he lived for an additional decade or two, his speculations might have succeeded because settlers eventually had to move onto his lands.

The author of Nicholson's obituary reflected that

> nature had bestowed talents, and he acquired by practice a facility in adjusting and settling the most intricate affairs with dispatch unequalled. Fortune smiled on his industry for a time and he acquired wealth; wealth afforded the opportunity (which he embraced to gratify the qualities and propensities of his mind. . . . Modest, unassuming and good tempered, he was a kind and affectionate husband and parent, a sincere friend and useful citizen.

Without being stimulated to avarice or ambition, he became too ardent (from habit) to the pursuit of wealth, and as many have done before by outstepping the bounds prescribed by prudence, he lost a fortune that ought to have contented him. . . .[19]

Perhaps this is the final historical verdict for John Nicholson.

NOTES

CHAPTER 1

1. Washington to William Crawford, 21 Sept. 1767 in John Fitzpatrick, ed., *The Writings of George Washington* (Washington, D.C.: Government Printing Office, 1931–1944), 2:468–69.

2. Nicholson to Dr. Enoch Edwards, 24 April 1795, John Nicholson Letterbooks 1 (Philadelphia: The Historical Society of Pennsylvania) (hereafter cited as NL, HSP).

3. Francis A. de La Rochefoucault-Liancourt, *Travels Through the United States of North America, the Country of the Iroquois, and Upper Canada, in the Years 1795, 1796, and 1797* . . . , 2d ed. (London: R. Phillips, 1800), 1:261 (hereafter cited as Liancourt, *Travels*), and Thomas Cooper, *Some Information Respecting America Collected by Thomas Cooper, Late of Manchester* (London: J. Johnson, 1794), p. 2.

4. For an evaluation of the land speculator see Paul Gates, "The Role of the Land Speculator in Western Development," *The Pennsylvania Magazine of History and Biography (PMHB)* 66 (July 1942): 314–33; Ray Allen Billington, *America's Frontier Heritage* (New York: Holt, Rinehart and Winston, 1966), pp. 44–45, 201–2; and Allan Bogue and Margaret Bogue, " 'Profits' and the Frontier Land Speculator," *Journal of Economic History* 17 (1957): 1–24.

5. Isaac Weld, *Travels Through the States of North America and the Provinces of Upper and Lower Canada During the Years 1795, 1796 and 1797*, 2d ed. (London: John Stockdale, 1799), 1:284–85 (hereafter cited as Weld, *Travels*).

6. John Cunningham to Nicholson, 14 Dec. 1796; Glause to Nicholson, 19 June 1795; and John Young to Nicholson, 25 Feb. 1794, John Nicholson General Correspondence, 1778–1800, John Nicholson Collection, Manuscript Group 96, Division of History and Archives, Pennsylvania Historical and Museum Commission, Harrisburg, Pennsylvania (hereafter cited as NC).

7. Nicholson to Samuel Nicholson, 29 May 1797, NL 7, HSP.

CHAPTER 2

1. The actual birthdate is unknown to authorities consulted and investigation of his letters did not reveal it. However, a reference was found

Notes

which indicated that a birthday greeting was sent from his mother at Carlisle which spoke of "twenty-two kisses." Sarah Nicholson to Nicholson, 6 June 1782, NC. This would approximate another account which gives his age as twenty-three in 1780. Thomas N. Page, *Washington and Its Romance* (New York: Doubleday, Page and Company, 1923), p. 80.

2. Family membership was gleaned from several letters in the Nicholson papers.

3. *Pennsylvania Archives*, 3d ser., 3:711. (Hereafter, references to the archives will be omitted in matters dealing with Nicholson's role as a state official.)

4. Nicholson to Brigadier General J. Gist, 27 Jan. 1780, John Nicholson Letter Books, 1779–1793, Pennsylvania Historical and Museum Commission, Public Records Division, William Penn Memorial Archives, Harrisburg, Pennsylvania (hereafter cited as NL, PRD).

5. Nicholson to Cornelius Comegys, 11 Jan. 1780, NC. He was still complaining in 1781 and wanted money due him at the rate of 40 to 1, taking into account depreciation. Nicholson to Board of Treasury, 18 Jan. 1781, NC.

6. Captain John Henderson to Nicholson, 23 Oct. 1780, NC.

7. Worthington C. Ford, ed., *Journals of the Continental Congress, 1774–1789* (Washington: Library of Congress, 1904–1937), 16:95–96.

8. John Bioren and Mathew Carey, comps., *Laws of the Commonwealth of Pennsylvania* (Philadelphia: Francis Bailey, 1803), 2:230. For a summary of this change see Joseph C. Ruddy, "The Policy of Land Distribution in Pennsylvania Since 1779" (M.A. thesis, The Pennsylvania State University, 1933), pp. 6–14, and Robert L. Brunhouse, *The Counter-Revolution in Pennsylvania, 1776–1790* (Harrisburg: Pennsylvania Historical Commission, 1942), pp. 79–80.

9. William B. Reed, ed. and comp., *The Life and Correspondence of Joseph Reed* (Philadelphia: Lindsay and Blakiston, 1847), 2:224.

10. Russell to Nicholson, 17 Jan. 1785, NC.

11. Edmund Hogan, ed., *The Pennsylvania State Trials: Containing the Impeachment, Trial, and Acquittal of Francis Hopkinson and John Nicholson . . .* (Philadelphia: Francis Bailey, 1794), passim; *Pennsylvania Archives*, 1st ser., 11:747.

12. *Pennsylvania Archives*, 1st ser., 2:702, 11:702, 3d ser., 3:711, 770–73; and *Pennsylvania Colonial Records* (Harrisburg: T. Fenn and Co., 1851–1853), 16:376.

13. Jared Sparks, ed., *Diplomatic Correspondence of the American Revolution* (Boston: Nathan Hale and Gray and Bowen, 1830), 3:242; Henry Cabot Lodge, ed., *The Works of Alexander Hamilton* (New York: G.P. Putnam's Sons, 1904), 3:83.

14. Edmund C. Burnett, ed., *Letters of Members of the Continental Congress* (Washington, D.C.: Carnegie Institution, 1921–1936), 5:439 n.; Reed, *Joseph Reed*, pp. 374–75.

15. John Nicholson, *A View of the Debts and Expenses of the Commonwealth of Pennsylvania . . .* (Philadelphia: R. Aitken and Son, 1786), reproduced in Evans, *Early American Imprints*, no. 19904, p. 25.

16. *Minutes of the Supreme Executive Council of Pennsylvania* (Harris-

Notes

burg: T. Fenn and Co., 1851–1853), 15:67, 16:326; *Pennsylvania Archives*, 1st ser., 9:663–64.

17. Nicholson to "My Dearest Girl," 9 Nov. 1781, NL, PRD.

18. Nicholson to Hannah Duncan, 24 Feb. 1782, ibid.

19. Ibid., 16, 28 April 1782.

20. Ibid., 25 Sept. 1784, 14 Oct. 1785.

21. Nicholson to Mrs. Hannah Nicholson, 1, 2 Aug. 1793, NL, PRD.

22. Ibid., 4 Aug. 1793.

23. John Nicholson, *An Address to the People of Pennsylvania*. Broadside reproduced in Evans, *Early American Imprints*, No. 22753 (Philadelphia: Francis Bailey, 1790), p. 10; *Pennsylvania Archives*, 1st ser., 11:90; Nicholson, *A View of Debts*, p. 25.

24. George Gibson to Nicholson, 30 April 1787, Dunning McNair Papers, 1786–1851, Darlington Memorial Library Manuscript Collections, University of Pittsburgh, Pittsburgh, Pennsylvania.

25. Nicholson to John Nixon, 26 April 1785, NL, PRD.

26. Captain James McLean to Nicholson, 12 Aug. 1786, NC.

27. Nicholson Accounts of Pennsylvania with the United States, Account Book No. 2, Box 3, PRD, p. 457.

28. Nicholson to John Dunlap, n.d., NC. This statement and Nicholson's reasons for opposing assumption verify Roland Baumann's contention that land speculators in Pennsylvania opposed assumption on the grounds that they benefited from the old formula whereby the state accepted state certificates in the Land Office and feared that cash would now be required. Roland Baumann, "The Democratic-Republicans of Philadelphia: The Origins, 1776–1797" (Ph.D. dissertation, The Pennsylvania State University, 1790), p. 282.

29. Joseph Horsfield to Nicholson, 2 Oct. 1791 and Esekiel Forman to Nicholson, 23 Jan. 1787, NC.

30. Morris to the president of the Supreme Executive Council, 5 Nov. 1783, Robert Morris, Private Letterbooks, 1793–1800, Library of Congress, Manuscript Division (hereafter cited as Morris Letterbooks, LC); Nourse to Nicholson, 6 May 1791, NC.

31. *Pennsylvania Colonial Records* (Harrisburg: T. Fenn and Co., 1851–1853), 16:68, 214; *Pennsylvania Archives*, 1st ser., 11:649–50; Christian Febiger to Nicholson, 3 Jan. 1790, McNair Papers; and Hogan, *Pennsylvania State Trials*, p. 71.

32. Nicholson to Henry Hill, 1 March 1784, NL, PRD.

33. Quoted in Allan Nevins, *The American States During and After The Revolution* (New York: The Macmillan Company, 1924), p. 514.

34. Nicholson, *An Address to the People of Pennsylvania*, p. 19.

CHAPTER 3

1. See Robert A. East, *Business Enterprise in the American Revolutionary Era* (New York: Columbia University Press, 1938), pp. 56–57, 206–25, 239–84, 315–24; E. James Ferguson, *Power of the Purse: A History of*

Notes

American Public Finance, 1776–1790 (Chapel Hill: University of North Carolina Press, 1961), pp. 70–105; and Stuart Bruchey, *The Roots of American Economic Growth, 1607–1861* (New York: Harper, 1968), pp. 54–57.

2. John Brodhead, ed., *Documents Relative to the Colonial History of the State of New York* (Albany: Weed, Parsons and Co., 1857), 7:297.

3. Hans Huth and Wilma Pugh, eds. and trans., *Talleyrand in America as a Financial Promoter, 1794–1796, Unpublished Letters and Memoirs, Annual Report of the American Historical Association for 1941, 2* (Washington, D.C.: Government Printing Office, 1942), p. 144.

4. See Joseph C. Ruddy, "The Policy of Land Distribution in Pennsylvania Since 1779" (M.A. thesis, Pennsylvania State College, 1933), ch. 5.

5. Emily Blackman, *History of Susquehanna County* (Philadelphia: Claxton, Remeson et al., 1873), p. 486. Nicholson to the Honorable James Wilson, 10 Aug. 1795, NL 2, HSP; Nicholson to Judge Wilson, 19 April 1796, Nicholson to James Wilson, 19 Aug. 1796, and Nicholson to the Honorable James Wilson, 8 March 1796, NL 4, HSP.

6. Nicholson to Morris, 23 Dec. 1796, NL 5, HSP.

7. James Gibson to Nicholson, 21 April 1795, NC; Nicholson to Susan Binney, 28 July 1795, NL 4, HSP.

8. *Pennsylvania Archives*, 3d. ser., 24:255, 262, 591; 25:142; 26:747.

9. Ibid., 23:718, Mr. Gross to Nicholson, 14 Feb. 1793, and John Young to Nicholson, 30 April, 25 July 1793, NC.

10. Robinson to Nicholson, 26 June, 1 July 1784, 3 Jan. 1785, and Williams to Nicholson, 5 June 1793 and 2 July 1794, NC.

11. Alexander Power to Nicholson, 19 July, 6 Nov. 1792, Alexander Power to Nicholson, 18 Nov. 1793, Francis Kirkpatrick to Nicholson, 29 June 1793, and Cadwallader Morris to Nicholson, 18 Nov. 1793, NC.

12. John Young to Nicholson, 13 Jan., 25 July 1793, and John Simpson to Nicholson, 19 Feb. 1793, NC.

13. *Pennsylvania Packet*, 12 March 1785.

14. Liancourt, *Travels*, 1:70–71.

15. *Pennsylvania Gazette*, 7 Sept. 1791.

16. Entries for 20 Oct., 19 Dec. 1792 in John Nicholson Diaries, 1792–1794, John Nicholson Collection, Manuscript Group 96, Division of History and Archives, Pennsylvania Historical and Museum Commission, Harrisburg, Pennsylvania (hereafter cited as Nicholson Diary).

17. Joseph H. Bausman, *History of Beaver County, Pennsylvania* (New York: The Knickerbocker Press, 1904), 2:665.

18. Nicholson to Samuel Nicholson, 2 Aug. 1793, NL, PRD.

19. Nicholson to Brodhead, 3 Oct. 1795, NL 3, HSP.

20. Brodhead to Nicholson, 13 Feb. 1796, NC.

21. Brodhead to Nicholson, 27 June 1794 and 23 March 1795, NC.

22. Brodhead to Nicholson, 9 Feb. 1796, NL 3, HSP.

23. Nicholson to Brodhead, 26 Dec. 1796, NL 5, HSP.

24. John Barron to Nicholson, 27, 29 Sept. 1793 and 10 Feb. 1794, NC; entry for 14 Nov. 1792, Nicholson Diary.

Notes

25. Barron to Nicholson, 20 Feb. 1794, NC; Nicholson to Barron, 24 March 1795, NL 1, HSP.

26. Nicholson to His Excellency Thomas Mifflin, 27 Oct. 1795, NL 3, HSP.

27. Nicholson to Samuel Nicholson, 31 Oct. 1795, ibid.

28. Charles Biddle, *Autobiography of Charles Biddle, Vice President of the Supreme Executive Council of Pennsylvania, 1745–1821*, ed. James S. Biddle (Philadelphia: E. Claxton and Co., 1883), pp. 266–67.

29. Washington to George Mason, 27 March 1779 in John Fitzpatrick, ed., *The Writings of George Washington* (Washington, D.C.: Government Printing Office, 1931–1944), 14:300.

30. Samuel Baird to Nicholson, 7 Oct. 1794, NC.

31. Samuel Baird to Nicholson, 4, 7, 19 Oct. 1794, NC.

32. *Laws of the Commonwealth of Pennsylvania (Smith's Laws)* (Philadelphia and Pittsburgh: n.p., 1810–1844), 4:133–38. See also Pennsylvania, *Annual Report of the Secretary of Internal Affairs, Land Office Bureau Bulletin* (1895), p. 25A.

33. Pennsylvania Department of Internal Affairs, *Bulletin* (1953), p. 30. See also Norman B. Wilkinson, "Land Policy and Speculation in Pennsylvania, 1779–1800" (Ph.D. dissertation, University of Pennsylvania, 1958), p. 221.

34. Ibid., Even though Bedford County was east of the real Indian disturbances, a prevention certificate gotten from any justice could be utilized.

35. Timothy Dwight, *Travels in New England and New York* (New Haven: T. Dwight, 1821–1822), 4:185.

36. Thomas Levis to Nicholson, 24 Sept. 1790, NL, PRD.

37. George Gibbs, ed., *Memoirs of the Administrations of Washington and John Adams Edited from the Papers of Oliver Wolcott* (New York: W. Van Norden, 1846), 2:231.

38. *Journals of the Senate of Pennsylvania, 1794–1795*, p. 116.

39. Nicholson to Mifflin, n.d., 1790, NL, PRD.

40. Andrew Russell to Nicholson, 5 Jan. 1791, Anthony Morrison to Nicholson, 19 July 1791, and John Morrison to Nicholson, 20 Nov. 1792, NC.

41. Entry for 13 April 1792, Nicholson Diary.

42. Nicholson to Thomas Mifflin, 28 Feb., 6 Sept., 11 Oct. 1792; Nicholson to Thomas Mifflin, 21 March and 15 May 1793, NL, PRD.

43. Nicholson to Governor Mifflin, 9 May 1793, 30 March 1796, NL, PRD; Nicholson to Thomas Mifflin, 29 July 1795, NL 2, HSP.

44. Dunbar to Nicholson, 1 Feb., 21 April, 19 July, 31 Sept. 1792, 3 Sept., 22 Dec. 1794, 16 Jan. 1796, NC; Nicholson to Dunbar, 17 Jan. 1796, NL 3, HSP.

45. Nicholson to McKissack, 1 Aug. 1796, NL 3, HSP.

46. John Donaldson to Nicholson, 15 April, 1 May, 14 July 1794, 2 March 1795, 12 March 1796, 27 May 1800, NC.

47. Samuel Bryan to Nicholson, 11, 18 Feb. 1795, 7 Dec. 1796, NC; Nicholson to Bryan, 13 April 1795, NL 1, HSP.

Notes

CHAPTER 4

1. *Pennsylvania Archives*, 4th ser., 4:237.

2. Wright to Nicholson, 6 Sept. 1789, NC.

3. See Harry M. Tinckom, *Republicans and Federalists in Pennsylvania, 1790–1801* (Harrisburg: Pennsylvania Historical and Museum Commission, 1950), pp. 1–17; Brunhouse, *The Counter-Revolution in Pennsylvania*, pp. 12–16.

4. See Robert Morris to Willink and Staphorst, n.d., Oct. 1782, Morris Letterbooks, LC; and Ferguson, *Power of the Purse*, p. 136.

5. Mathew Carey, ed., *Debates and Proceedings of the General Assembly of Pennsylvania on the Memorials Praying a Repeal or Suspension of the Law Annulling the Charter of the Bank* (Philadelphia: Seddon and Pritchard, 1786), pp. 52, 57, 61–62, 65–66.

6. For the Acts, Debates, and Republican charges of Constitutonialist speculations see *Pennsylvania House Minutes*, 2d sess., 9th assembly, pp. 335, 348; *Pennsylvania Archives*, 4th ser., 3:1,004; and *Pennsylvania Gazette*, 16, 23 Feb. 1785. For the implications of these measures in regard to land speculators see the *Pennsylvania Packet*, 31 March, 1 April 1785.

7. Sergeant quoted in Burton Konkle, *Thomas Willing and the First American Financial System* (Philadelphia: University of Pennsylvania Press, 1937), p. 111.

8. Moncure D. Conway, ed., *The Writings of Thomas Paine* (New York and London: G.P. Putnam, 1894–1896), 2:178.

9. Philip S. Foner, ed., *The Complete Writings of Thomas Paine* (New York: Citadel Press, 1945), 2:434–35.

10. Adonijah Stanburrough to Nicholson, 21 June 1794, NC.

11. For Hamilton's views on the National Bank and the Bank of North America see Harold C. Syrett et al., *The Papers of Alexander Hamilton* (New York: Columbia University Press, 1961–1969), 7:280–84; see also Philadelphia *General Advertiser*, 21 Feb. 1791.

12. *Minutes of the House of Representatives of the Commonwealth of Pennsylvania, 1776–1790* (Philadelphia: State Printers, 1776–1790), 1st sess., 7th assembly, p. 801; Joseph Nourse to Nicholson, 7 Dec. 1783, Sharp Delany to Nicholson, 24 Feb., 11 March 1784, and Richard Dallam to Nicholson, 11 March 1784, NC.

13. Henry Hill to Nicholson, 29 Feb. 1784, NC.

14. Nicholson to Henry Hill, 1 March 1784, NL, PRD.

15. See *Freeman's Journal*, 26 Dec. 1787, 9 Jan. 1788, and Baird to Nicholson, 7 Jan. 1788, NC.

16. *Pennsylvania House Minutes*, 2d sess., 12th assembly, pp. 182–83. See also Brooke Hindle, *David Rittenhouse* (Princeton: Princeton University Press, 1964), p. 298, and *Freeman's Journal*, 5 Nov. 1788.

17. John Simpson to Nicholson, 26 May 1789, NC.

18. Ibid., 11 June 1789.

19. Nicholson to Philadelphia printer John Dunlap, n.d., July 1789, NC. See also the *Pennsylvania Packet*, 25 Aug. 1789.

Notes

20. John Simpson to Nicholson, 10 July 1789, NC.

21. *Minutes of the Supreme Executive Council of Pennsylvania*, 16:318–91, 323, 328–29, 329–32, 343. There was evidence that Nicholson encouraged others to oppose the Constitution's revision but not through violent means.

22. Nicholson, *An address to the People of Pennsylvania*, p. 49. It is interesting to note that Francis Bailey, a noted publisher in Philadelphia and the publisher of Nicholson's Broadside, was financed by Nicholson and gave him advice as to when to sign his articles and when to use a pseudonym. Francis Bailey to Nicholson, 15 Feb., 10 Jan., 15 Jan. 1790, NC. The charges against Nicholson were published by Miles and the others, see *Pennsylvania Packet*, 22 April 1790.

23. Samuel Bryan to Nicholson, 4 April, 8 May 1790, NC.

24. Scott to Nicholson, 18 June 1790, NC.

25. For examples see George Logue to Nicholson, 28 Oct. 1788, Captain James McLean to Nicholson, 20 Aug. 1789, Edward Pole to Nicholson, 31 Oct. 1789, and Samuel Postlewaite to Nicholson, 22 Jan. 1789, NC.

26. John Irwin to Nicholson, 24 Aug. 1790, NC.

27. Simpson to Nicholson, 30 Sept. 1790, NC. See also the *Pennsylvania Packet*, 6, 9, 18 Sept. 1790. John Jordan to Nicholson, 14 April 1790, NC.

28. Tinkcom, *Republicans and the Federalists in Pennsylvania*, p. 31.

29. Nicholson to Meade, 1 June 1793, NL, PRD.

30. Nicholson to Andrew Summers, 31 May, 1 June 1793, NL, PRD; John Oldden to Nicholson, 30 April 1794, Joseph Ball to Nicholson, 30 Sept. 1794, and Mordicai Lewis to Nicholson, 3 Dec. 1794, NC.

31. Notice of 5 Aug. 1793 in NC.

32. Nicholson to John Swanwick, 24 June 1793, NL, PRD.

33. Jonathan Mifflin to Nicholson, 11 Aug., 30 Dec. 1794, NC.

34. Chauncey Goodrich to Senator Oliver Wolcott, 13 Dec. 1796 in Gibbs, *Memoirs of the Administration of Washington and Adams*, p. 410.

35. James Gibson to Nicholson, 12 Dec. 1794, NC; Nicholson to James Gibson, 16 Dec. 1794, NL 4, HSP.

36. John Young to Nicholson, n.d., Peter Ickes to Nicholson, 7 April 1788, Robert Hooper to Nicholson, 28 Feb. 1789, and Andrew Summers to Nicholson, 17 Dec. 1791, NC; Nicholson to Oliver Wolcott, 12 July 1797, NL 7, HSP.

37. *Pennsylvania Gazette*, 6 April 1785.

38. Nicholson to Christian Febiger, 31 May 1791, NC.

39. John Simpson to Nicholson, 13 Feb. 1793, NC.

40. Hogan, *Pennsylvania State Trials*, p. 85.

41. Nicholson to Samuel Powell, Speaker of the Senate of Pennsylvania, 5 Jan. 1797, Impeachment File, 1779–1794, Public Records Division, Pennsylvania Historical and Museum Commission (hereafter cited as Impeachment File, PRD).

42. Pennsylvania, *House Journal*, 1791–1792, p. 157; Pennsylvania, *Senate Journal*, 1794–1795, p. 116.

43. Jared Ingersoll to Nicholson, 19 April 1793, NC; Hogan, *Pennsylvania*

State Trials, p. 695; Raymond Walters, Jr., "The Making of a Financier: Albert Gallatin in the Pennsylvania Assembly," *PMHB* 70 (July 1946): 267; Philadelphia *General Advertiser*, 4, 6, 9 April 1793; *Gazette of the United States*, 17 April 1793; see also, Nicholson to the printers of "The General Advertiser" and "The Gazette," 23 April 1793, NC.

44. Hogan, *Pennsylvania State Trials*, p. 107.

45. Nicholson to Hoge, 5 April 1793, and Nicholson to Edie, 4 April 1793, NL, PRD; Albert Gallatin to Thomas Clare, 3 May 1793, Impeachment File, PRD; Nicholson to Matthew Clarkson, 29 June 1793, NL, PRD; and Hogan, *Pennsylvania State Trials*, p. 410.

46. Soloman Marache to Nicholson, 12 Sept. 1793, NC.

47. *Pennsylvania Archives*, 1st ser., 11:702. See also the *Pennsylvania Colonial Records*, 16:376.

48. Nicholson to Aaron Burr, 27 April 1793, NL, PRD.

49. Edmund Randolph to Nicholson, 7 Aug. 1793, NC.

50. Defense speech given during the trial. Hogan, *Pennsylvania State Trials*, p. 617.

51. Nicholson to Major John Clark, 29 June 1793, NL, PRD. See, for example, Philadelphia *General Advertiser*, 21 March 1794.

52. E. Hogan to Nicholson, 26 Feb., 12 April 1794, 11 June, 7 July 1795, 7 March 1796, NC.

53. Speech by William Lewis, 22 March 1794, Impeachment File, PRD.

54. Jacob Hiltzheimer, *Extracts from the Diary of Jacob Hiltzheimer, of Philadelphia, 1765–1798*, ed. Jacob Cox Parsons (Philadelphia: W.F. Fell and Co., 1893), p. 203.

55. Hogan, *Pennsylvania State Trials*, p. 160. See Philadephia *Aurora General Advertiser*, 18 April 1795.

56. Hogan, *Pennsylvania State Trials*, p. 764.

57. Entry for 29 Jan. 1794, Nicholson Diary.

CHAPTER 5

1. Richard Bard to Nicholson, 1 Feb. 1788, NC.

2. John Jordan to Nicholson, 26 Jan. 1788, and John Simpson to Nicholson, 20 Feb. 1789, NC.

3. Hamilton, "Report on Public Credit," in *American State Papers, Documents, Legislative and Executive of the Congress of the United States, Finance*, ed. Walter Lowrie and Matthew Clarke (Washington, D.C.: Gales and Seaton, 1832–1861), 1:15–37, and Ferguson, *Power of the Purse*, p. 294.

4. Matthew McConnell to Nicholson, 20 Jan. 1790, NC.

5. Nicholson to Thomas Hartley, 15 Feb. 1790, NL, PRD.

6. *Gazette of the United States*, 27 Jan. 1790.

7. Nicholson to Thomas Hartley, 7 Feb. 1790, NL, PRD.

8. Nicholson to James Madison, 17 Feb. 1790, NL, PRD.

9. *Freeman's Journal*, 28, 29 Jan., 8 Feb. 1790, Daniel Hiester to

Nicholson, 25 Feb. 1790, and Nicholson to William Maclay, 29 Jan. 1790, NC.

10. Nicholson to William Maclay, n.d., NC. See also Whitney Bates, "Assumption of State Debts, 1783–1793" (Ph.D. dissertation, University of Wisconsin, 1951), pp. 230–32.

11. "A customer" in the *Pennsylvania Gazette*, 3 Feb. 1790; see also *Pennsylvania Packet*, 10 Dec. 1790; Lodge, *The Works of Hamilton*, 2:265.

12. William Maclay, *The Journal of William Maclay: United States Senator from Pennsylvania 1789–1791*, ed. Edgar S. Maclay (New York: D. Appleton Co., 1890), pp. 174–75, 177–78, 231.

13. John C. Miller, *Alexander Hamilton and the Growth of the New Nation* (New York: Harper and Row, 1964), p. 243. Miller confuses Nicholson with a John Nicholson of Maryland.

14. Benjamin Rush to Thomas Fitzsimmons, 5 Aug. 1790 in Lyman H. Butterfield, ed., *Letters of Benjamin Rush* (Princeton: Princeton University Press, 1951), 1:569.

15. George Barclay and Company to Nicholson, 2, 14 July 1792, NC.

16. Nicholson to Oliver Wolcott, 12 July 1797, NL 7, HSP.

17. *National Gazette*, 17 July 1793; *Gazette of the United States*, 17 July 1793.

18. Henry Wansey, *The Journal of an Excursion to the United States of North America in the Summer of 1794* (Salisbury: J. Easton, 1796), p. 207.

19. George M. Dallas, ed. and comp., *The Life and Writings of Alexander J. Dallas* (Philadelphia: J.B. Lippincott, 1871), p. 223.

20. James D. Richardson, ed., *A Compilation of the Messages and Papers of the Presidents of the United States* (New York: Bureau of National Literature, 1897), pp. 155–58.

21. Seth Ames, ed., *The Works of Fisher Ames* (Boston: Little, Brown and Co., 1854), 1:143.

22. Budden to Nicholson, 29 Sept. 1794, NC. See Leland D. Baldwin, *Whiskey Rebels, The Story of a Frontier Uprising* (Pittsburgh: University of Pittsburgh Press, 1939), pp. 221, 301; Eugene Perry Link, *Democratic-Republican Societies, 1790–1830* (New York: Columbia University Press, 1942), p. 202; and Congressman John Kittera to Nicholson, 26 July 1793, 9 April 1794, NC.

23. Baird to Nicholson, 8 Oct. 1794, and Budden to Nicholson, 19 Nov. 1794, NC.

24. Philadelphia *General Advertiser*, 19 May 1794.

25. Nicholson to Morris, 15 May 1795, NL 1, HSP.

26. Gibbs, *Memoirs of the Administrations of Washington and Adams*, 1:218; Philadelphia *Aurora General Advertiser*, 29 July 1795. The complete text of the treaty can be found in Samuel Flagg Bemis, *Jay's Treaty: A Study in Commerce and Diplomacy* (New Haven: Yale University Press, rev. ed., 1962), Appendix B, pp. 453–88.

27. Nicholson to Griffith Evans, 27 June 1795, NL 2, HSP.

28. Nicholson to Griffith Evans, 29 Oct. 1795, NL 3, HSP.

Notes

CHAPTER 6

1. *Gazette of the United States,* 15 April 1789; Huth and Pugh, *Talley-rand in America,* pp. 161, 162.

2. For Irvine's efforts see C.W. Butterfield, ed., *Washington-Irvine Correspondence* (Madison, Wis.: David Atwood Co., 1882), p. 69. See "Northern Boundary of Pennsylvania—Middle of Lake Erie," Pennsylvania Department of Internal Affairs, *Bulletin* 13, no. 11, p. 18. On Nicholson's appointment see *Pennsylvania Archives,* 1st ser., 7:91. *Statutes at Large of Pennsylvania,* 2:454–86; *Pennsylvania Archives,* 4th ser., 3:991–1,012 and 4:225.

3. Entry for 21 Feb. 1795, Pennsylvania Population Company Minute Books, 1792–1815, Crawford County Historical Society Papers, Meadville, Pennsylvania (hereafter cited as PCMB).

4. Nicholson to Edward Robinson, 27 April 1793, NL, PRD.

5. Theophilus Cazenove to Nicholson, 6 Dec. 1792, NL, PRD.

6. Quoted in Joseph Dorfman, *The Economic Mind in American Civilization, 1606–1865* (New York: The Viking Press, 1953), p. 245. The quote applies to speculators throughout the United States.

7. Prince de Talleyrand, *Memoirs,* ed. Le Duc de Broglie (London: Griffith, Farren, Okedon and Welsh, 1891), 1:175; Harm Jan Huidekoper, *Remarks on the Late Proceedings of the Nicholson Commissioners and on the Nicholson Lien in Relation to Lands Formerly of the Pennsylvania Population Company* (Meadville, Pa.: The Author, 1842), pp. 3, 4.

8. William Duncan to Nicholson, 3 May 1796, NC.

9. *Smith's Laws,* 4:133–34; Dunlop, *The General Laws of Pennsylvania,* pp. 135–38.

10. *Population Company Minute Books,* Booklet 2, p. 42; Nicholson to General William Irvine, 27 May 1796, NL 4, HSP.

11. Nicholson to Mifflin, 25 May 1792, NC.

12. James T. Mitchell and Henry Flanders, eds., *The Statutes at Large of Pennsylvania from 1682 to 1801* (Harrisburg: n.p., 1896–1915), 14:233.

13. Ebenezer Denny, *Military Journal of Major Ebenezer Denny* (Philadelphia: J.B. Lippincott and Company, 1859), p. 263.

14. Nicholson to Burr, 29 June 1793, NL, PRD.

15. "A Pennsylvanian" in Philadelphia *General Advertiser,* 1 Aug. 1794.

16. Thomas Rees to Nicholson, 14 Nov. 1794, NC.

17. Weld, *Travels,* 2:93.

18. Gouverneur Morris, *A Diary of the French Revolution by Gouverneur Morris, 1752–1816,* ed. Beatrix Davenport (Boston: Houghton-Mifflin Company, 1939), 2:49.

19. Griffith Evans to Nicholson, 27 Aug., 21 Sept. 1795, NC.

20. Enoch Edwards to Nicholson, 1, 26 Aug. 1795, NC.

21. Andrew A. Lipscomb, ed., *The Writings of Thomas Jefferson* (Washington, D.C.: Thomas Jefferson Memorial Association, 1903), 2:118.

22. Entry for 19 May 1795, PCMB.

23. Liancourt, *Travels,* 4:74.

Notes

24. William Power to Nicholson, 12 June 1796, NC.

25. Morris to Thomas Morris, 22 March 1796, Morris Letterbooks, LC; entry for 19 April 1796, PCMB; Judah Colt, "Judah Colt's Narrative," *Publications of the Buffalo Historical Society* (Buffalo: Historical Society, 1904), pp. 18–19; Pennsylvania Population Company, Plan of Association, Booklet 1, p. 150, in Pennsylvania Population Company Papers Francis Spencer Estate Collection, Erie Public Museum Manuscript Collection, Erie, Pennsylvania (hereafter cited as EPM).

26. Entry for 22 Aug. 1796, Blotter of Judah Colt, 1804, Pattee Library, The Pennsylvania State University, University Park, Pennsylvania (hereafter cited as PL).

27. Entry for 17 Feb. 1797, PCMB.

28. *Population Company Minute Book*, Booklet 2, p. 80.

29. "Judah Colt's Narrative," p. 347.

30. Nicholson to Morris, 13 Jan. 1795, NL 1, HSP; Morris to Nicholson, 17 Jan. 1795, Morris Letterbooks, LC.

31. Nicholson to William Crammond, 23 Feb. 1797, NL 7, HSP.

32. Nicholson to Managers of the Population Company, 1 March 1797, NL 5, HSP.

33. Huidekoper, "Remarks on the Nicholson Commissioners," p. 11.

CHAPTER 7

1. William Priest, *Travels in the United States of America* (London: J. Johnson, 1802), p. 132.

2. Gibbs, *Memoirs of the Administrations of Washington and Adams*, 1:102–3.

3. Paul L. Ford, *The Writings of Thomas Jefferson* (New York: G.P. Putnam's Sons, 1892–1899), 7:345.

4. Moreau de St. Mery and Company to Nicholson, 1 Nov. 1794, NC.

5. Nicholson to the Committee for the Relief of Sufferers of Cape Francois, 1 Aug. 1793, NL, PRD.

6. Enoch Edwards to William Russell, 7 Dec. 1793, NC.

7. Charles Sherrill, *French Memoirs of the Eighteenth Century* (New York: Charles Scribner's Sons, 1915), p. 34; Louise Welles Murray, *The Story of Some French Refugees and Their "Azilum," 1793–1800* (Athens, Pa.: Tioga Point Historical Society, 1903), p. 16; David Craft, "The French Settlement of Asylum," *Proceedings of the Wyoming Historical and Geological Society* 5 (1900): 78–79; Wansey, *Journal*, p. 142; Samuel Breck, *Recollections of Samuel Breck with Passages from His Note Books, 1771–1862*, ed. H.E. Scudder (Philadelphia: Porter and Coates, 1877), pp. 165–66.

8. Philadelphia *General Advertiser*, 8 May 1793.

9. Breck, *Recollections*, pp. 199–200.

10. Elsie Murray, *Azilum, French Refugee Colony of 1793* (Athens, Pa.: Tioga Point Museum, 1940), p. 24; Mildred Jordan, *Asylum for the Queen* (New York: Alfred Knopf, 1948), p. 230; Elsie Singmaster,

Notes

Pennsylvania's Susquehanna (Harrisburg: J: Horace McFarland Co., 1950), pp. 33–34.

11. Alexander Graydon, *Memoirs of a Life Chiefly Passed in Pennsylvania within the Last Sixty Years* (Harrisburg: John Wyeth, 1811), pp. 397–98.

12. William Egle, ed., "Documents Relating to the Connecticut Settlement in the Wyoming Valley," *Pennsylvania Archives*, 2d ser., 18:629, 660–64, 682–83.

13. Samuel Baird to Nicholson, 11 Sept. 1787, NC.

14. Various entries, Mathias Hollenback Account Book, 1788–1789, PRD.

15. See Murray, *Azilum, French Refugee Colony of 1793*, p. 8; T. Wood Clarke, *Emigrés in the Wilderness* (New York: Macmillan Co., 1941), pp. 58, 83; Murray, *The Story of Some French Refugees and Their "Azilum,"* pp. 36–38; Carl Carmer, *The Susquehanna* (New York: Rinehart and Co., 1955), p. 233; and Craft, "The French Settlement at Asylum," pp. 90–95. See also Lucille Zoller, "The French Settlement of Asylum, Pennsylvania" M.A. thesis (University of Pittsburgh, 1919), p. 37.

16. Huth and Pugh, *Talleyrand in America*, p. 25.

17. Ibid., pp. 25, 39.

18. Clarke, *Emigrés in the Wilderness*, p. 58.

19. Samuel Baird to Nicholson, 30 June 1793 and 30 June 1795, NC.

20. N. DeBroval on behalf of Mm. Boulogne, 2 Aug. 1796, NC.

21. John Keating to Nicholson, 1, 20 Aug. 1795 and 16 April 1796, NC.

22. Morris to Nicholson, 10 Feb., 2 May 1796, Morris Letterbooks, LC; Deed, John Nicholson, and wife Hannah to James Donatianus Le Ray Chaumont, 1797 in Reverend David Craft Papers, Tioga Point Museum Manuscript Collections, Athens, Pennsylvania; Morris to William Morris, 1 May 1795, Morris Lettersbooks, LC.

23. Liancourt, *Travels*, 1:162. See Nicholson to William Crammond, 11 April 1795, NL 1, HSP.

24. Nicholson to M. Cadigan, 18 June 1795, and Nicholson to David Allison, 5 Dec. 1795, NL 2, 3, HSP.

25. Nicholson to James Gibson, 20 Jan. 1797, and Nicholson to Talon, 13 May, 26 Sept. 1795, NL 1, 3, 5, HSP. See also Talon to Nicholson, 4 Dec., 24 July 1795, NC, and Morris to Talon, 8 June, 4 July, 12 Aug. 1796, Morris Letterbooks, LC.

26. Nicholson to Edwards, 2 June 1796, NL 4, HSP.

27. Charles Cadignan to Nicholson, 14 Sept. 1795, NC.

28. Huth and Pugh, *Talleyrand in America*, p. 25.

29. *Gazette of the United States*, 3 July 1793; Philadelphia *General Advertiser*, 29 Jan. 1796.

30. Adam Hoops to Nicholson, 5 July 1794, NC.

31. Francis Baily, *Journal of a Tour in Unsettled Parts of North America in 1796 and 1797*, 3d ed. (London: James Ridgway, 1818), p. 182.

32. Benjamin Rush, *Essays, Literary, Moral and Philosophical* (Philadelphia: Thomas and William Bradford, 1794), p. 287.

33. William Winterbotham, *An Historical, Geographical, Commercial and Philosophical View of the United States of America and of the European Settlements in America and the West Indies* (London: J. Ridgway, H.D. Symonds and D. Holt, 1795), 3:493–94.

34. J. Montoulle to Nicholson, 16 July 1797, NC.

35. Liancourt, *Travels*, 4:103, 160–73, 177–78.

36. Morris to Nicholson, 24 Nov. 1796, Morris to James Marshall, 1, 24 May 1796, Morris to Edward Tilghman, 1, 2 June 1797, and Morris to T. Cazenove, 5 July 1797, Morris Letterbooks, LC.

37. Talleyrand to Morris, 16 March 1795, Morris Letterbooks, LC.

38. Huth and Pugh, *Talleyrand in America*, p. 94.

39. Philadelphia *General Advertiser*, 25 July 1794; see also Frances Childs, *French Refugee Life in the United States, 1790–1800* (Baltimore: Johns Hopkins Press, 1940), pp. 133–35.

40. Pierre Egron to Nicholson, 28 July 1794, NC.

41. Prospectus of 1794 in NC.

42. Boissiere to Nicholson, 21 April, 18 Dec. 1795, 13 Jan. 1796, NC.

43. "Conference with President Washington," 6 Aug. 1793, in Lipscomb, *The Writings of Jefferson*, 1:388.

44. Nicholson to Randolph, 27 March, 31 March, 21 April, 27, 30 May 1795, NL 1, HSP.

45. Liancourt, *Travels*, 1:170; Hoops to Nicholson, 5 July 1794, NC.

46. James Gibson to Nicholson, 30 Nov. 1796, NC. See Robert J. Taylor, ed., *The Susquehannah Company Papers* (Ithaca, N.Y.: Cornell University Press, 1969), 8:104, 256, 274, 399, 400.

47. See A.J. Dallas, comp., *Laws of Pennsylvania, 1781–1790* (Philadelphia: Hall and Sellers, 1795), 2:304; Nicholson to Joseph Duncan, 13 May 1795, Nicholson to James Gibson, 12 July 1796, and Nicholson to Joseph Duncan, 13 May 1795, NL 1, 4, HSP.

48. Nicholson to Morris, 12 July 1796, NL 4, HSP.

49. Weld, *Travels*, 2:450–51.

50. Liancourt, *Travels*, 1:168–69.

51. Plan of Association of the Asylum Company, 26 Oct. 1801, Tioga Museum, Athens, Pennsylvania.

52. Murray, *The Story of Some French Refugees and Their "Azilum,"* pp. 65–66; Craft, "The French Settlement at Asylum," p. 103; Shaw Livermore, *Early American Land Companies* (New York: Oxford Press, 1939), p. 174.

53. Edwards to Nicholson, 15, 16, 17 Aug. 1793; Edwards wrote on 24 Oct. 1793, "I never saw a man more taken by any thing in my life than the Doctor is over that place," NC.

54. Nicholson to John Simpson, 13 Dec. 1793, Nicholson to Col. John Myer, 13 Dec. 1793, and Nicholson to Benjamin Morris, 13 Dec. 1793, NC.

55. Cooper, *Some Information Respecting America*, p. 105.

56. Wansey, *Journal*, p. 173; Wansey was a participant in the project.

57. Nicholson to Bird, Savage and Bird, Merchants of London, 2 April

1795, NL 1, HSP; Joseph Priestley, *The Memoirs of Dr. Joseph Priestley*, ed. John Boyer (Washington, D.C.: Barcroft Press, 1964), p. 131.

58. Carmer, *The Susquehanna*, pp. 209–15.

59. Thomas Cooper to Nicholson, 21 April 1794, NC; Cooper, *Some Information Respecting America*, pp. 16, 39, 73, 74.

60. Wansey, *Journal*, p. 77.

61. Priestley, *Memoirs*, pp. 131–32.

62. For examples see Thomas Russell to Nicholson, 3 May 1796, and Dr. Joseph Priestley to Nicholson, 23 Feb. 1797, NC; Nicholson to William Eichbaum, 4, 5 May 1796, NL 4, HSP.

CHAPTER 8

1. The capital was officially designated Washington, D.C., in September 1791 by the commissioners of the proposed new capital. However, it was not until 1 January 1794 that the commissioners began using Washington, D.C. on their official letters. Throughout the 1790s, the name used most often for the district was the Federal City. See Constance Green, *Washington: Village and Capital, 1800–1878* (Princeton: Princeton University Press, 1962), p. 14; Wilhelmus Bogart Bryan, *A History of the National Capital from Its Foundation Through the Period of the Adoption of the Organic Act* (New York: Macmillan Co., 1914–1916), 1:226.

2. Allen C. Clark, *Greenleaf and Law in the Federal City* (Washington, D.C.: W.F. Roberts, 1901), p. 13; James Edward Greenleaf, *Genealogy of the Greenleaf Family* (Boston: Privately Printed, 1896), pp. 80–81, 217–18; Emily Ellsworth Ford, ed., *Notes on the Life of Noah Webster* (New York: Privately Printed, 1912), 1:186, 205; Harry Warfel, ed., *Letters of Noah Webster* (New York: Library Publishing Company, 1953), p. 104.

3. Liancourt, *Travels*, 3:622.

4. Morris to Nicholson, 2 Sept. 1793, Morris Letterbooks, LC.

5. Nicholson to Barrell and Servante, London, 25 Nov. 1796, NL 4, HSP.

6. Washington to Jefferson, 31 March 1791, in Saul K. Padover, *Thomas Jefferson and the National Capital* (Washington, D.C.: Government Printing Office, 1946), p. 54; John Fitzpatrick, ed., *Diaries of George Washington* (Boston and New York: Houghton-Mifflin Co., 1925), 4:154–55.

7. Elizabeth S. Kite, *L'Enfant and Washington, 1791–1792* (Baltimore: Johns Hopkins Press, 1929), pp. 57–58.

8. Winterbotham, *View of the United States*, 3:72.

9. Morris to Nicholson, 2 Sept. 1793, Morris Letterbooks, LC.

10. Isaac Roberdeau to Nicholson, 30 May 1793, NC; Nicholson to Samuel Davidson, 29 June 1793, NL, PRD.

11. Clark, *Greenleaf and Law*, pp. 68–71; Liancourt, *Travels*, 3:623, 624; Bryan, *A History of the National Capital*, 1:219; Page, *Washington and Its Romance*, pp. 80, 85.

12. Morris to Sylvanius Bourne, 8 Oct. 1795; Nicholson and Morris to James Marshall, 16 Oct. 1795, Morris Letterbooks, LC. See also Warfel, *Letters of Webster*, p. 540.

13. Nicholson and Morris to James Marshall, 16 Oct. 1795, and Morris to Marshall, 24 May 1796, Morris Letterbooks, LC.

14. Weld, *Travels*, 1:80.

15. Nicholson and Morris to William King and William Tunnicliff, 20 Aug. 1796, NL 4, HSP. Morris and Nicholson to the trustees of the Aggregate Fund, 24 Aug. 1797, and Morris to William Cranch, 13 Nov., 14 Dec. 1795, Morris Letterbooks, LC.

16. *Gazette of the United States*, 29 Oct. 1791; Wansey, *Journal*, pp. 220–22; Weld, *Travels*, 1:83–84; Winterbotham, *View of the United States*, 3:70.

17. See Thomas Twining, *Travels in America 100 Years Ago* (New York: Harper and Brothers, 1893), pp. 58, 87, 104; Gibbs, *Memoirs of the Administrations of Washington and Adams*, 2:377–78; Liancourt, *Travels*, 3:561–62.

18. Twining, *Travels*, pp. 109–10.

19. Thomas Law to Nicholson and Morris, 20 Sept., 4 Nov. 1796, NC; Liancourt, *Travels*, 3:625; and Nicholson to Aaron Burr, 25 June 1795, NL 2, HSP.

20. Nicholson to Morris, 16, 18, 23, 27 Nov., 8, 12 Dec. 1796, NL 4, HSP.

21. Nicholson to the Commissioners of the Federal City, 12 Sept. 1795, NL 3, HSP; Morris to Nicholson, 22 Nov. 1796, Morris Letterbooks, LC; Clark, *Greenleaf and Law*, pp. 104, 186, 263–64, 274, 283; Stuart Mitchell, ed., *Some Letters of Abigail Adams, 1788–1801* (Boston: Houghton-Mifflin, 1947), p. 203.

22. Morris to Greenleaf, 27 May 1795, Morris Letterbooks, LC.

23. Morris to His Excellency, George Washington, 21 Sept. 1795, Morris Letterbooks, LC.

24. Morris to Nicholson, 24 July 1795, Morris Letterbooks, LC.

25. Morris to Greenleaf, 24 April 1795, ibid.

26. Morris to Wilhelm and Jan Willink, 19 April 1797, and Morris to William T. Franklin, 18 July 1795, Morris Letterbooks, LC.

27. Morris to Thomas Russell, 28 July, 18 Sept. 1795, Morris to William Cranch, 20 July 1795, ibid.

28. Mitchell, *Letters of Abigail Adams*, pp. 102, 140; Clark, *Greenleaf and Law*, pp. 47–66 gives a sketch of Cranch's career; see also Greenleaf, *Genealogy of the Greenleaf Family*, pp. 217–18, and Morris to Cranch, 9 Nov. 1796, Morris Letterbooks, LC.

29. Morris to Nicholson, 8 Feb. 1797, Morris Letterbooks, LC.

30. Weld, *Travels*, 1:84.

31. Nicholson to Lewis Deblois, 21 April 1795, Nicholson to Henderson, Loving, and Clark, 21 April 1795, and Nicholson to Morris, 24 April 1795, NL 1, HSP.

32. Nicholson to Greenleaf, 12 April 1795, and Nicholson to Morris, NL 1, HSP.

33. Nicholson to William Lovering, 17 Aug. 1795, and Nicholson to Lewis Deblois, 16 Sept. 1795, NL 1, 3, HSP.

34. Nicholson to John Henry Cazenove Nephew and Company, 1 Sept. 1795, and Nicholson to Lewis Deblois, 17 Nov. 1795, NL 3, HSP.

35. Nicholson to William Lovering, 17 Aug. 1795, NL 2, HSP; Morris to William Cranch, 14 Dec. 1795, Morris Letterbooks, LC.

36. Deblois to Nicholson, 30 Sept. 1795, NC.

37. Liancourt, *Travels,* 3:633. For a list of their lots see Nicholson to the Commissioners of the Federal City, 12 Sept. 1795, NL 3, HSP. The list can also be found in Washington, D.C., Legal Papers, 1795–1796, Box 4, PRD. The lots are listed by number on the "Plan of Washington by Andrew Ellicott, 1792," which is reproduced in John Reps, *Monumental Washington: the Planning and Development of the Capital Center* (Princeton: Princeton University Press, 1967), pp. 23–24.

38. Weld, *Travels,* 1:85.

39. Ibid., p. 86; and Winterbotham, *View of the United States,* 3:72.

40. Liancourt, *Travels,* 3:629–32.

41. Prentiss to Nicholson, 19 May, 11 Aug., 26 Oct. 1797, NC.

42. Lewis Deblois to Nicholson, 20 March 1795, NC.

43. Nicholson to Deblois, 23 March 1795, NL 1, HSP.

44. Notice of Meeting and Petition, 9 Nov. 1795 in Washington, D.C., Legal Papers, 1795–1796, Box 4, PRD.

45. Nicholson to Morris, 16 Nov. 1796, NL 4, HSP.

46. Nicholson to Morris, 23 Jan. 1797, NL 5, HSP.

47. William White to Nicholson, 3 Sept. 1794, and Lewis Deblois to Nicholson, 9 Nov. 1795, NC; Nicholson to Deblois, 18 Dec. 1795, NL 3, HSP; Morris to Thomas Law, 18 July 1795, Morris Letterbooks, LC.

48. Benjamin Freeman to Nicholson, 20 May 1795, and T.B. Freeman and Company to Nicholson, 22 Jan., 11 April, 23 March 1797, NC; William Prentiss to T.B. Freeman and Company, 26 April 1796, and William Budden to T.B. Freeman and Company, 18 Sept. 1796, T.B. Freeman and Co. Correspondence, PRD; and Nicholson to Freeman and Company, 9 Sept. 1796, NL 4, HSP.

49. Nicholson to Peter Miller, 27 Nov., 5 Dec. 1796, and Nicholson to Morris, 1 Jan. 1797, NL 4, 5, HSP; Henry Sheaff to Nicholson, 31 March 1797, William Lovering to Nicholson, 26 March 1799, William Tunnicliff to Nicholson, 16 Feb. 1797, and James Pusey to Nicholson, 15 Feb. 1797, NC.

50. Mark Ward to Nicholson, 28 Sept. 1796 and 31 Aug. 1797, NC; Nicholson to William Tunnicliff, 7 March 1797, NL 5, HSP.

51. For the partners' stock purchases see George Gilpin to James Greenleaf, 17 June 1794, and William Deakins to Nicholson, 5 Dec. 1794, NC; Nicholson to Robert Smith, 4 Oct. 1795, NL 3, HSP; Morris to William Cranch, 25 July 1796, Morris Letterbooks, LC.

52. Walter Smith to Nicholson, 25 Sept., 21 Nov. 1796, and Thomas Clark to Nicholson, 9 May 1796, NC; Morris to Walter Smith, 27 March 1797, Morris Letterbooks, LC.

53. George Gilpin to James Greenleaf, 26 July 1794, and Garret Cottringer to Nicholson, 2 Sept. 1796, NC; Nicholson to Greenleaf, 15 April, 22 May 1795, and Nicholson to Henry Lee, 5 July 1795, NL 1, 2, HSP. See also Clark, *Greenleaf and Law,* p. 115.

54. Bartholomew Dandridge to Nicholson, 25 Feb. 1796, NC.

55. Morris to James Marshall, 1 Nov. 1796, Morris Letterbooks, LC.

56. Twining, *Travels*, pp. 100–101.

57. Bailey, *Journal of a Tour*, pp. 28, 127.

58. Twining, *Travels*, p. 110.

59. Philip Nicklin to Nicholson, 27 Nov. 1795, and Isaac Polock to Nicholson, 18 Jan. 1797, NC.

60. Fitzpatrick, *The Writings of Washington*, 34:254. See Nicholson and Morris to Commissioners of the City of Washington, 29 Aug. 1796, NL 6, HSP; Morris to J. Watson, 22 April 1795, and Morris to Washington, 21 Sept., 7 Dec. 1795, Morris Letterbooks, LC.

61. Alexander White to Nicholson, 9 May 1796, NC; Morris to President George Washington, 21 Sept. 1795, and Morris to William Cranch, 19 Aug. 1795, Morris letterbooks, LC.

62. *American State Papers, Miscellaneous*, 1:136; Morris to James Marshall, 20 March, 3 April, 24 May 1796, Morris Letterbooks, LC; Weld, *Travels*, 1:87; Morris to Lewis Deblois, 6 May 1796, NL 4, HSP.

63. Ford, *Notes on Webster*, 1:385. See Liancourt's criticisms in *Travels*, 3:629, 632, and Nicholson to Morris, 18 Jan. 1797, NL 5, HSP.

64. For examples see Gustavus Scott, William Thorton, and Alexander White to Nicholson, 1 Oct. 1795, NC; Nicholson to Andrew Moore, 3 June 1796 and 21 Feb. 1797, and Nicholson to William Thornton, 17 Jan. 1797, NL 4, 5, HSP; Morris to Gustavus Scott, 7 Jan. 1797, Morris Letterbooks, LC.

65. Morris to Thomas Law, 4 July, 11 Dec. 1796, and Morris to Nicholson, 18 Jan. 1796, Morris Letterbooks, LC.

66. See Nicholson to Carroll, 1 July, 5 Oct. 1796, NL 3, HSP; *Washington Gazette*, 28 Sept. 1796; and Robert D. Arbuckle, "John Nicholson, 1757–1800, A Case Study of an Early American Land Speculator, Financier and Entrepreneur" (Ph.D. dissertation, The Pennsylvania State University, 1972), pp. 359–63.

67. Nicholson to Morris, 16 Jan. 1797, NL 5, HSP.

68. Nicholson to Morris, 8 Feb. 1797, NL 5, HSP; Morris to Joseph Boone, 24 Oct. 1797, Morris Letterbooks, LC. See also Nicholson to William Hunt, the creditor who was hounding Boone, 16 May 1797, NL 6, HSP.

69. Joseph Boone to Nicholson, 13 Oct. 1797, NC.

70. For examples see Garret Cottringer to Nicholson, 2 Oct. 1795, and Lewis Deblois to Nicholson, 12 Oct. 1796 and 19 June 1797, NC; Nicholson to Morris, 5 April, 22 Aug. 1796, Nicholson to James Jarvis, 4 Aug. 1796, Nicholson to James Greenleaf, 12 Jan. 1796, Nicholson to John Vaughan, 15 July 1797, and Nicholson to Jared Ingersoll, 24 Feb. 1797, NL 2, 4, 5, 7, HSP; Morris to trustees of the Aggregate Fund, 28 Sept. 1797, Morris Letterbooks, LC.

71. Nicholson to Morris, 16 Jan. 1797, NL 5, HSP.

72. Morris and Nicholson to the trustees of the Aggregate Fund, 24 Aug. 1797, Morris Letterbooks, LC; trustees of the Aggregate Fund to Nicholson, 30 July 1797, NC.

73. Morris to Nicholson, 15 Oct. 1797, and Morris and Nicholson to the

trustees of the Aggregate Fund, 24 Oct. 1797, Morris Letterbooks, LC. See also Clark, *Greenleaf and Law*, p. 74.

74. Morris to Nicholson, 21, 23 Nov. 1797, Morris Letterbooks, LC.

75. *Washington Gazette*, 31 May 1797, and William Tunnicliff to Nicholson, 2 June 1797, NC; Morris to trustees, 27 Oct. 1797, Morris Letterbooks, LC.

76. Morris to Marshall, 1 Nov. 1796, and Morris to Nicholson, 12, 13 Dec. 1796, Morris Letterbooks, LC. See also Aaron Sakolski, *The Great American Land Bubble: The Amazing Story of Land-Grabbing, Speculations, and Booms from Colonial Days to the Present Time* (New York: Harper and Brothers, 1932), pp. 167–68.

77. Philadelphia *Aurora General Advertiser*, 3 Oct. 1796; *Washington Gazette*, 23 Jan. 1797; this Broadside was actually written on 23 Sept. 1796 for future publication. It can be found in Washington, D.C., Legal Papers, 1793–1800, Nicholson Papers, PRD.

78. Hamilton to Greenleaf, 30 July 1796 in Gertrude Atherton, *A Few of Hamilton's Letters* (New York: Macmillan Co., 1903), p. 193.

79. Nicholson to Greenleaf, 9, 19 Oct. 1796, NL 4, HSP.

80. Nicholson to Gibson, 3 Dec. 1796, NL 5, HSP.

81. Philadelphia *Aurora General Advertiser*, 12 Oct. 1796; Morris and Nicholson to Luther Martin, 31 Aug. 1797, Morris Letterbooks, LC; Morris and Nicholson to trustees of Aggregate Fund, 13 July 1797, NL 7, HSP.

82. Morris to Gustavus Scott, 8, 10 May 1797, Morris Letterbooks, LC.

83. Greenleaf to Nicholson and Morris, 2 July 1799, NC.

84. Green, *Washington: Village and Capital*, p. 15. The author mistakenly refers to Nicholson as James, as does John Reps in his *Monumental Washington*, p. 26.

CHAPTER 9

1. Alexander Hamilton, "Report on Manufactures," in *American State Papers, Finance*, 1:123–44.

2. "Plan of Society" in *American Museum* (1787), 2:167–69. For the election of the officers see *Pennsylvania Gazette*, 12 Sept. 1787.

3. Victor S. Clark, *History of Manufactures in the United States, 1607–1860* (1929); Reprint. New York: Peter Smith, 1949), p. 535; Curtis Nettles, *The Emergence of a National Economy, 1775–1815* (New York: Holt, Rinehart and Winston, 1962), p. 275; William R. Bagnall, *The Textile Industries of the United States* (Cambridge, Mass.: H.O. Houghton and Co., 1893), pp. 89, 96–98. Slater was directly lured by the Pennsylvania Society's offer of financial rewards. See Harold Hutcheson, *Tench Coxe, A Study in American Economic Development* (Baltimore: Johns Hopkins Press, 1938), pp. 160–61.

4. Joseph S. Davis, *Essays in the Earlier History of American Corporations* (Cambridge: Harvard University Press, 1917), 1:356–58, 381–405, 473–74; Miller, *Alexander Hamilton*, pp. 300–301; Philadelphia *General Advertiser*, 15 Aug. 1791; *Gazette of the United States*, 10 Sept. 1791.

5. Low, Duer, Constable, Hammond, et al. to Hamilton, 9 Aug. 1791;

Syrett, *Papers of Alexander Hamilton*, 9:24–25; and Davis, *Earlier History of American Corporations*, 1:399–401.

6. William Duer was a major stockholder in S.U.M., and his failure caused widespread disillusionment. He was governor of S.U.M. in 1791. See *Gazette of the United States*, 3 Dec. 1791. See also Davis, *Earlier History of American Corporations*, 1:410; Miller, *Alexander Hamilton*, pp. 304–5, 308; Hutcheson, **Tench Coxe**, p. 109.

7. See *National Gazette*, 1 Sept. 1792; *Gazette of the United States*, 22 Sept. 1792; Philadelphia *General Advertiser*, 17 April 1792; and Davis, *Earlier History of American Corporations*, 1:303–8.

8. "Agreement with John Campbell," 9 Nov. 1792, Syrett, *Papers of Alexander Hamilton*, 13:31–32; Hamilton to Nicholas Low, 14 June 1793, ibid., 14:546.

9. Wansey, *Journal*, pp. 69–70, 76.

10. Moreau de St. Mery, *Moreau de St. Mery's American Journey, 1793–1798*, trans. and ed. Kenneth Roberts and Anna M. Roberts (Garden City, N.Y.: Doubleday and Co., 1947), pp. 113–14.

11. Liancourt, *Travels*, 4:192.

12. John Campbell to William Pollard, 30 Jan., 6 Feb. 1794, NC.

13. Ibid., 6 Feb. 1794.

14. The agreement was found among the Nicholson manuscripts at the PRD, Harrisburg. It has now been published by the editors of the Hamilton Papers, Syrett and Cooke.

15. *Gazette of the United States*, 22 Sept. 1792; Tench Coxe, *A View of the United States of America . . . 1787–1794* (Philadelphia: Wrigley and Berriman, 1794), pp. 52, 385. See also Hutcheson, **Tench Coxe**, pp. 118–19.

16. Nicholson to Edwards, 8 May 1793, NL, PRD.

17. William Pollard to Nicholson, 28 March, 4 Aug., 1 Oct. 1794, NC.

18. James Trenchard to Nicholson, 14 Nov. 1794, 11 Feb., 5 May, 15 July 1795, NC.

19. John Lithgow to Nicholson, 12, 24 Oct., 7, 17 Nov. 1794, 10, 20 April 1795, NC.

20. Wansey, *Journal*, p. 157; see also Liancourt, *Travels*, 1:7.

21. Liancourt, *Travels*, 1:8–9.

22. Nicholson to Joubert, 11 April 1796, NL 4, HSP.

23. Nicholson to George Slackpool, 24 July 1797, NL 7, HSP.

24. Thomas Bedwell to Nicholson, 3 July 1793, and William Eichbaum to Nicholson, 9 July 1795, NC; Nicholson to M. Kepple, 14 Dec. 1795, NL 3, HSP.

25. Nicholson Papers, Glass Works Accounts, Aug. 1796 through Feb. 1797, in Individual Business Accounts 1787–1800, PRD.

26. Clark, *History of Manufactories*, p. 524; John and Jonathan Mix to Nicholson, 10 Nov. n.y., NC.

27. Jonathan Mix to Nicholson, 17 July 1795, and Nathaniel Mix to Nicholson, 18 April 1795, NC; Nicholson to Mr. Mix, 29 May 1795, Nicholson to Lewis Deblois, 30 May 1795, and Nicholson to General Walter Stewart, 23 May 1795, NL 1, HSP; Button Works Accounts 1794–1797, PRD.

28. Jonathan Mix to Nicholson, 20 Feb. 1796 and 26 April 1798, and Thomas Joubert to Nicholson, 25, 29 May 1797, NC.

29. John Campbell to Nicholson, 10 April 1795, NC.

30. Pollard to Nicholson, 14 July, 29 Aug., 15 Sept. 1795, NL 1, 2, HSP; see also letters of 5 June, 18 July, 7 March 1795, NL 1, 2, HSP.

31. Nicholson to Bayard, 14 Sept. 1795; also Nicholson to Pollard, 7, 11 Sept. 1795, NL 2, 3, HSP.

32. Nicholson to Taylor, 18 Sept. 1795, NL 3, HSP; Taylor to Nicholson, 30 May, 2, 14 Nov. 1796, 6 April, 1, 25 May 1797, NC; Nicholson to Taylor, 4 Nov. 1796, NL 4, HSP.

33. Nicholson to Thomas Potts, 31 March 1795, NL 4, HSP; Thomas Flood to Nicholson, 19 June 1795, NC; Thomas Flood Account Book, 1795, PRD.

34. Nicholson to Samuel Bayard, 17 June 1795, NL 2, HSP; Articles of Agreement, 9 May 1795 in T.B. Freeman and Company Accounts, 1795–1800, PRD and in T.B. Freeman and Company Correspondence, 1794–1799, PRD.

35. Nicholson to James Trenchard, 28 July, 5 Sept. 1795; Notice of Dissolution, 3 Aug. 1797, NL 2, 7, HSP; William Nichols to Nicholson, 8 Dec. 1797, and George Slackpoole to Nicholson, 12 Jan. 1798, NC.

36. George Hughes, "The Pioneer Iron Industry in Western Pennsylvania," *Western Pennsylvania Historical Magazine* 14 (1931): 208. Hayden, near Uniontown, is named for John Hayden.

37. Alexander McClean to Nicholson, 14 Feb. 1793 and 13 March 1794, and also Francis Bryan to Nicholson, 16, 29 Nov. 1797, NC.

38. Jessee Evans to Nicholson, 26 July, 27 Aug. 1794, 14, 22 Oct. 1796, 30 Nov., 23 June, 18 Oct. 1797, NC.

39. Ibid., 15 March 1798; John Lyon, Hayden's attorney, to Nicholson, 14 July 1799, NC.

40. General Chambers to Nicholson, 25 Oct. 1796, NC.

41. Nicholson to General James Chambers, 21 April 1797, NL 6, HSP.

42. William Henry to Nicholson, 28 Sept. 1794, NC; Nicholson to Michael Hillegas, 12 June 1795, NL 2, HSP. Henry Spering to Nicholson, 27 Feb. 1798, and John Waddington to Nicholson, 6 March 1798, NC.

43. Nicholson to John Nancarrow and Thomas Bedwell, 3 April 1793, NL, PRD; John Nancarrow to Nicholson, 10 March 1793, NC.

44. For examples see Joshua Percival to Nicholson, 1 March 1797, and John Evans to Nicholson, 25 Aug. 1797, NC.

45. Nicholson to Garder and Towell, 16 Nov. 1796, NL 4, HSP.

46. Morris to Nicholson, 22 Nov. 1796, Morris Letterbrooks, LC.

47. Liancourt, *Travels*, 1:9–10.

48. Tench Coxe to Nicholson, 6 March 1788, NC.

49. Nicholson to James McLane, 26 March 1788, NL, PRD.

50. Journal of the Society for the Improvement of Roads and Inland Navigation, p. 1, PRD.

51. Wansey, *Journal*, p. 155.

52. *Statutes at Large of Pennsylvania,* 14:279–94; *Pennsylvania Gazette,* 25 April, 2 May, 1, 22 Aug. 1792; Charles I. Landis, "History of the Philadelphia and Lancaster Turnpike," *PMHB* 42 (1918): passim; Account Entry of 2 May 1792, Nicholson Business Accounts, 1792–1793, Box 3, PRD; Charles Pettit to Nicholson, 3 Oct. 1792, NC.

53. William Pollard to Nicholson, 13 Jan. 1793, NC.

54. Cooper, *Some Information Respecting America,* pp. 138–39; Wansey, *Journal,* p. 211, and Baily, *Journal of a Tour,* p. 107.

55. Nicholson to Thomas Mifflin, 23, 27 April 1795, and Nicholson to John Kitland, 29 July 1795, NL 1, HSP.

56. *Pennsylvania House Journal, 1790–1791,* p. 13.

57. Nicholson to J. Dunlap, 15 Nov. 1791, NC; *The Pennsylvania Packet,* 17 Nov. 1791.

58. Liancourt, *Travels,* 1:9.

59. Pollard to Nicholson, 17 May 1795, NC.

60. *Gazette of the United States,* 20 June 1791.

61. Philadelphia *Aurora General Advertiser,* 10 Jan. 1794; *Pennsylvania Archives,* 9th ser., 1:201, 421; William Smith, *An Historical Account of the Rise, Progress and Present State of Canal Navigation in Pennsylvania* (Philadelphia: Zachariah Poulson, Jr., 1805), pp. 44, 67.

62. The complete accounts of Nicholson's association with the Delaware and Schuylkill Company can be found in the Delaware and Schuylkill Navigation Canal Company Accounts, 1792–1795, PRD.

63. Liancourt, *Travels,* 1:28–29.

64. Philadelphia *Aurora General Advertiser,* 30 May 1795, 19 Jan. 1796, 5 July 1797; *Pennsylvania Archives,* 9th ser., 2:978–83, 1,021.

65. Philadelphia *General Advertiser,* 15 April 1793.

66. In Dorothy Bathe and Grenville Bathe, *Oliver Evans, A Chronicle of Early American Engineering* (Philadelphia: Historical Society of Pennsylvania, 1935), p. 47. See also Nicholson to Evans, 24, 26 May, 30 June 1797, NL 7, HSP.

67. Sherrill, *French Memoirs of the Eighteenth Century,* pp. 303–4; see also Huth and Pugh, *Talleyrand in America,* pp. 121–32.

68. Nicholson to Dr. E. Edwards, 31 March 1795, NL 1, HSP.

69. Washington testimony, 22 Nov. 1787, James A. Padgett, ed., "Rumsey Documents," *Maryland Historical Magazine* (MHM) 31 (1936): 185–88.

70. Padgett, "Rumsey Documents," *MHM* 32:141–42; Ella May Turner, *James Rumsey, Pioneer in Steam Navigation* (Scottdale, Pa.: Mennonite Publishing Company, 1930), pp. 16, 75–76; George M. Beltzhoover, Jr., *James Rumsey, the Inventor of the Steamboat* (Philadelphia: J.B. Lippincott and Company for the West Virginia Historical and Antiquarian Society, 1900), p. 16.

71. Padgett, "Rumsey Documents," *MHM* 31:189; Beltzhoover, *Rumsey,* p. 16; Turner, *Rumsey,* p. 69; H.A. Gosnell, "The First American Steamboat: James Rumsey Its Inventor Not John Fitch," *Virginia Magazine of History and Biography* 40 (April 1932): 125.

72. Washington to Rumsey, 31 Jan. 1786, Jared Sparks, ed., *The Writings*

of George Washington (Boston: Russell, Odeorne and Metcalf, 1835), 12:19; Ford, *Writings of Jefferson*, 7:328; Henry W. Dickinson, *Robert Fulton, Engineer and Artist* (New York: The Century Co., 1925), p. 127.

73. Padgett, "Rumsey Documents," *MHM* 32:145; Philadelphia *General Advertiser*, 8 March 1793; Westcott, *Life of Fitch*, pp. 186–87.

74. Padgett, "Rumsey Documents," *MHM* 32:146–50. See also *Pennsylvania Packet*, 23 Oct. 1789.

75. J.P. Brissot de Warville, *New Travels in the United States of America Performed in 1788* (Boston: J. Bumstead, 1797), 1:197.

76. Padgett, "Rumsey Documents," *MHM* 32:279–81; James Rumsey to Joseph Barnes, 3 Feb., 10 Oct. 1790, NC; Philadelphia *General Advertiser*, 8 March 1793.

77. Nicholson to Barnes, 7 July 1795, NL 2, HSP; Benjamin Wynkoop to Nicholson, 17 June 1798, NC.

78. Nicholson to Fitch, 5 July 1795, NL 2, HSP.

79. Thomas Clark, *Frontier America: The Story of the Westward Movement*, 2d ed. (New York: Charles Scribner's Sons, 1969), p. 348.

CHAPTER 10

1. See Sakolski, *The Great American Land Bubble*, p. 48; Livermore, *Early American Land Companies*, p. 168.

2. Plan of Association of the North American Land Company (Philadelphia: R. Aitken and Son, 1795). Copies can be found in the Gratz Collection, HSP, and in Evans, *Early American Imprints*, no. 29220.

3. Barclay and Nixon to Nicholson, March 1795, NC.

4. Nicholson to Colborn Barrel and Henry Servanti, 2 April 1795, NL 1, HSP. The press also publicized the fact that aliens could hold title to the land in the state. See *Gazette of the United States*, 15 May 1790.

5. Schedule of Lands, 6 Jan. 1795, in Morris Letterbooks, LC; list of lands also in Nicholson to Morris, 28 April, 17, 22 June 1795, NL 1, 2, HSP. These acreages were based on the county boundaries of that period.

6. Nicholson to Greenleaf, 18 Feb., 2 May 1796, NL 3, 4, HSP. See also Ruddy, "The Policy of Land Distribution in Pennsylvania," pp. 77–79, and Moses Levy to Nicholson and Morris, 18 March 1795, NC.

7. Morris to Wilhelm and Jan Willink, 16 March 1795, Morris Letterbooks, LC.

8. Nicholson to Barrell and Servanti, 2 April 1795, NL 1, HSP.

9. Weld, *Travels*, 2:336–37.

10. Morris to Wilhelm and Jan Willinks, 16 March 1796, Morris Letterbooks, LC.

11. S.G. McLendon, *History of the Public Domain of Georgia* (Atlanta: Foote and Davis Co., 1924), p. 171.

12. The specific locations of the first three Yazoo Company tracts are described in *American State Papers, Indian Affairs*, 1:113–14.

13. John Wade to Nicholson, 12, 17, 24 Feb., 14 April 1791, 20 Dec. 1792, 12 Jan. 1793, and Sarah Wade to Nicholson, 8 Nov. 1792, NC.

14. Stockdale to Nicholson, 26 Dec. 1794, NC.

15. Moultrie to Nicholson, 15 May 1796, NC.

16. Moultrie to Nicholson, 1 Nov. 1796, NC.

17. Benjamin Wright, *The Contract Clause of the Constitution* (Cambridge: Harvard University Press, 1938), pp. 21–23; Miller, *Alexander Hamilton*, pp. 547–48. See also Gibbs, *Memoirs of the Administrations of Washington and Adams*, p. 305.

18. Mouultrie to Nicholson, 27 Feb. 1797, NC.

19. *American State Papers, Public Lands*, 1:133.

20. See Morris to James Marshall, 10 Nov. 1795, Morris Letterbooks, LC.

21. E. Merton Coulter, *Georgia, A Short History*, rev. ed. (Chapel Hill: University of North Carolina Press, 1947), p. 198.

22. Daniel Carthy to Nicholson and Morris, 2 Aug. 1794, NC.

23. Stockdale to Nicholson, 26 Dec. 1794, NC.

24. Hall to Nicholson, 4 Aug. 1794, and Sarah Wade to Nicholson, 9 Jan. 1793, NC; entry for 10 Feb. 1794, Nicholson Diary, 1793–1794, PRD.

25. Cox to Nicholson, Morris, and Greenleaf, 20 Oct. 1794, NC.

26. Stockdale to Nicholson, 26 Dec. 1794, NC.

27. Morris to Hampton, 17 March 1795, Morris Letterbooks, LC.

28. Morris to Constable, 22 Sept. 1795, ibid.

29. Hampton to Morris, 8 Jan. 1795, ibid.

30. Stockdale to Nicholson, 26 Dec. 1794, and Cox to Nicholson, 19 Jan. 1794, NC.

31. Cox to Nicholson, 13 Jan. 1795, NC.

32. Nicholson to Cox, 22, 28 March, 14 April 1795, NL 1, HSP.

33. Hampton to Morris, 8 Jan. 1795, NC.

34. Abraham Bishop, *Georgia Speculations Unveiled* (Hartford, Conn.: Elisha Babcock, 1797), pp. 7, 26.

35. Moultrie to Nicholson, 15 May 1796, NC.

36. Morris to Nicholson, 3 Nov. 1795, Morris Letterbooks, LC.

37. Bishop, *Georgia Speculations Unveiled*, p. 16.

38. Blount to Nicholson, 18 Aug. 1794, NC.

39. John Reps, in his *Making of Urban America* (Princeton: Princeton University Press, 1965), gives a description of these towns based on Winterbotham's account and reproduces, on pp. 356–57, the sketches of the town plans of Franklinville and Lystra, included in Winterbotham's travel log in vol. 3, on pp. 124–25, 140–41. However, he does not mention Nicholson, the company, or Barber.

40. Winterbotham, *View of the United States*, 3:145, 147.

41. Barber to Nicholson, 16 April, 30 Dec. 1796, NC.

42. Barber to Nicholson, 24 March, 30 May, 17 Sept. 1798, 29 May, 14 June, 25 Oct. 1799, NC.

43. Nicholson to Greenleaf, 20 March 1795, NL 1, HSP.

44. Morris to Thomas Hall, 23 Feb. 1795, Morris Letterbooks, LC; Matthew McConnel to Nicholson, 9 April 1798, NC.

45. Morris to S. Bean, 10 June 1797, Morris Letterbooks, LC.

CHAPTER 11

1. Nicholson to unnamed correspondent, 19 May 1797, NL 6, HSP.

2. Plan of Association of the Pennsylvania Property Company (Philadelphia: R. Aitken and Son, 1797). Reproduced in Evans, *Early American Imprints*, no. 32658.

3. Mrs. Susan Woodrow to Nicholson, 29 May 1797, and Robert Porter to Nicholson, 23 May 1797, NC.

4. Joseph Ball to Nicholson, 13 July 1797, NC.

5. Anthony, "Report against Nicholson," p. 6.

6. Ibid., p. 11; Huidekoper, "Remarks on the Nicholson Commissioners," p. 15.

7. Anthony, "Report against Nicholson," p. 11.

8. Ibid., pp. 5, 6, 14.

9. William Prentiss to Nicholson, 1, 3, 6, 7, 10 June 1798, NC.

10. William Duncan to Nicholson, 16 Oct. 1796, NC.

11. For examples see Abraham Morehouse to Nicholson, 17 May 1797, Benjamin Stevens to Nicholson, 18 Feb. 1797, John Taylor to Nicholson, 28 April 1799, and James McCally to Nicholson, 3 May 1798, NC.

12. Nicholson to Fitzsimmons, 13 April, 9, 25 May 1795, NL 2, HSP; Fitzsimmons to Nicholson, 10 Jan. 1795 and 12 June 1797, NC.

13. Morris to Nicholson, 1, 24 Jan. 1795, 12 Aug. 1796, Morris Letterbooks, LC.

14. Anthony, "Report against Nicholson," p. 5; Morris to Nicholson, 4 Dec. 1796, Morris Letterbooks, LC.

15. Jonas Phillips to Nicholson, 12 June 1795, Richard Parrot to Nicholson, 28 Dec. 1797, John Stockdale to Nicholson, 6 April 1797, 4, 6 April, 28 May, 3 June 1795, and B. Storrs to Nicholson, 13 Aug. 1796, NC.

16. Jonas Phillips to Nicholson, 23 Feb. 1797, and Moulder to Nicholson, 7 Feb. 1797, NC.

17. Joseph Clark to Nicholson, 5 Feb. 1797, NC.

18. Nicholson to James Gibson, 28 May 1797, NL 7, HSP.

19. Nicholson to John McCulloch, 27 May, 10 June 1797, Nicholson to trustees of the African Church, 7 April 1797, Nicholson to Higbee, 29 Sept. 1797, and Nicholson to Thomas Fitzsimmons, 7 Oct. 1797, NL 6, 7, HSP.

20. Morris to Nicholson, 22 Nov. 1796, Morris Letterbooks, LC.

21. Mary Ann McPherson to Nicholson, 18 Jan. 1798, NC.

22. Quoted in Bathe, *Oliver Evans*, p. 60.

23. Morris to Nicholson, 25 Oct. 1797, Morris Letterbooks, LC.

24. Morris to Nicholson, 13 Sept., 3 Oct. 1797, Morris Letterbooks, LC.

25. Nicholson to Morris, 1 Feb. 1797, NL 5, HSP; Morris to Nicholson, 1 Nov. 1797, Morris Letterbooks, LC.

26. Morris to Nicholson, 30 Dec. 1797, ibid.

27. William Nichols to Nicholson, 3 Jan. 1798, NC; Morris to Nicholson, 6 March 1797, Morris Letterbooks, LC.

28. Nicholson to Joseph Higbee, 29 Sept. 1797, and Nicholson to Morris, 30 Dec. 1796, NL 5, 7, HSP.

29. Morris to Nicholson, 1 Nov. 1797, Morris Letterbooks, LC.

30. Nicholson to Morris, 14 Dec. 1796, NL 4, HSP; Benjamin Rush, *The Autobiography of Benjamin Rush: His Travels Through Life Together with His "Commonplace Book" for 1789–1813*, edited with an introduction and notes by George W. Corner (Princeton: Princeton University Press, 1948), pp. 235–36; Gibbs, *Memoirs of the Administrations of Washington and Adams*, p. 410.

31. Morris to Nicholson, 11, 12, 18 Dec. 1797, 5 Feb. 1798, Morris Letterbooks, LC. See also Eleanor Young, *Forgotten Patriot, Robert Morris* (New York: Macmillan Co., 1950), pp. 203–4.

32. Morris to Nicholson, 12 Feb. 1798, Morris Letterbooks, LC.

33. Morris to Nicholson, 15 Feb. 1798, Morris Letterbooks, LC.

34. Morris to Nicholson, 13 March 1797, ibid.

35. Ibid., 2 Feb. 1798.

36. Nicholson to Samuel Nicholson, 21 April 1797, NL 6, HSP; Morris to Nicholson, 8 Feb. 1798, Morris Letterbooks, LC.

37. Abigail Adams to Mary Cranch, 11 Dec. 1799, in Mitchell, *Letters of Abigail Adams*, p. 220.

38. Morris to Nicholson, 14 Dec. 1797, Morris Letterbooks, LC.

39. William Wood, *Personal Recollections of the Stage, Embracing Notices of Actors, Authors, and Auditors During a Period of Forty Years* (Philadelphia: Henry Carey Baird, 1855), p. 39.

40. Oberholtzer, *Robert Morris*, p. 347.

41. St. Mery, *Journey*, p. 354.

42. Moses Castello to Nicholson, 4 Nov. 1800, and Samuel Seely to Nicholson, 14 March 1800, NC.

43. Anne C. Morris, ed., *The Diary and Letters of Gouverneur Morris* (New York: Charles Scribner's Sons, 1882), 2:378; Elizabeth Drinker, *Extracts from the Journal of Elizabeth Drinker*, ed. Henry Biddle (Philadelphia: J.B. Lippincott Co., 1899), p. 362.

CHAPTER 12

1. *Poulson's American Daily Advertiser*, 8 Dec. 1800.

2. Biddle, *Journal of Elizabeth Drinker*, p. 366.

3. See *Reports of Cases Adjudged in the Supreme Court of Pennsylvania by the Honorable Jasper Yeates, one of the Judges of the Supreme Court of Pennsylvania* (Philadelphia: John Bioren, 1818), 2:15; Huidekoper, "Remarks on the Nicholson Commissioners," pp. 8, 11, 16.

4. Anthony, "Report against Nicholson," p. 5.

5. Improvements of the liability of the debtor and of the prisons were made by the state from 1800 to 1842. Then in 1842 a law was passed which abolished imprisonment for debt. See *Statutes at Large of Pennsylvania*, 14:267–69, 16:98–106; Frank Carleton, "The Abolition of Imprisonment for Debt in the United States," *The Yale Review* 17 (1908–1909): 338–44; George Bauer, "The Movement against Imprisonment for Debt in the United States" (Ph.D. dissertation, Harvard University, 1935), pp. 119–29.

6. John Ely to Nicholson, 16 July 1799, NC.

7. Adams to Mary Cranch, 13 March 1798, in Mitchell, *Letters of Abigail Adams*, pp. 142–43.

8. Ralph Mather to Nicholson, 10 May 1797, NC.

9. Nicholson to Lewis Deblois, 14 Dec. 1795, NL 3, HSP.

10. Nicholson to George Harrison, 29 Oct. 1796, NL 4, HSP.

11. Ewing to Nicholson, 19 April 1796, NC.

12. Defense Speech by William Lewis, 19 March 1793, in Nicholson Papers, Impeachment File, 1779–1794, PRD.

13. Breck, *Recollections*, p. 204.

14. Samuel McKee, ed., *Alexander Hamilton's Papers on Public Credit, Commerce, and Finance* (New York: Putnam, 1957), p. 233.

15. Lymen Butterfield, ed., *Letters of Benjamin Rush* (Princeton: Princeton University Press, 1951), 2:636, 637.

16. Benjamin Rush, *A Memorial Containing Travels Through Life or Sundry Incidents in the Life of Dr. Benjamin Rush* (Philadelphia: Louis Biddle, 1905), p. 146.

17. Anthony Fowler to Nicholson, 6 Aug. 1797, Absalom Jones and William Gray to Nicholson, 3 Dec. 1792, 7 Feb., 11 May, 13 Aug. 1793, and William Budden to Nicholson, 14 March 1795, NC; Nicholson to Jones and Gray, 26 Jan., 26 March 1795, NL 1, HSP.

18. John Shippen to Nicholson, 12 Jan. 1795, and Stephen Boisbrun to Nicholson, 25 March 1795, NC.

19. *Poulson's American Daily Advertiser*, 8 Dec. 1800.

LIST OF SOURCES

PRIMARY SOURCES

MANUSCRIPTS

Crawford County Historical Society Papers, Meadville, Pennsylvania: Holland Land Company, Day Book, 1795–1800; Pennsylvania Population Company, Minute Books, 1792–1815.

Darlington Memorial Library Manuscript Collections, The University of Pittsburgh, Pittsburgh, Pennsylvania: Dunning McNair Papers, 1786–1851.

Erie Public Museum Manuscript Collections, Erie, Pennsylvania: Francis Spencer Estate Papers—Colt, Judah, Accounts and Letters, 1796–1799, and Journal; Pennsylvania Population Company, Papers.

Historical Society of Pennsylvania, Philadelphia, Pennsylvania: Democratic Society of Pennsylvania, Minutes; Gratz Collection; Nicholson, John, Correspondence, 1792–1796, and Letterbooks, 1791–1798.

Historical Society of Western Pennsylvania, Pittsburgh, Pennsylvania: McNair Papers.

Library of Congress, Manuscript Division: Morris, Robert, Diary, 1781–1783 (on microfilm), and Private Letterbooks, 1793–1800 (on microfilm).

Pattee Library Manuscript Collections, The Pennsylvania State University, University Park, Pennsylvania: Blotter of Judah Colt, 1803 and 1804.

Pennsylvania Historical and Museum Commission, Public Records Division, William Penn Memorial Archives, Harrisburg, Pennsylvania: The Delaware and Schuylkill Navigation Canal Company Accounts, 1792–1795; Journal of the Society for the Improvement of Roads and Inland Navigation; Moulder, William, Jr., Correspondence, 1794–1800; New Loan Certificate Accounts, vol. A, nos. 1, 2, 3, 60, 225, 230, 262.

Nicholson, John, Papers*: Accounts of Pennsylvania with the United States, Account Book No. 2; Asylum Company Business Accounts, 1793–1794—Business Accounts, 1787–1800 and 1792–1793; Individual Business Accounts, 1787–1800; Button Works Accounts, 1794–1797;

*The Nicholson Papers, designated as Manuscript Group 96 in the state archives, consist of 32,000 items, 26,000 of which have now been microfilmed. This collection is distinct from Record Group 4, Records of the Office of the Comptroller-General, 1762–1810, which includes much of Nicholson's record while serving in public office.

List of Sources

Diaries, 1792–1794; General Correspondence, 1778–1800; Glass Works Accounts, 1796–1797; Impeachment File, 1779–1794; Letter Books, 1779–1793; *The Supporter,* or *Daily Repast* Accounts, 1799–1800; Washington, D.C., Business Accounts, 1794; Washington, D.C., Legal Papers, 1795–1796.

Henry Elouis Account Book, 1794–1797.
Thomas Flood Account Book, 1795.
Mathias Hollenback Account Book, 1788–1789.

Nicholson, Samuel, Correspondence, 1793–1794; Petitions to Exchange New Loan Certificates, 1785–1788; T.B. Freeman and Company, Papers, Accounts, 1795–1800, and Correspondence, 1794–1799.
Tioga Point Museum Collections, Athens, Pennsylvania: Reverend David Craft, Papers.

NEWSPAPERS AND PERIODICALS

Philadelphia: *American Daily Advertiser* (Dunlap); *American Museum; Freeman's Journal,* or *North-American Intelligencer; Gazette of the United States; General Advertiser,* or *Aurora; Independent Gazetter,* or *Chronicle of Freedom; National Gazette; Pennsylvania Gazette; Pennsylvania Packet,* or *General Advertiser; Poulson's Daily American Advertiser.*
Also: *The Pittsburgh Press,* 27 September 1970; *Washington Gazette.*

PUBLIC DOCUMENTS, LAWS, AND RECORDS OF THE UNITED STATES

Carter, Clarence E., ed. and comp. *The Territorial Papers of the United States.* 24 vols. Washington, D. C.: Government Printing Office, 1934–1959.
Fletcher v. *Peck.* 6 Cranch (U.S.), 87, 128 (1810).
Ford, Worthington, ed. *Journals of the Continental Congress, 1774–1789.* 34 vols. Washington, D.C.: Library of Congress, 1904–1937.
Gales, Joseph, and Seaton, W.W., comps. *Annals of Congress.* 42 vols. Washington, D.C.: Government Printing Office, 1834–1856.
Huidekoper's Lesse v. *Douglass.* 4 Dallas (U.S.), 897 (1805).
Jowitt, Earl, ed. *The Dictionary of English Law.* London: Sweet and Maxwell, 1959.
Lowrie, Walter, and Clark, M.S.C., eds. *American State Papers . . . : Finance, Indian Affairs, Public Lands, Miscellaneous.* 38 vols. Washington, D.C.: Gales and Seaton, 1832–1861.
Peters, Richard, ed. *The Public Statutes at Large of the United States . . . .* Boston: Little, Brown and Co., 1854.
Thorpe, Francis Newton, ed. *The Federal and State Constitutions, Colonial Charters, and Other Organic Laws of the States, Territories, and Colonies . . . ,* 5. Washington, D.C.: Government Printing Office, 1909.
U.S. Board of Treasury. *Resolutions,* 1778–1779. Reproduced in Evans. *Early American Imprints.* No. 16642.
U.S. Bureau of the Census. *Historical Statistics of the United States, Colonial Times to 1957.* Washington, D.C.: Government Printing Office, 1961.
Vanhorne's Lessee v. *Dorrance.* 2 Dallas (U.S.), 304 (1795).
Wharton, Francis, ed. *The Revolutionary and Diplomatic Correspondence of the United States.* 6 vols. Washington, D.C.: Government Printing Office, 1889.

List of Sources

PUBLIC DOCUMENTS, LAWS, AND RECORDS OF
THE COMMONWEALTH OF PENNSYLVANIA

Acts of the Legislature of Pennsylvania Relating to the Schuylkill Navigation Company. Philadelphia: L.R. Bailey, 1826.

Bioren, John, and Carey, Matthew, comps. *Laws of the Commonwealth of Pennsylvania.* 8 vols. Philadelphia: Francis Bailey, 1803.

Carey, Matthew, ed. *Debates and Proceedings of the General Assembly of Pennsylvania on the Memorials Praying a Repeal or Suspension of the Law Annulling the Charter of the Bank.* Philadelphia: Seddon and Pritchard, 1786.

Dallas, A.J., comp. *Laws of Pennsylvania, 1781–1790.* 3 vols. Philadelphia: Hall and Sellers, 1795.

Dunlop, James, comp. *The General Laws of Pennsylvania from the Year 1700 to 1846.* Philadelphia: T. and J.W. Johnson, 1847.

Fertig, John H., comp. *Constitutions of Pennsylvania.* Harrisburg: Legislative Reference Bureau, 1926.

Hogan, Edmund. *The Pennsylvania State Trials: Containing the Impeachment, Trial, and Acquittal of Francis Hopkinson and John Nicholson* . . . . Philadelphia: Francis Bailey, 1794.

Journals of the House of Representatives of the Commonwealth of Pennsylvania, 1776–1790 . . . . Philadelphia: State Printers, 1776–1790.

Journal of the Pennsylvania House of Representatives, 1790–1801. Philadelphia, Lancaster, and Harrisburg: State Printers, 1790–1932.

Journals of the Pennsylvania Senate, 1794–1795. Philadelphia: State Printers, 1795.

Journal of the Senate of the State of Pennsylvania, 1842. Harrisburg: State Printer, 1843.

Laws of the Commonwealth of Pennsylvania. (*Smith's Laws*). 10 vols. Philadelphia and Pittsburgh: n.p., 1810–1844.

Laws of the General Assembly of the Commonwealth of Pennsylvania, 1842. Harrisburg: Printed by McKinley and Lescure, 1842.

Minutes of the . . . General Assembly of the Commonwealth of Pennsylvania . . . . Philadelphia: n.p., 1781–1790.

Minutes of the House of Representatives of the Commonwealth of Pennsylvania, 1776–1790. Philadelphia: State Printers, 1776–1790.

Minutes of the Supreme Executive Council of Pennsylvania. Harrisburg: T. Fenn and Co., 1851–1853.

Mitchell, James T., and Flanders, Henry, eds. *The Statutes at Large of Pennsylvania from 1682 to 1801.* 17 vols. Harrisburg: n.p., 1896–1915.

Nicholson, John. *Abstract from a Digest of John Nicholson, Comptroller-General, of the Laws of Pennsylvania Now in Force, Relative to Excise, July, 1786.* Philadelphia: n.p., 1786.

Pennsylvania Archives. 120 vols. Philadelphia and Harrisburg: State Printers, 1852–1935.

Pennsylvania. Annual Reports of the Secretary of Internal Affairs, Land Office Bureau *Bulletin*, 1892, 1893, 1895, 1898, 1945, 1953.

Pennsylvania Colonial Records. 16 vols. Harrisburg: T. Fenn and Co., 1851–1853.

Proceedings Relative to Calling the Conventions of 1776 and 1790, and the Minutes of the Convention . . . and of the Council. Harrisburg: J.S. Wiestling, printer, 1825.

Reports of Cases Adjudged in the Supreme Court of Pennsylvania, by the Honorable Jasper Yeates, One of the Judges of the Supreme Court of Pennsylvania. Philadelphia: John Bioren, 1818.

List of Sources

Sergeant, Thomas. *A Treatise Upon the Law of Pennsylvania Relative to the Proceedings of Foreign Attachment*. Philadelphia: Farrant and Nichols, 1811.

————. *A View of the Land Laws of Pennsylvania* . . . . Philadelphia: James Kay, Jun and Brother, 1838.

U.S. Bureau of the Census. *Heads of Families at the First Census of the United States Taken in the Year 1790—Pennsylvania*. Washington, D.C.: Government Printing Office, 1907–1908.

PUBLISHED WRITINGS

—Collections

Adams, Charles Francis, ed. *Letters of Mrs. Adams, the Wife of John Adams*. 2 vols. Boston: Little, Brown and Co., 1848.

Ames, Seth, ed. *The Works of Fisher Ames*. 2 vols. Boston: Little, Brown and Co., 1854.

Atherton, Gertrude, ed. *A Few of Hamilton's Letters*. New York: Macmillan Co., 1903.

Baker, William Spohn, comp. *Washington after the Revolution, 1784–1799*. Philadelphia: J.B. Lippincott Co., 1898.

Boyd, Julian P., et al., eds. *The Papers of Thomas Jefferson*. 18 vols. Princeton: Princeton University Press, 1952–1965.

Brodhead, John, ed. *Documents Relative to the Colonial History of the State of New York*. Vol. 8. Albany: Weed, Parsons and Co., 1857.

Burnett, Edmund C., ed. *Letters of Members of the Continental Congress*. 8 vols. Washington, D.C.: Carnegie Institution, 1921–1936.

Butterfield, C.W., ed. *Washington-Irving Correspondence*. Madison, Wis.: David Atwood Co., 1882.

Butterfield, Lyman, ed. *Letters of Benjamin Rush*. 2 vols. Princeton: Princeton University Press, 1951.

Byars, William, ed. *Gratz Papers*. Jefferson City, Mo.: Hugh Stephens Co., 1916.

Cole, Arthur H., ed. *The Industrial and Commercial Correspondence of Alexander Hamilton* . . . . Boston: The Business Historical Society, 1928.

Conway, Moncure, ed. *The Writings of Thomas Paine*. 4 vols. New York and London: G.P. Putnam's Sons, 1894–1896.

Cutler, William, and Cutler, Julia, eds. and comps. *The Life, Journals and Correspondence of Reverend Manasseh Cutler*. 2 vols. Cincinnati: Robert Clarke, 1888.

Dallas, George M., ed. and comp. *The Life and Writings of Alexander J. Dallas*. Philadelphia: J.B. Lippincott Co., 1871.

Day, Sherman, ed. *Historical Collections of the State of Pennsylvania*. Philadelphia: George Gorton, 1843.

Donnan, Elizabeth, ed. "Papers of James A. Bayard, 1796–1815." *Annual Report of the American Historical Association for the Year 1913 2*. Washington, D.C.: Government Printing Office, 1915.

Egle, William, ed. "Documents Relating to the Connecticut Settlement in the Wyoming Valley." *Pennsylvania Archives*. 2d ser., vol. 8, 1–123, 629–683.

Fitzpatrick, John, ed. *Diaries of George Washington*. 4 vols. Boston: Houghton-Mifflin Co., 1925.

————, ed. *The Writings of George Washington*. 39 vols. Washington, D.C.: Government Printing Office, 1931–1944.

Foner, Philip S., ed. *The Complete Writings of Thomas Paine*. 2 vols. New York: Citadel Press, 1945.

List of Sources

Ford, Emily Ellsworth, ed. *Notes on the Life of Noah Webster*. 2 vols. New York: Privately Printed, 1912.

Ford, Paul L., comp. *Pamphlets on the Constitution of the United States*. 1888. Reprint. New York: Da Capo Press, 1968.

———, ed. *The Writings of Thomas Jefferson*. 10 vols. New York: G.P. Putnam's Sons, 1892–1899.

Ford, Worthington C., ed. "Some Papers of Aaron Burr." *Proceedings of the American Antiquarian Society* 29 (April–October, 1919): 43–128.

Gibbs, George, ed. *Memoirs of the Administrations of Washington and John Adams Edited from the Papers of Oliver Wolcott*. 2 vols. New York: W. Van Norden, 1846.

Gilpin, H.D., ed. *James Madison's Letters and Other Writings*. 4 vols. Philadelphia: J.B. Lippincott Co., 1865.

Hamer, Philip, ed. "Letters of Governor William Blount." *East Tennessee Historical Society Publications* 4 (1932): 122–37.

Hamilton, John, ed. *The Works of Alexander Hamilton*. Vol. 5. New York: Francis and Co., 1851.

Hamilton, Stanislaus M., ed. *The Writings of James Monroe*. 7 vols. New York: G.P. Putnam's Sons, 1898–1903.

Henkels, Stan V., ed. *The Confidential Correspondence of Robert Morris* .... Philadelphia: Powler Co., 1917.

Hunt, Gaillard, ed. *The First Forty Years of Washington Society in the Family Letters of Margaret Bayard Smith*. 1906. Reprint. New York: Frederick Ungar Publishing Co., 1965.

———. *The Writings of James Madison*. 9 vols. New York: G.P. Putnam's Sons, 1900–1910.

Huth, Hans, and Pugh, Wilma, eds. and trans. *Talleyrand in America as a Financial Promoter, 1794–1796, Unpublished Letters and Memoirs, Annual Report of the American Historical Association for 1941*. 2 vols. Washington, D.C.: Government Printing Office, 1942.

Jameson, J.F., ed. "Letters of Phineas Bond . . . , 1790–1794." *Annual Report of the American Historical Association for the Year 1896*. Washington, D.C.: Government Printing Office, 1897.

Keith, Alice Barnwell, ed. *The John Gray Blount Papers*. 2 vols. Raleigh: North Carolina Department of Archives and History, 1952.

King, Charles R., ed. *The Life and Correspondence of Rufus King*. 2 vols. New York: G.P. Putnam's Sons, 1894–1900.

Lipscomb, Andrew A., ed. *The Writings of Thomas Jefferson*. 20 vols. Washington, D.C.: Thomas Jefferson Memorial Association, 1905.

Lodge, Henry Cabot, ed. *The Works of Alexander Hamilton*. 12 vols. New York: G.P. Putnam's Sons, 1904.

McKee, Samuel, ed. *Alexander Hamilton's Papers on Public Credit, Commerce and Finance*. New York: Putnam, 1957.

Mathews, Catherine Van Cortlandt, ed. and comp. *Andrew Ellicott, His Life and Letters*. New York: Grafton Press, 1908.

Melville, Lewis, ed. and comp. *The Life and Letters of William Cobbett*. 2 vols. London: John Lane, 1913.

Mitchell, Stuart, ed. *Some Letters of Abigail Adams, 1788–1801*. Boston: Houghton-Mifflin, 1947.

Montgomery, Thomas, ed. *Frontier Forts of Pennsylvania*. 2 vols. Harrisburg: W.S. Ray, 1916.

Morris, Anne C., ed. *The Diary and Letters of Gouverneur Morris*. 2 vols. New York: Charles Scribner's Sons, 1882.

"Notes and Queries." *Pennsylvania Magazine of History and Biography* 37 (1913): 379–84.

List of Sources

Padgett, James A., ed. "Rumsey Documents." *Maryland Historical Magazine* 31 (1936): 185–89; 32 (1937): 10–28, 136–55, 271–85.

Padover, Saul K., ed. *Thomas Jefferson and the National Capital.* Washington, D.C.: Government Printing Office, 1946.

Reed, William B., ed. and comp. *The Life and Correspondence of Joseph Reed.* 2 vols. Philadelphia: Lindsay and Blakeston, 1847.

Richardson, James D., ed. *A Compilation of the Messages and Papers of the Presidents of the United States.* Vol. 1. New York: Bureau of National Literature, 1897.

Rutt, John T., ed. and comp. *Life and Correspondence of Joseph Priestley.* 2 vols. London: R. Hunter, et al., 1831–1832.

Silveus, Marian, ed. "McNair Correspondence: Land Problems in Northwestern Pennsylvania." *Western Pennsylvania Historical Magazine* 17 (1935): 237–54.

Smyth, Albert H., ed. *Writings of Benjamin Franklin.* 10 vols. New York: Macmillan Co., 1905–1907.

Sparks, Jared, ed. *Diplomatic Correspondence of the American Revolution.* 12 vols. Boston: Nathan Hale and Gray and Bowen, 1830.

————, ed. *The Writings of George Washington.* Vol. 12. Boston: Russell, Odeorne and Metcalf, 1835.

Syrett, Harold C., et al., eds. *The Papers of Alexander Hamilton.* 15 vols. New York: Columbia University Press, 1961–1969.

Turner, Frederick J., ed. "Correspondence of the French Ministers to the United States, 1791–1797." *Annual Report of the American Historical Association for the Year 1903* 2. Washington, D.C.: Government Printing Office, 1904.

Warfel, Harry, ed. *Letters of Noah Webster.* New York: Library Publishing Co., 1953.

"The Writings of George Washington Relating to the National Capital." *Columbia Historical Society Records* 17 (1914): 3–232.

Young, John R., ed. *Memorial History of the City of Philadelphia, 1681–1895.* New York: New York History Co., 1895–1898.

—Travel Accounts

Bailey, Francis. *Journal of a Tour in Unsettled Parts of North America in 1796 and 1797.* London: Bailey Brothers, 1856.

Birkbeck, Morris. *Notes on a Journey in America from the Coast of Virginia to the Territory of Illinois.* 3d ed. London: James Ridgway, 1818.

Brissot de Warville, J.P. *New Travels in the United States of America Performed in 1788.* Boston: J. Bumstead, 1797.

Cooper, Thomas. *Some Information Respecting America Collected by Thomas Cooper, Late of Manchester.* London: J. Johnson, 1794.

Crevecoeur, St. John de. *Eighteenth Century Travels in Pennsylvania and New York.* Translated and edited by Percy Adams. Lexington: University of Kentucky Press, 1961.

Dwight, Timothy. *Travels in New England and New York.* 4 vols. New Haven: T. Dwight, 1821–1822.

Imlay, Gilbert. *A Topographical Description of the Western Territory of North America.* New York: Samuel Campbell, 1796.

La Rochefoucault-Liancourt, Francis A. de. *Travels Through the United States of North America, the Country of the Iroquois and Upper Canada in the Years 1795, 1796, and 1797* . . . . 2d ed., 4 vols. London: T. Gillet, 1800.

Priest, William. *Travels in the United States of America.* London: J. Johnson, 1802.

List of Sources

St. Mery, Moreau de. *Moreau de St. Mery's American Journey (1793–1798)*. Translated and edited by Kenneth Roberts and Anna M. Roberts. Garden City, N.Y.: Doubleday and Co., 1947.

Twining, Thomas. *Travels in America 100 Years Ago*. New York: Harper and Brothers, 1893.

Wansey, Henry. *The Journal of an Excursion to the United States of North America in the Summer of 1794*. Salisbury: J. Easton, 1796.

Weld, Isaac. *Travels Through the States of North America and the Provinces of Upper and Lower Canada During the Years 1795, 1796 and 1797*. 2d ed., 2 vols. London: John Stockdale, 1799.

Winterbotham, William. *An Historical, Geographical, Commercial and Philosophical View of the United States of America and of the European Settlements in America and the West Indies*. 4 vols. London: J. Ridgway, H.D. Symonds and D. Holt, 1795.

—Reminiscences and Writings

Barton, William. *Memoirs of the Life of David Rittenhouse*. Philadelphia: Edward Parker, 1813.

Biddle, Charles. *Autobiography of Charles Biddle, Vice President of the Supreme Executive Council of Pennsylvania, 1745–1821*. Edited by James S. Biddle. Philadelphia: E. Claxton and Co., 1883.

Breck, Samuel. *Recollections of Samuel Breck with Passages from His Note Books, 1771–1862*. Edited by H.E. Scudder. Philadelphia: Porter and Coates, 1877.

Cazenove, Theophilus. *Cazenove Journal, 1794*. Edited by Rayner Kelsey. Haverford: Pennsylvania Historical Press, 1922.

Colt, Judah. "Judah Colt's Narrative." *Publications of the Buffalo Historical Society* 7 (1904).

Coxe, Tench. *A View of the United States of America . . . .* Philadelphia: Wrigley and Berriman, 1794.

Denny, Ebenezer. *Military Journal of Major Ebenezer Denny*. Philadelphia: J.B. Lippincott Co., 1859.

Drinker, Elizabeth. *Extracts from the Journal of Elizabeth Drinker*. Edited by Henry Biddle. Philadelphia: J.B. Lippincott Co., 1899.

Febiger, Christian. "Extracts of a Merchant's Letters, 1784–1786." *Magazine of American History* 7 (1882): 345–58.

Findley, William. "An Autobiographical Letter." *Pennsylvania Magazine of History and Biography* 5 (1881): 440–50.

Fisher, Joshua Francis. *Recollections*. Edited by Sophia Cadwalader. Boston: Privately Printed, 1929.

Graydon, Alexander. *Memoirs of a Life Chiefly Passed in Pennsylvania within the Last Sixty Years*. Harrisburg: John Wyeth, 1811.

Hiltzheimer, Jacob. *Extracts from the Diary of Jacob Hiltzheimer, of Philadelphia, 1765–1798*. Edited by Jacob Cox Parsons. Philadelphia: W.F. Fell and Co., 1893.

Latrobe, Benjamin H. *The Journal of Latrobe . . . .* Introduction by J.H.B. Latrobe. New York: Appleton Co., 1905.

Lincklaen, John. *Journals of John Lincklaen, Agent of the Holland Land Company*. New York: G.P. Putnam's Sons, 1897.

Maclay, William. *The Journal of William Maclay: United States Senator from Pennsylvania 1789–1791*. Edited by Edgar S. Maclay. New York: D. Appleton Co., 1890.

———. *Sketches of Debate in the First Senate of the United States*. Harrisburg: Lane S. Hart, 1880

Morris, Gouverneur. *A Diary of the French Revolution by Gouverneur*

List of Sources

Morris, 1752–1816. 2 vols. Edited by Beatrix Davenport. Boston: Houghton-Mifflin Co., 1939.

Priestley, Joseph. *Memoirs.* 2 vols. 1809. Reprint. London: Piper and Carter, 1893.

————. *The Memoirs of Dr. Joseph Priestley.* Edited by John Boyer. Washington: Barcroft Press, 1964.

Rush, Benjamin. *The Autobiography of Benjamin Rush: His Travels Through Life Together with His "Commonplace Book" for 1789–1813.* Edited with an introduction and notes by George W. Corner. Princeton: Princeton University Press, 1948.

————. *Essays, Literary, Moral and Philosophical.* Philadelphia: Thomas and William Bradford, 1794.

————. *A Memorial Containing Travels Through Life or Sundry Incidents in the Life of Dr. Benjamin Rush.* Philadelphia: Louis Biddle, 1905.

Smith, William L. "Journal of William Loughton Smith, 1790–1791." *Massachusetts Historical Society Proceedings* 51 (1917): 20–88.

Talleyrand, Prince de. *Memoirs.* 2 vols. Edited by Le Duc de Broglie. London: Griffith, Farren, Okedon and Welsh, 1891.

Webster, Pelatiah. *Political Essays on the Nature and Operation of Money, Public Finances.* Philadelphia: Cruckshank, 1791.

Wilkinson, General James. *Memoirs of My Own Times.* 3 vols. Philadelphia: Abraham Small, 1816.

Wood, William. *Personal Recollections of the Stage, Embracing Notices of Actors, Authors, and Auditors During a Period of Forty Years.* Philadelphia: Henry Carey Baird, 1855.

—Broadsides and Pamphlets

Bishop, Abraham. *Georgia Speculation Unveiled.* Hartford, Conn.: Elisha Babcock, 1797.

Georgia-Mississippi Company. *State of Facts Showing the Right of Certain Companies to the Lands Lately Purchased by Them for the State of Georgia.* Philadelphia: R. Aitken, 1795.

Harper, Robert Goodloe. *The Case of the Georgia Sales on the Mississippi, Considered with a Reference to Law Authorities and Public Acts.* Philadelphia: Francis Bailey, 1799.

Huidekoper, Harm Jan. *Remarks on the Late Proceedings of the Nicholson Commissioners, and on the Nicholson Lien in Relation to the Lands Formerly of the Pennsylvania Population Company.* Meadville, Pa.: The Author, 1842.

Nicholson, John. *An Address to the People of Pennsylvania.* Broadside reproduced in Evans, *Early American Imprints.* Philadelphia: Francis Bailey, 1790.

————. *Observations of the Committee of Land Owners . . . .* Philadelphia: Joseph James, 1788.

————. *A View of the Debts and Expenses of the Commonwealth of Pennsylvania.* Reproduced in Evans, *Early American Imprints.* Philadelphia: R. Aitken, 1786.

————. *A View of the Proposed Constitution of the United States.* Philadelphia: R. Aitken and Son, 1787.

Randolph, Edmund. *Interesting State Papers . . . .* London: J. Owen and W. Richardson, 1796.

————. *Political Truth: or Animadversions on the Past and Present State of Public Affairs with an Inquiry into the Truth of the Charges Preferred against Mr. Randolph.* Philadelphia: Samuel H. Smith, 1796.

List of Sources

————. *A Vindication of Mr. Randolph's Resignation.* Philadelphia: Samuel H. Smith, 1795.

—Corporation Accounts and Reports

Anthony, J.B. "Report of the Investigation of the Claims of the Commonwealth against the Estate of John Nicholson and Peter Baynton." *The Journal of Law* 1 (1830).

Bingham, R.W., ed. "Holland Land Company Papers, Reports of Joseph Ellicott." *Buffalo Historical Society Publications* (1937).

Pennsylvania Population Company Minute Books and Plan of Association. Compiled by the Works Progress Administration. Harrisburg: Pennsylvania Historical Commission, n.d.

"Plan of Association of the Asylum Company." Philadelphia: R. Aitken, 1797.

"Plan of Association of the North American Land Company." Philadelphia: R. Aitken and Son, 1795.

"Plan of Association of the Pennsylvania Land Company." Philadelphia: R. Aitken, 1797.

"Plan of Association of the Pennsylvania Property Company." Philadelphia: R. Aitken and Son, 1797.

"Plan of Association of the Territorial Land Company." Philadelphia: R. Aitken, 1795.

Smith, William. *An Historical Account of the Rise, Progress and Present State of Canal Navigation in Pennsylvania.* Philadelphia: Zachariah Poulson, Jr., 1805.

Taylor, Robert J., ed. *The Susquehannah Company Papers.* Vol. 7, 8. Ithaca, N.Y.: Cornell University Press, 1969.

SECONDARY SOURCES

GENERAL HISTORIES OF THE UNITED STATES

Billington, Ray Allen. *Westward Expansion, A History of the American Frontier.* 2d ed. New York: Macmillan Co., 1960.

————. *America's Frontier Heritage.* New York: Holt, Rinehart and Winston, 1966.

Breuning, Charles. *The Age of Revolution and Reaction, 1789–1850.* New York: W.W. Norton and Co., 1970.

Bruchey, Stuart. *The Roots of American Economic Growth, 1607–1861.* New York: Harper, 1968.

Channing, Edward. *A History of the United States.* Vol. 4. New York: Macmillan Co., 1917.

Clark, Thomas. *Frontier America: The Story of the Westward Movement.* 2d ed. New York: Charles Scribner's Sons, 1969.

Hession, Charles, and Sardy, Hyman. *Ascent to Affluence: A History of American Economic Development.* Boston: Allyn and Bacon, 1969.

Hildreth, Richard. *The History of the United States of America.* 6 vols. New York: Harpers, 1877–1900.

Kirkland, Edward. *A History of American Economic Life.* 4th ed. New York: Appleton-Century-Crofts, 1961.

McMaster, John Bach. *A History of the People of the United States, from Revolution to the Civil War.* 8 vols. New York: Appleton and Co., 1895.

List of Sources

Palmer, Robert R. *The Age of the Democratic Revolution, A Political History of Europe and America, 1760–1800.* 2 vols. Princeton: Princeton University Press, 1964.

MONOGRAPHS AND SPECIAL STUDIES ON THE UNITED STATES

Abernethy, Thomas P. *From Frontier to Plantation in Tennessee.* Chapel Hill: University of North Carolina Press, 1932.
————. *Western Lands and the American Revolution.* New York: D. Appleton-Century Co., 1937.
Bagnall, William R. *The Textile Industries of the United States.* Cambridge, Mass.: H.O. Houghton and Co., 1893.
Beard, Charles A. *The Economic Origins of Jeffersonian Democracy.* New York: Macmillan Co., 1915.
Bemis, Samuel Flagg. *Jay's Treaty: A Study in Commerce and Diplomacy.* 2d ed. New Haven: Yale University Press, 1962.
Bond, Beverley. *The Civilization of the Old Northwest: A Study of Political, Social, and Economic Development, 1788–1812.* New York: Macmillan Co., 1934.
Bowen, Catherine D. *Miracle at Philadelphia: The Story of the Constitutional Convention.* Boston: Little, Brown and Co., 1966.
Bryan, Wilhelmus Bogart. *A History of the National Capital from Its Foundation Through the Period of the Adoption of the Organic Act.* 2 vols. New York: Macmillan Co., 1914–1916.
Caemmerer, H. Paul. *Washington, the National Capital.* Washington, D.C.: Government Printing Office, 1932.
Childs, Frances. *French Refugee Life in the United States, 1790–1800.* Baltimore: Johns Hopkins Press, 1940.
Clark, Allen C. *Greenleaf and Law in the Federal City.* Washington, D.C.: W.F. Roberts, 1901.
Clark, Victor S. *History of Manufactures in the United States, 1607–1860.* Vol. 1. Washington, D.C.: Carnegie Institution of Washington, 1921.
Clarke, T. Wood. *Emigrés in the Wilderness.* New York: Macmillan Co., 1941.
Cleland, George. *George Washington in the Ohio Valley.* Pittsburgh: University of Pittsburgh Press, 1955.
Cook, Roy Bird. *Washington's Western Lands.* Strasburg, Va.: Shenandoah Publishing House, 1930.
Coulter, E. Merton. *Georgia: A Short History.* Rev. ed. Chapel Hill: University of North Carolina Press, 1947.
Cunningham, Noble E. *The Jeffersonian Republicans: the Formation of Party Organization, 1789–1801.* Chapel Hill: University of North Carolina Press, 1957.
Davis, Joseph S. *Essays in the Earlier History of American Corporations.* 2 vols. Cambridge: Harvard University Press, 1917.
Dorfman, Joseph. *The Economic Mind in American Civilization, 1606–1865.* Vol 1. New York: The Viking Press, 1953.
Durrenberger, Joseph A. *Turnpikes: A Study of the Toll Road Movement in the Middle Atlantic States and Maryland.* 1931. Reprint. Cos Cob, Conn.: John E. Edwards, 1968.
East, Robert A. *Business Enterprise in the American Revolutionary Era.* New York: Columbia University Press, 1938.
Eberlein, Harold D., and Hubbard, Cortlandt Van Dyke. *Diary of Independence Hall.* Philadelphia: J.B. Lippincott Co., 1948.

List of Sources

Evans, Paul D. *The Holland Land Company*. Buffalo: Buffalo Historical Society, 1924.

Faris, John. *The Romance of Forgotten Towns*. New York: Harper and Brothers, 1924.

Fay, Bernard. *The Revolutionary Spirit in France and America*. New York: Harcourt, Brace and Co., 1927.

Ferguson, E. James. *The Power of the Purse: A History of American Public Finance, 1776–1790*. Chapel Hill: University of North Carolina Press, 1961.

Flexner, James T. *Steamboats Come True: American Inventors in Action*. New York: The Viking Press, 1944.

Goodrich, Carter. *Government Promotion of American Canals and Railroads, 1800–1890*. New York: Columbia University Press, 1960.

Green, Constance. *Washington: Village and Capital, 1800–1878*. Vol. 1. Princeton: Princeton University Press, 1962.

Griswold, Rufus W. *The Republican Court or American Society in the Days of Washington*. New York: D. Appleton and Co., 1855.

Gutheim, Frederick. *The Potomac*. New York: Rinehart and Co., 1949.

Hammond, Bray. *Banks and Politics in America, from the Revolution to the Civil War*. Princeton: Princeton University Press, 1957.

Haskins, Charles. *The Yazoo Land Companies*. New York: The Knickbocker Press, 1891.

Hazen, Charles. *Contemporary American Opinion of the French Revolution*. 1897. Reprint. Gloucester, Mass.: Peter Smith, 1964.

Hibbard, Benjamin H. *A History of the Public Land Policies*. New York: Peter Smith, 1939.

Hidy, Ralph W. *The House of Baring in American Trade and Finance*. Cambridge: Harvard University Press, 1949.

Jensen, Merrill. *The New Nation, a History of the United States During the Confederation, 1781–1789*. New York: Alfred Knopf, 1958.

Kite, Elizabeth S. *L'Enfant and Washington, 1791–1792*. Baltimore: Johns Hopkins Press, 1929.

Krout, John Allen, and Fox, Dixon. *The Completion of Independence, 1790–1830*. New York: Macmillan Co., 1944.

Link, Eugene Perry. *Democratic-Republican Societies, 1790–1830*. New York: Columbia University Press, 1942.

Livermore, Shaw. *Early American Land Companies*. New York: Oxford Press, 1939.

McDonald, Forrest. *E Pluribus Unum: The Formation of the American Republic, 1776–1790*. Boston: Houghton-Mifflin Co., 1965.

————. *We the People: The Economic Origins of the Constitution*. Chicago: University of Chicago Press, 1958.

McLendon, S.G. *History of the Public Domain of Georgia*. Atlanta: Foote and Davis Co., 1924.

McNall, Neil A. *An Agricultural History of the Genesee Valley, 1790–1860*. Philadelphia: University of Pennsylvania Press, 1952.

Magrath, C. Peter. *Yazoo: Law and Politics in the New Republic, The Case of Fletcher v. Peck*. Providence, R.I.: Brown University Press, 1966.

Main, Jackson T. *The Anti-Federalists, Critics of the Constitution, 1781–1788*. Chapel Hill: University of North Carolina Press, 1961.

Mathews, Alfred. *Ohio and Her Western Reserve*. New York: D. Appleton and Co., 1902.

Miller, John C. *The Federalist Era, 1789–1801*. New York: Harper and Row, 1963.

List of Sources

Morrison, John. *History of American Steam Navigation.* New York: Stephen Daye Press, 1958.

Nettels, Curtis. *The Emergence of a National Economy, 1775–1815.* New York: Holt, Rinehart and Winston, 1962.

Nevins, Allan. *The American States During and After the Revolution.* New York: Macmillan Co., 1924.

Newell, Frederick H. *Planning and Building the City of Washington.* Washington, D.C.: Washington Society of Engineers, 1932.

Nicolay, Helen. *Our Capital on the Potomac.* New York: The Century Co., 1924.

Page, Thomas N. *Washington and Its Romance.* New York: Doubleday, Page and Company, 1923.

Philbrick, Francis S. *The Rise of the West, 1754–1830.* New York: Harper and Row, 1965.

Phillips, P. Lee. *The Beginnings of Washington as Described in Books, Maps and Views.* Washington, D.C.: The Author, 1917.

Prucha, Francis Paul. *The Sword of the Republic, The United States Army on the Frontier, 1783–1846.* Toronto: Collier-Macmillan Co., 1969.

Reps, John. *The Making of Urban America.* Princeton: Princeton University Press, 1965.

———. *Monumental Washington: the Planning and Development of the Capital Center.* Princeton: Princeton University Press, 1967.

Robbins, Roy M. *Our Landed Heritage: The Public Domain, 1776–1936.* Princeton: Princeton University Press, 1942.

Rose, Lisle A. *Prologue to Democracy, the Federalists in the South 1789–1800.* Lexington: University of Kentucky Press, 1968.

Rosengarten, J.G. *French Colonists and Exiles in the United States.* Philadelphia: J.B. Lippincott Co., 1907.

Rossiter, Clinton. *1787: The Grand Convention.* New York: Macmillan Co., 1966.

Rutland, Robert A. *The Ordeal of the Constitution, the Anti-Federalists and the Ratification Struggle of 1787–1788.* Norman: University of Oklahoma Press, 1965.

Sakolski, Aaron M. *The Great American Land Bubble: The Amazing Story of Land-Grabbing, Speculations, and Booms from Colonial Days to the Present Time.* New York: Harper and Brothers, 1932.

Sherrill, Charles. *French Memoirs of the Eighteenth Century.* New York: Charles Scribner's Sons, 1915.

Smith, George. *The Story of Georgia and the Georgia People, 1732 to 1800.* Macon, Ga.: George Smith, 1900.

Stanwood, Edward. *A History of the Presidency from 1788–1897.* 2 vols. 4th ed. Boston: Charles Bolton, 1928.

Stewart, Donald. *The Opposition Press of the Federalist Period.* Albany: State University of New York Press, 1969.

Swiggett, Howard. *The Forgotten Leaders of the Revolution.* New York: Doubleday and Co., 1955.

Thompson, Holland. *The Age of Invention: A Chronicle of Mechanical Conquest. Yale Chronicles of America Series,* vol. 38. New Haven: Yale University Press, 1921.

Tindall, William. *Origins and Government of the District of Columbia.* Washington, D.C.: Government Printing Office, 1908.

Treat, Payson Jackson. *The National Land System, 1785–1820.* New York: E.B. Treat and Co., 1910.

List of Sources

Tryon, Rolla M. *Household Manufactures in the United States, 1640–1860.* 1917. Reprint. New York: August Kelley, 1966.

Turner, Orasmus. *History of the Pioneer Settlement of Phelps and Gorham's Purchase and Morris Reserve.* Rochester, New York: William Alling, 1851.

Van Doren, Carl. *The Great Rehearsal, the Story of the Making and Ratifying of the Constitution of the United States.* New York: Viking Press, 1948.

Van Every, Dale. *Ark of Empire: The American Frontier, 1784–1803.* New York: William Morrow and Co., 1963.

Warren, Charles. *The Supreme Court in United States History.* 2 vols. Rev. ed. Boston: Little, Brown and Co., 1935.

Wharton, Anne H. *Social Life in the Early Republic.* Philadelphia: J.B. Lippincott Co., 1902.

Whitaker, Arthur P. *The Spanish American Frontier, 1783–1795.* Boston: Houghton-Mifflin, 1927.

Wright, Benjamin. *The Contract Clause of the Constitution.* Cambridge: Harvard University Press, 1938.

Young, Alfred F. *The Democratic-Republicans of New York: The Origins, 1763–1797.* Chapel Hill: University of North Carolina Press, 1967.

BIOGRAPHIES

Beltzhoover, George M., Jr. *James Rumsey, the Inventor of the Steamboat.* Philadelphia: J.B. Lippincott and Company for the West Virginia Historical and Antiquarian Society, 1900.

Bernhard, Winfred E.A. *Fisher Ames, Federalist and Statesman, 1758–1808.* Chapel Hill: University of North Carolina Press, 1965.

Beveridge, Albert J. *The Life of John Marshall.* 4 vols. Boston: Houghton-Mifflin Co., 1916–1919.

Bowers, Claude G. *Jefferson and Hamilton: The Struggle for Democracy in America.* Boston: Houghton-Mifflin Co., 1925.

Boyd, Thomas. *Poor John Fitch, Inventor of the Steamboat.* New York: G.P. Putnam's Sons, 1935.

Brant, Irving. *James Madison.* 6 vols. Indianapolis: Bobbs-Merrill, 1950.

Caemmerer, H. Paul. *The Life of Pierre Charles L'Enfant, Planner of the City Beautiful, The City of Washington.* Washington, D.C.: National Republic Publishing Co., 1950.

Clarifield, Gerard H. *Timothy Pickering and American Diplomacy, 1795–1800.* Columbia: University of Missouri Press, 1969.

Conway, Moncure D. *Omitted Chapters of History Disclosed in the Life and Papers of Edmund Randolph.* New York: G.P. Putnam's Sons, 1888.

Cooke, Jacob, ed. *Alexander Hamilton: A Profile.* New York: Hill and Wang, 1967.

Cowan, Helen I. *Charles Williamson, Genesee Promoter–Friend of Anglo-American Rapprochemont.* Rochester: Rochester Historical Society, 1941.

Destler, Chester. *Joshua Coit, American Federalist, 1758–1798.* Middletown, Conn.: Wesleyan University Press, 1962.

Dickinson, Henry W. *Robert Fulton, Engineer and Artist.* New York: The Century Co., 1925.

Freeman, Douglas S. *George Washington, A Biography.* 7 vols., the last

volume completed by John A. Carroll and Mary W. Ashworth. New
York: Charles Scribner's Sons, 1948–1957.
Greenleaf, James Edward. *Genealogy of the Greenleaf Family.* Boston:
Privately Printed, 1896.
Malone, Dumas, *Jefferson and His Time.* 5 vols. Boston: Little, Brown
and Co., 1948–1971.
Masterson, William Henry. *William Blount.* Baton Rouge: Louisiana
State University Press, 1954.
Miller, John C. *Alexander Hamilton and the Growth of the New Nation.*
New York: Harper and Row, 1964.
Neel, Joanne Loewe. *Phineas Bond, A Study in Anglo-American Relations,
1786–1812.* Philadelphia: University of Pennsylvania Press, 1968.
Parmet, Herbert, and Hecht, Marie. *Aaron Burr, Portrait of an Ambitious
Man.* New York: Macmillan Co., 1967.
Sutcliffe, Alice Crary. *Robert Fulton and the Clermont.* New York: The
Century Co., 1909.
Turner, Ella May. *James Rumsey, Pioneer in Steam Navigation.* Scottdale,
Pa.: Mennonite Publishing Company, 1930.
Wandell, Samuel, and Minningerode, Meade. *Aaron Burr.* New York:
G.P. Putnam's Sons, 1927.
Welch, Richard. *Theodore Sedgwick, Federalist: A Political Portrait.*
Middletown, Conn.: Wesleyan University Press, 1965.
Westcott, Thompson. *Life of John Fitch, the Inventor of the Steamboat.*
Philadelphia: J.B. Lippincott Co., 1857.
Woodward, W.E. *George Washington: The Image and the Man.* New
York: Harper and Brothers, 1926.

ARTICLES ON UNITED STATES HISTORY

Adams, Herbert. "Washington's Interest in Western Lands." *Johns Hop-
kins University Studies in Historical and Political Science* 3. Baltimore,
1885.
Bates, Whitney. "Northern Speculators and Southern State Debts: 1790."
William and Mary Quarterly 19. 3d ser. 19 (January 1962): 30–48.
Belote, Theodore T. "The Scioto Speculation and the French Settlement at
Gallipolis." *University of Cincinnati Studies* 3. 2d ser. (1907).
Billington, Ray A. "The Origin of the Land Speculator as a Frontier
Type." *Agricultural History* 19 (1948): 204–12.
Bishop, Morris. "Louis Philippe in America." *American Heritage* 20
(April 1969): 43–45, 90–97.
Bogue, Allan, and Bogue, Margaret. " 'Profits' and the Frontier Land
Speculator." *Journal of Economic History* 17 (1957): 1–24.
Brant, Irving. "Edmund Randolph, Not Guilty!" *William and Mary Quar-
terly* 7. 3d ser. (April 1950): 180–98.
Brock, W.R. "The Ideas and Influence of Alexander Hamilton." In *The
American Scene* 1, edited by Robert Marcus and David Burnes. New
York: Appleton-Century-Crofts, 1971.
Bruchey, Stuart. "Alexander Hamilton and the State Banks, 1789 to
1795." *William and Mary Quarterly* 27 (July 1970): 347–78.
Carleton, Frank. "The Abolition of Imprisonment for Debt in the United
States." *The Yale Review* 17 (1908–1909): 338–44.
Charles, Joseph. "Hamilton and Washington: The Origins of the American

Party System." *William and Mary Quarterly* 12. 3d ser. (1955): 217–67.

Clark, Allen C. "Daniel Carroll of Duddington." *Records of the Columbia Historical Society* 39 (1938): 1–48.

——. "Origin of the Federal City." *Records of the Columbia Historical Society* 36 (1935): 1–97.

Cotterill, R.S. "The National Land System in the South, 1803–1812." *Mississippi Valley Historical Review* 16 (March 1930): 495–506.

Elkins, Stanley, and McKitrick, Eric. "The Founding Fathers: Young Men of the Revolution." *Political Science Quarterly* 76 (June 1961): 181–216.

Evans, Paul D. "The Pulteney Purchase." *Quarterly Journal of the New York State Historical Association* 3 (April 1922): 83–104.

Ferguson, E. James. "State Assumption of the Federal Debt During the Confederation." *Mississippi Valley Historical Review* 38 (December 1951): 403–24.

Gates, Paul. "The Role of the Land Speculator in Western Development." *The Pennsylvania Magazine of History and Biography* 66 (July 1942): 314–33.

Gosnell, H.A. "The First American Steamboat: James Rumsey Its Inventor Not John Fitch." *Virginia Magazine of History and Biography* 40 (1932): 14–22,

Haskins, Charles. "The Yazoo Land Companies." *American Historical Association Papers* 5 (January, April 1891): 395–437.

Hulbert, Archer. "The Methods and Operations of the Scioto Group of Speculators." *Mississippi Valley Historical Review* 1 (March 1915): 502–15; and 2 (June 1915): 56–73.

Kenny, Lawrence. "The Gallipolis Colony." *Catholic Historical Review* 4 (1918–1919): 415–51.

Kenyon, Cecelia. "Men of Little Faith: The Anti-Federalists on the Nature of Representative Government." *William and Mary Quarterly* 12. 3d ser. (January 1955): 3–43.

Mason, Bernard. "Alexander Hamilton and the Report on Manufactures: A Suggestion!" *Pennsylvania History* 32 (1965): 288–94.

Miller, William. "First Fruits of Republican Organization." *Pennsylvania Magazine of History and Biography* 63 (April 1939): 118–43.

Rezneck, Samuel. "The Rise and Early Development of Industrial Consciousness in the United States, 1760–1830." *Journal of Economic and Business History* 4 (1932): 784–811.

Werner, Raymond C. "War Scare and Politics, 1794." *Quarterly Journal of the New York State Historical Association* 11 (1930): 324–34.

Wettereau, James O. "Letters From Two Business Men to Alexander Hamilton on Federal Fiscal Policy, November 1789." *Journal of Economic and Business History* 3 (August 1931): 667–86.

GENERAL HISTORIES OF THE COMMONWEALTH OF PENNSYLVANIA

Bolles, Albert S. *Pennsylvania, Province and State, a History From 1609 to 1790.* 2 vols. New York: J. Wanamaker, 1899.

Dunaway, Wayland. *A History of Pennsylvania.* New York: Prentice-Hall, 1948.

Works Progress Association. *Pennsylvania: A Guide to the Keystone State.* New York: Oxford University Press, 1940.

List of Sources

COUNTY AND REGIONAL HISTORIES

Agnew, Daniel. *A History of the Region of Pennsylvania North of the Ohio and West of the Allegheny River* . . . . Philadelphia: Kay and Brothers, 1887.

Bausman, Joseph H. *History of Beaver County, Pennsylvania.* 2 vols. New York: The Knickerbocker Press, 1904.

Blackman, Emily C. *History of Susquehanna County.* Philadelphia: Claxton, Remsen et al., 1873.

Bradsby, H.C. *History of Bradford County, Pennsylvania.* Chicago: S.B. Nelson and Co., 1891.

Brenckman, Fred. *History of Carbon County.* Harrisburg: J.J. Nungesser, 1913.

Buck, Solon, and Buck, Elizabeth. *The Planting of Civilization in Western Pennsylvania.* Pittsburgh: University of Pittsburgh Press, 1939.

Craft, David. *History of Bradford County, Pennsylvania.* Philadelphia: J.B. Lippincott Co., 1878.

Downes, Randolph. *Council Fires on the Upper Ohio.* Pittsburgh: University of Pittsburgh Press, 1940.

Huidekoper, Alfred. *Incidents in the Early History of Crawford County.* Philadelphia: Pennsylvania Historical Society, 1850.

Jackson, Joseph. *Encyclopedia of Philadelphia.* 4 vols. Harrisburg: National Historical Association, 1931–1933.

Mombert, J.I. *Authentic History of Lancaster County in the State of Pennsylvania.* Lancaster, Pa.: Lancaster County Historical Society, 1868.

Montgomery, Morton. *History of Berks County in the Revolution From 1774–1783.* Philadelphia: Everts, Peck and Richards, 1886.

Nolan, J. Bennett. *Early Narratives of Berks County.* Reading, Pa.: Historical Society of Berks County, 1927 .

Oberholtzer, Ellis P. *Philadedphia, A History of the City and Its People, A Record of 255 Years.* 4 vols. Philadelphia: S.J. Clarke Co., 1911.

Reynolds, John Earle. *In French Creek Valley.* Meadville, Pa.: Crawford County Historical Society, 1938.

Riesenman, Joseph. *History of Northwestern Pennsylvania.* Vol. 1. New York: Lewis Historical Publishing Co., 1943.

Westcott, Thompson. *The Historic Mansions and Buildings of Philadelphia.* Philadelphia: Porter and Coates, 1877.

MONOGRAPHS AND SPECIAL STUDIES
ON THE COMMONWEALTH OF PENNSYLVANIA

Baldwin, Leland D. *Whiskey Rebels, The Story of a Frontier Uprising.* Pittsburgh: University of Pittsburgh Press, 1939.

Barnes, Harry. *The Evolution of Penology in Pennsylvania.* Indianapolis: Bobbs-Merrill, 1927.

Bining, Arthur. *Pennsylvania Iron Manufacture in the Eighteenth Century.* Harrisburg: Pennsylvania Historical Commission, 1938.

Brunhouse, Robert L. *The Counter-Revolution in Pennsylvania, 1776–1790.* Harrisburg: Pennsylvania Historical Commission, 1942.

Carmer, Carl. *The Susquehanna.* New York: Rinehart and Co., 1955.

Ferguson, Russell. *Early Western Pennsylvania Politics.* Pittsburgh: University of Pittsburgh Press, 1938.

Hartz, Louis. *Economic Policy and Democratic Thought: Pennsylvania, 1776–1860.* Cambridge: Harvard University Press, 1948.

List of Sources

Jordan, Mildred. *Asylum for the Queen*. New York: Alfred Knopf, 1948.
Kehl, James. *Ill Feeling in an Era of Good Feeling*. Pittsburgh: University of Pittsburgh Press, 1951.
Klein, Theodore B. *The Canals of Pennsylvania and the System of Internal Improvements*. Harrisburg: Pennsylvania Historical Commission, 1901.
Kussart, S. *The Allegheny River*. Pittsburgh: Burgum Printing Co., 1938.
Lewis, John F. *An Old Philadelphia Land Title*. Philadelphia: Patterson and White Co., 1934.
Lewis, Lawrence. *History of the Bank of North America*. Philadelphia: J.B. Lippincott Co., 1882.
Livingood, James Weston. *The Philadelphia-Baltimore Trade Rivalry, 1780–1860*. Harrisburg: The Pennsylvania Historical Commission, 1947.
McMaster, John Bach and Stone, Frederick D. *Pennsylvania and the Federal Constitution*. Philadelphia: Historical Society of Pennsylvania, 1888.
Murray, Elsie. *Azilum, French Refugee Colony of 1793*. Athens, Pa.: Tioga Point Museum, 1940.
———. *A Frontier Trianon*. Athens, Pa.: Tioga Point Museum, 1955.
Murray, Louise Welles. *The Story of Some French Refugees and Their "Azilum," 1793–1800*. Athens, Pa.: Tioga Point Historical Society, 1903.
Myers, Richmond E. *The Long Crooked River*. Boston: Christopher Publishing House, 1949.
Nolan, J. Bennett. *The Schuylkill*. New Brunswick, N.J.: Rutgers University Press, 1951.
Plummer, Wilbur C. *Road Policy of Pennsylvania*. Philadelphia: University of Pennsylvania Press, 1925.
Powell, John H. *Bring Out Your Dead: The Great Plague of Yellow Fever in Philadelphia in 1793*. Philadelphia: University of Pennsylvania Press, 1949.
Selsam, J. Paul. *The Pennsylvania Constitution of 1776*. Philadelphia: University of Pennsylvania Press, 1936.
Shepard, William R. *The Land System of Provincial Pennsylvania*. Washington, D.C.: The American Historical Association, 1895.
Singmaster, Elsie. *Pennsylvania's Susquehanna*. Harrisburg: J. Horace McFarland Co., 1950.
Sipe, C. Hale. *The Indian Wars of Pennsylvania*. Harrisburg: The Telegraph Press, 1931.
Thayer, Theodore. *Pennsylvania Politics and the Growth of Democracy, 1740–1776*. Harrisburg: Pennsylvania Historical and Museum Commission, 1953.
Thomas, E. Bruce. *Political Tendencies in Pennsylvania, 1738–1794*. Philadelphia: n.p., 1938.
Tinkcom, Harry M. *Republicans and Federalists in Pennsylvania, 1790–1801*. Harrisburg: Pennsylvania Historical and Museum Commission, 1950.

BIOGRAPHIES OF PENNSYLVANIANS

Adams, Henry. *The Life of Albert Gallatin*. Philadelphia: J.B. Lippincott Co., 1879.
Alberts, Robert C. *The Golden Voyage: The Life and Times of William Bingham, 1752–1804*. Boston: Houghton-Mifflin Co., 1969.

List of Sources

Bathe, Dorothy, and Bathe, Grenville. *Oliver Evans, A Chronicle of Early American Engineering*. Philadelphia: Historical Society of Pennsylvania, 1935.

Biner, Carl. *Revolutionary Doctor, Benjamin Rush (1746–1831)*. New York: W.W. Norton, 1966.

Burt, Nathaniel, *The Perennial Philadelphians*. Boston: Little, Brown and Co., 1963.

Fay, Bernard. *The Two Franklins: Fathers of American Democracy*. Boston: Little, Brown and Co., 1933.

Hindle, Brooke. *David Rittenhouse*. Princeton: Princeton University Press, 1964.

Hutcheson, Harold. *Tench Coxe: A Study in American Economic Development*. Baltimore: Johns Hopkins Press, 1938.

Konkle, Burton. *George Bryan and the Constitution of Pennsylvania, 1731–1791*. Philadelphia: University of Pennsylvania Press, 1922.

———. *Joseph Hopkinson*. Philadelphia: University of Pennsylvania Press, 1931.

———. *The Life and Times of Thomas Smith, 1745–1809*. Philadelphia: Champion and Co., 1904.

———. *Thomas Willing and the First American Financial System*. Philadelphia: University of Pennsylvania Press, 1937.

Malone, Dumas. *The Public Life of Thomas Cooper*. New Haven: Yale University Press, 1926.

Oberholtzer, Ellis P. *Robert Morris, Patriot and Financier*. New York: Macmillan Co., 1903.

Roche, John F. *Joseph Reed, A Moderate in the American Revolution*. New York: Columbia University Press, 1957.

Rossman, Kenneth R. *Thomas Mifflin and the Politics of the American Revolution*. Chapel Hill: University of North Carolina Press, 1952.

Simpson, Henry. *The Lives of Eminent Philadelphians*. Philadelphia: William Brotherhead, 1859.

Smith, Charles P. *James Wilson: Founding Father, 1742–1798*. Chapel Hill: University of North Carolina Press, 1956.

Stevens, John. *The Life of Albert Gallatin*. Boston: Houghton-Mifflin Co., 1898.

Sumner, William G. *The Financier and the Finances of the American Revolution*. 2 vols. New York: Dodd, Mead and Co., 1892.

Tiffany, Nina, and Tiffany, Francis. *Harm Jan Huidekoper*. Cambridge: Riverside Press, 1904.

Tolles, Frederick. *George Logan of Philadelphia*. New York: Oxford University Press, 1953.

Ver Steeg, Clarence L. *Robert Morris, Revolutionary Financier*. Philadelphia: University of Pennsylvania Press, 1954.

Walters, Raymond. *Alexander James Dallas: Lawyer-Politician-Financier*. Philadelphia: University of Pennsylvania Press, 1943.

———. *Albert Gallatin, Jeffersonian Financier and Diplomat*. New York: Macmillan Co., 1957.

Young, Eleanor. *Forgotten Patriot, Robert Morris*. New York: Macmillan Co., 1950.

ARTICLES ON PENNSYLVANIA HISTORY

Anspach, Marshall. "The Sunbury Case." *Northumberland County Historical Society Proceedings* 19 (1952): 103–18.

List of Sources

Baldridge, Edwin R., Jr. "Talleyrand's Visit to Pennsylvania, 1794–1796." *Pennsylvania History* 36 (April 1969): 145–60.

Brown, Margaret L. "William Bingham, Eighteenth Century Magnate." *Pennsylvania Magazine of History and Biography* 61 (October 1937): 387–434.

Butterfield, Lyman H. "The Milliner's Mission in 1775; Or the British Seize a Treasonable Letter from Dr. Benjamin Rush." *William and Mary Quarterly* 7. 3d ser., (1951): 192–203.

Craft, David. "A Day at Asylum, Pennsylvania." *Proceedings and Collections of the Wyoming Historical and Geological Society* 7 (1902): 1–10.

———. "The French Settlement of Asylum" *Proceedings and Collections of the Wyoming Historical and Geological Society* 5 (1900): 75–110.

Cumming, John. "George Burges and the Erie Triangle." *Western Pennsylvania Historical Magazine* 49 (July 1966): 231–50.

Daniel, Warren. "Large Areas of Unpatented Land in Pennsylvania." *Pennsylvania Department of Internal Affairs Bulletin* 13 (1945): 9–15.

Earl, John L., III. "Talleyrand in Philadelphia, 1794–1796." *Pennsylvania Magazine of History and Biography* 91 (July 1967): 282–98.

Hale, R. Nelson. "The Pennsylvania Population Company." *Pennsylvania History* 16 (1949): 122–30.

Hartman, J. Lee. "Pennsylvania's Grand Plan of Post-Revolutionary Internal Improvements." *Pennsylvania Magazine of History and Biography* 65 (October 1941): 439–57.

Henderson, Elizabeth K. "The Northwestern Lands of Pennsylvania." *Pennsylvania Magazine of History and Biography* 60 (1936): 131–60.

Hughes, George. "The Pioneer Iron Industry in Western Pennsylvania." *Western Pennsylvania Historical Magazine* 14 (1931): 207–24.

Klein, Philip S. "Senator William Maclay." *Pennsylvania History* 10 (April 1943): 83–93.

Landis, Charles I. "The First Long Turnpike in the United States." *Papers of the Lancaster Historical Society* 20 (1916): 205–58.

———. "History of the Philadelphia and Lancaster Turnpike." *Pennsylvania Magazine of History and Biography* 42 (1918): passim.

McClintock, Walter. "Title Difficulties of the Holland Land Company in Northwestern Pennsylvania." *Western Pennsylvania Historical Magazine* 21 (1938): 119–38.

Malone, Dumas. "The First Years of Thomas Cooper in America." *South Atlantic Quarterly* 22 (April 1923): 139–56.

Miller, William. "The Democratic Societies and the Whiskey Insurrection." *Pennsylvania Magazine of History and Biography* 62 (July 1938): 324–49.

Murray, Elsie. "Early Land Companies and Titles of Northumberland County." *The Northumberland County Historical Society Proceedings* 20 (1954): 16–33.

"Northern Boundary of Pennsylvania—Middle of Lake Erie." *Pennsylvania Department of Internal Affairs Bulletin* 13 (1945): 17–19.

Oberholtzer, Ellis P. "A Great Philadelphian: Robert Morris." *Pennsylvania Magazine of History and Biography* 28 (1904): 273–94.

Peeling, James H. "Governor McKean and the Pennsylvania Jacobins, 1779–1808." *Pennsylvania Magazine of History and Biography* 54 (1930): 320–54.

Risch, Erna. "Immigrant Aid Societies Before 1820." *Pennsylvania Magazine of History and Biography* 60 (January 1936): 16–27.

List of Sources

Rossman, Kenneth. "Thomas Mifflin—Revolutionary Patriot." *Pennsylvania History* 15 (1948): 9–23.
Sakolski, Aaron M. "Robert Morris, Patriot and Bankrupt." *Nation's Business* 18 (April 1930): 36–38, 302–6.
Walters, Raymond, Jr. "The Making of a Financier: Albert Gallatin in the Pennsylvania Assembly." *Pennsylvania Magazine of History and Biography* 70 (July 1946): 258–69.
———. "The Origins of the Jeffersonian Party in Pennsylvania." *Pennsylvania Magazine of History and Biography* 61 (October 1942): 440–58.
Winner, John E. "Depreciation and Donation Lands." *Western Pennsylvania Historical Magazine* 8 (1925): 1–11.
Woodbury, Margaret. "Public Opinion in Philadelphia, 1789–1801." *Smith College Studies* 5. Northampton, Mass., 1920.

UNPUBLISHED DISSERTATIONS AND THESES

Arbuckle, Robert D. "John Nicholson, 1757–1800, A Case Study of an Early American Land Speculator, Financier and Entrepreneur." Ph.D. dissertation, The Pennsylvania State University, 1972.
Bates, Whitney. "The Assumption of State Debts, 1783–1793." Ph.D. dissertation, University of Wisconsin, 1951.
Bauer, George. "The Movement Against Imprisonment for Debt in the United States." Ph.D. dissertation, Harvard University, 1935.
Baumann, Roland. "The Democratic-Republicans of Philadelphia: The Origins, 1776–1797." Ph.D. dissertation, The Pennsylvania State University, 1970.
Bivens, Harry R. "The Disposition of Lands in Provincial Pennsylvania." M.A. thesis, Pennsylvania State College, 1932.
Felton, Paul. "Alexander Hamilton's Indebtedness to Robert Morris For His Financial Policy." M.A. thesis, University of Pittsburgh, 1932.
Filippelli, Ronald Lee. "The Schuylkill Navigation Company and Its Role in the Development of the Anthracite Coal Trade and Schuylkill County." M.A. thesis, The Pennsylvania State University, 1966.
Fullerton, Elizabeth M. "Colonel Daniel Brodhead." M.A. thesis, University of Pittsburgh, 1931.
Hale, Robert N. "Pennsylvania Population Company." Ph.D. dissertation, University of Pittsburgh, 1951.
Ireland, Owen. "The Ratification of the Federal Constitution in Pennsylvania." Ph.D. dissertation, University of Pittsburgh, 1966.
Keith, Alice Barnwell. "Three North Carolina Blount Brothers in Business and Politics." Ph.D. dissertation, University of North Carolina, 1940.
Keller, William F. "American Politics and the Genet Mission." Ph.D. dissertation, University of Pittsburgh, 1951.
Peeling, James H. "The Public Life of Thomas McKean, 1734–1817." Ph.D. dissertation, University of Chicago, 1929.
Peters, Barbara. "Judah Colt, Connecticut Yankee in the Erie Triangle." M.A. thesis, University of Pittsburgh, 1937.
Quattrocchi, Anna. "James Wilson, A Study in Portraits." M.A. thesis, University of Pittsburgh, 1931.
Ritchie, Carey. "A Study of Some Important Laws Enacted By the Pennsylvania Legislature, 1790–1801." M.A. thesis, University of Pittsburgh, 1930.

List of Sources

Ruddy, Joseph C. "The Policy of Land Distribution in Pennsylvania Since 1779." M.A. thesis, Pennsylvania State College, 1933.

Walsh, Mary L. "The Legal and Public Career of Alexander James Dallas." M.A. thesis, University of Pittsburgh, 1935.

Wilkinson, Norman B. "Land Policy and Speculation in Pennsylvania, 1779–1800." Ph.D. dissertation, University of Pennsylvania, 1958.

Winpenny, Thomas. "William Bingham's Pennsylvania Land Operations, 1792–1804." M.A. thesis, Pennsylvania State University, 1965.

Zoller, Lucille. "The French Settlement of Asylum, Pennsylvania." M.A. thesis, University of Pittsburgh, 1919.

INDEX

Index

Index

Huntingdon County, 23–24, 167
Hutchinson, James, 103

Ihril, Charles, 48
Indians, 95, 172, 174, 176, 182, 192; activities in Pennsylvania, 15–16, 21, 33–34, 71, 76, 82–83, 87, 96, 167, 207
Ingersoll, Jared, 23, 51, 54–56, 59, 87–88, 99, 166, 168, 174, 180
Ireland, 149, 169, 182
Iroquois Nation, 76, 83, 87
Irvine, General William, 17, 28, 76–77, 80–83
Irwin, John, 49
Irwin, Matthew, 188

Jack, Samuel, 175–76
Jackson, Dr. David, 188
Jackson, Senator James, 179
James, Robert, 168
Jay, John, 72–73
Jay Treaty, 70, 72–73, 170
Jefferson, Thomas, 57, 85, 93, 106–7, 114–15, 160, 181
Jefferson County, 35
Jessup, William, 109
Johnson, Thomas, 115
Joubert, Thomas, 146, 149

Karrick, Joseph, 168
Keating, John, 98–101
Kensington Mill, 144
Kentucky, 135–36, 147; land speculations in, 167–68, 181–83
Kentucky Land Company, 183
King, William, 116, 119
Knox, General Henry, 26

Lancaster County, 13
Lancaster-Philadelphia Turnpike, 149, 154–55, 205
Land speculation, 1–2, 20–21, 32, 75, 104–5, chapter 8, chapter 10; in Pennsylvania, 154, 186, 190, 207; chapters 6–7, 10
Laporte, 109
Laporte, Bartholemew, 109
Lardner, John, 55
Law, Thomas, 120–22, 128, 131, 133
Lawrence County, 10, 35
Lehigh Coal Company, 151, 155
Lehigh Navigation Company, 151
Lehigh Portage Road, 155

Lehigh River, 151, 153, 155
Lee, Arthur, 11, 15
Lee, Henry, 71, 122, 129, 130
Leet, Daniel, 25, 28, 78, 80
L'Enfant, Pierre Charles, 115–17
Level of Europe and North America, 106, 170
Levy, Moses, 88, 168
Lewis, Mordecai, 62, 137
Lewis, William, 58–59, 88, 205
Lincoln, Levi, 174
Lithgrow, John, 145–46
Livingston, Robert, 11
Livingston, Walter, 15
Louis Philippe, 104
Lovering, William, 125, 127, 133
Low, Nicholas, 140–43
Loyalsock Creek, 110–11, 113
Lukens, John, 25
Luzerne County, 23–24, 100, 153, 167
Lycoming County, 99
Lystra, 182

McCall, Archibald, 109
McClean, Captain James, 16
McCleanachan, Blair, 62, 73, 188, 196
McConnell, Matthew, 62
McKean, Thomas, 29, 34–35, 48, 77, 150, 188, 193
McKean County, 35
McLane, James, 153
McNair Brothers, 89–90
Maclay, Samuel, 49
Maclay, William, 65–67
Macomb, Alexander, 20, 88
Madison, James, 62–64, 66–67, 174
Mahoning Creek, 10
Maple sugar production, 103–4
Marbury, William, 134
Marshall, Humphrey, 181
Marshall, James, 119, 131, 136, 169
Marshall, John, 119, 180, 207
Marshall, Thomas, 140
Maryland, 117, 127, 133–35, 160, 193
Mason, John, 152
Massachusetts, 20, 42, 64
Matthews, Governor George, 177
Meade, George, 50, 67–68, 78, 80
Mercer County, 10, 35
Mifflin, Jonathan, 52, 54, 59, 77, 196
Mifflin, Thomas, 10, 12, 21–23, 27,

129, 145–46, 149, 158, 160–63,
205; stone quarries of, 145–46,
149, 155, 157; supply stores of,
128, 145–46, 149–50, 186; support of, Bank of Pennsylvania,
50–52, 68; Blacks, 194, 206;
English refugees, 109–13, 182–
83; French émigrés, 93–94, 98,
106; internal improvements, 82–
84, 100, 129, 149, 153–58, 205,
207; manufacturing, 102–4, 128–
30, chapter 9. *See also* T.B.
Freeman and Company, 193,
205, 207; and the Territorial
Land Company, 107, 179, 185–
86; and textile production, 3,
110, 139–40, 142–46, 148–49;
and the Whiskey Rebellion, 70–
71; Virginia land speculations of,
167–68, 181
Nicholson, Samuel, 5, 23, 25, 28,
31, 64, 188
Nicholson Township, 188–89
Nixon, John, 15, 77, 166
Noailles, Count Louis de, 69, 94–
101, 104–5, 109, 185
North American Land Company,
31, 88, 101–2, 113, 119, 121,
123–24, 135, 153, chapter 10,
192
North Carolina, 66–67, 178; land
speculations in, 167–68, 180–81
Northampton County, 17, 48, 100,
152–53, 167
Northern Road, 153
Northumberland, 110–13
Northumberland County, 23–25,
32, 46, 49, 100, 104–5, 167
Nourse, Joseph, 18, 44, 76–77

Ohio River, 10, 34, 77–78, 156,
167–68, 182
Ohiopiomingo, 182
Oldden, John, 51
Osgood, Samuel, 15
Oswald, Eleazer, 48

Paine, Thomas, 42–43
Pantisocracy, 111
Parker, Daniel, 161–62
Parrish, Charles, 150
Parrish, John, 170
Parsons, Benjamin, 169

Paterson, New Jersey, 3, 141–45,
148
Paterson, William, 144
Peale, Charles Willson, 147
Pearce, William, 140
Penn, William, 3
Penn family, 7, 22
Pennsylvania, boundary of, 76; confiscated estates in, 7, 11–12, 16,
23, 40; debtor's law of, 200; General Assembly of, 7, 31–32, 83,
153–54, 156, 158; internal improvements in, 82–84, 100, 112,
149, 153–58, 161, 205; land disputes of, 22–23, 30, 87–89, 91–
92, 96–97, 104, 107–8, 168,
193; land laws of, 7, 22, 32–34,
40, 76–77, 80, 86–88, 90, 105,
107–8, 167, 188, 193; land office
of, 7, 21–30, 34–37, 53, 77; land
speculations in, 17, 21, 24–30,
32–38, 42, 51, 53, 64, 75–76,
105, 112, 167–68, 186, 192–93.
See also Asylum Company, North
American Land Company, Pennsylvania Land Company, Pennsylvania Population Company,
liens on John Nicholson's lands,
60, 91–92, 109, 151–52, 184,
187–88, 202–3; mining in, 150–
52; 154, 186; population of, 85–
86; Revolutionary War debts of,
16–17, 42, 53–54, 62–65
Pennsylvania Constitution of 1776,
7, 39–40, 46–47; of 1790, 22,
49
Pennsylvania Land Company, 149,
151, 186–87, 190
Pennsylvania Population Company,
36, 57, 71, 74, chapter 6, 101,
135, 154, 186, 203
Pennsylvania Property Company,
186
Pennsylvania Society for the Encouragement of Manufactures
and Useful Arts, 139–40
Pennsylvania Society for the Information and Assistance of Emigrants and Persons Emigrating
from Europe, 86. *See also* Nicholson, John, aid to immigrants
Peters, Richard, 46
Pettit, Charles, 42, 51, 77
Phelps, Oliver, 20, 64, 95

Index